I0796539

AUTOBIOGRAPHY OF A PUNK ROCKER

EDWARD TUDOR POLE

Oldcastle Books

First published in 2025
by Oldcastle Books Ltd,
Harpenden, UK

oldcastlebooks.co.uk
@OldcastleBooks

A CIP catalogue record for this book is available from the British Library.

ISBN
978-0-85730-605-0 (Hardcover)
978-0-85730-606-7 (eBook)

2 4 6 8 10 9 7 5 3 1

Typeset in 11.75 on 14.8pt Goudy Old Style
by Avocet Typeset, Bideford, Devon, EX39 2BP
Printed and bound in Great Britain by
TJ Books Ltd, Padstow, Cornwall

The manufacturer's authorised representative in the EU for product safety is Easy Access System Europe, Mustamäe tee 50, 10621 Tallinn, Estonia
gpsr.requests@easproject.com

The Pen is Mightier

Do what thy manhood bids thee do,
From none but self expect applause.
He noblest lives and noblest dies
Who makes and keeps his self-made laws.

Richard Burton, 1821–1890

For Sue

With thanks to: Alex Cox, Dave Twigg, Henry Tudor Pole, Dan Morrow, Mick Mercer, Andy Muscroft, Josephine Pembroke, Steve Sweeney, David Shaw-Parker, Stuart Eliot, Ellie Lavender and Ion Mills for their help in getting this book together.

Contents

PRELUDE

The Death of Rock and Roll Show

I'd think of ways to break the conventional boundaries of the rock show, constantly striving to make it more interesting, theatrical and original. Our most elaborate concert was 'The Death of Rock and Roll' show, performed in 1984 in a student hall near the Post Office Tower in London.

The place was packed, we were headlining, and the show begins with me coming on with a guitar and singing a couple of songs. Then I greet the crowd.

'Hang on, this would be much better if we had a proper band, wouldn't it?' I say.

'Yes!' they agree.

'I know, let's form a band! Can anyone play the drums?'

This question always elicits volunteers but Sarah was in the audience, planted and primed, and the first to make it onto the stage.

'But you're a girl!' I say, 'girls can't play drums!'

Sarah punches me indignantly and realistically to the floor using the stage-fight movements we'd rehearsed. I get up, concede her point and she gets the job as drummer.

'As we've got a girl drummer, let's form an ALL GIRL GROUP!' I now say to the audience. 'Is there a girl bassist and guitarist and sax player in the house?'

As hoped for and expected, no one volunteers, so I say,

'We've got some girls in our dressing room. Let's get them on stage and we'll ask them if they can play anything.'

Enter Matt Fisher, Sean Poe and Mick O'Donnell stage left, dressed up as women with wigs, make-up, false eyelashes and padded white blouses. The costumes affect them differently: Matt looks very pretty, Sean looks like the girl-next-door while Mick looks like an old charlady. Briefly interviewing them in turn, I ask about their hobbies and interests, and discovering they were all musicians I invite them to join the band for a few Chuck Berry rockers. After which I spot a copy of *Melody Maker* on one of the amps and pick it up.

'Let's see if we've got a review,' I say to the audience, bending time, as I leaf through the pages. Suddenly I see something that makes me freeze. Eyes wide in shock I look out to the crowd, appalled.

'Oi! It says here that rock and roll is dead! Why didn't anybody tell me?!' I demand. There's an awkward silence. I am not amused.

My anger building, I pull out a Stanley knife and approach the girls. I grab Sean from behind with my arm around his neck waving the blade in his face.

'Oi Sharon, why didn't you tell me rock and roll was dead?'

'I'm sorry!' sobs Sean, whereupon I start stabbing the red paint-filled condom strapped to his chest beneath his white blouse, until it bursts, flooding it blood-red, and Sean falls dying to the floor.

I then kill Matt in similar fashion and more blood pours. By now pre-prepared and spooky music is playing over the PA.

As I cross the stage to do Mick I suddenly turn upon the audience and gave a quick thrust of the dripping blade in their direction.

I was astonished by how quickly these rough-looking men down the front recoiled sharply backwards, creating a space between us as if they were in real danger. Surely they didn't believe my homicidal maniac act was genuine? I was acting! We're performing on a stage; don't they realise? Evidently not...

After I did Mick, only Sarah was left. I mowed her down with an invisible audible machine-gun and she kicked over the drums in her death spasms.

Then the music changed to Mozart's *Requiem* as I faced the audience, now horrified at what I had done.

Lit by a single spotlight in a sea of black I plunged the knife into my own blood pack, strapped on to a biscuit tin lid that I wore around my neck under the shirt like a bib. I have a scar that marks the night I learned the wisdom of wearing body armour when trying that stunt (it can be surprisingly tricky to pierce the rubber).

I freely admit that all these theatrics are borrowed wholesale from Lindsay Kemp's *Flowers*, a show that blew my mind in 1975. I took the lads to see it in the eighties and it blew theirs too, but the Tenpole Tudor audience was never going to go to Sadler's Wells in a million years to see Lindsay Kemp, so let's bring the best bits to them.

I bit down on a blood capsule, and imitating Munch's *The Scream*, blood dripped out of my mouth in the shrinking spotlight, until only my face was lit. The music climaxed and the light faded to blackout...and a stunned silence.

This show took much preparation in creating the intro and outro tapes, the costumes, and getting the make-up, wigs, and false eyelashes etc. My regret is that we only performed it once.

PART ONE

1
Crossfire Hurricane

I was forged on the anvil of a mother's rage. It wasn't a happy beginning and there's no getting round it. And I am immediately faced with a problem: which is how to describe my early life without making both you and me quite miserable.

Inner dialogue
Me: I really don't want to relate all the ghastly details of my childhood: it's too much of a downer.
Ed: Well, you can't avoid talking about your mother altogether, man: she had a formative influence.
Me: But it's a trap! The more vividly I evoke it the more depressing it will be. My aim is to amuse and entertain the reader, not to bring them down.
Ed: Well, simply give a bare-bones account and move swiftly on.
Me: But what about...
Ed: For goodness' sake man, get on with it!

The fact is, dear reader, being raised by my mother was a terrifying experience about which I shall be as succinct as possible.

Emerging at 8.30 on Monday morning, on 6 December, 1954 in the maternity hospital in York Way by Waterloo Station, my life began like one of those action films that open with maximum white-knuckle tension and trepidation. My mother was a very beautiful woman consumed by an anger she was compelled to unleash upon me daily.

My introduction to the world was to find myself being punished on a daily basis by rage for an unspecified offence of which I knew

I couldn't be guilty, having only recently been born. All I could do was protest my innocence.

The earliest years were spent in trying to understand my mother's illogical behaviour, with very little success. It's extremely alarming for a toddler to conclude he's got more sense than his guardian, whilst also realising he's too young to seize the reins of control to do anything about it.

The worst thing about being under daily attack is it leaves precious little time for anything else. Fear predominates causing learning ability and mental development to be severely hampered. It's why I am a slow learner.

Every day, after her rage had abated, she would apologise for the unfairness of the attack and give me a quick consolatory hug before putting me down again. It was clear she didn't like holding me: you can always tell. The repetition of this ritual eventually rendered it meaningless.

Reprimanded for breaking rules of behaviour I hadn't been taught in the first place, yet given none to follow to keep out of trouble, I had no safe corridor of travel. I was trapped in a lawless world.

By the time I was four, after a life of study and experiment, it became impossible not to infer that Mum was either a moron or insane. It was daily torture in a loveless tyranny, a laughter-free zone, with no place to flee except my mind.

In her defence my mother's behaviour was impersonal thus without conscious malice: she couldn't help it. And you could argue her parenting technique shaped my character and career and gave me an edge. You could suggest, dear reader, that any aspects of personality which make me interesting, if I am at all, are a direct result of her influence. For instance, without such an early diet of psychic violence there's no way a chap of my background could possibly have got into the Sex Pistols – not in a million years, old chap. And look where that led.

How persuasive this argument is and how much of a bargain it turned out to be will be up to the reader to decide.

Although my mother wasn't horrid round the clock, I learned early on never to drop my guard. In between the daily rages she could act normally and sometimes bought me a plastic knight to add to my collection from Lottie's sweet shop by Shepherd's Bush roundabout, near where we lived at 14, Addison Crescent, Kensington – in the late 1950s when everything was still in black and white.

I remember sitting on Mum's lap being taught to read; a warm and cosy spot, in the lee of which I could play my part, decipher words correctly and meet with approval. The mistake was in learning to read, for thereafter such closeness ceased.

Mum was always most insistent on speaking properly and instructed me as a drama teacher would. I was drilled in good manners and how to behave when having tea with the Queen, for instance. All easily learned, like a part in a play. It's all about appearances with the middle classes. When we went out, my mother could put on a superb show and act like a princess, and with her natural beauty, gracious manner and hundred-watt-smile, could charm the birds off the trees.

One example: years later whilst driving, when she was pulled over by the police for having a filthy rear-windscreen, she managed to talk the policeman into cleaning it for her, handing him the stuff to do it from the glove box.

My mother had a few love affairs, not many, and all with rather grand people, (with the splendid exception of Dave Jones the greengrocer) the most significant of whom was the First Sea Lord of the Navy, Sir Caspar John, son of the painter Augustus John. In Caspar's defence, his wife had turned sapphic during all the years he was at sea and had a girlfriend of her own by then.

It was a brief and passionate love affair that produced my brother Tom, when I was three. Despite being unmarried to the father, still something of a stigma in those days, the overriding reason, she told me, for deciding to have the baby was to give me a brother. This was her greatest move, for Tom is not only a boon to the world, he would go on to save my life.

Shortly after Tom was born, on our daily walk to Holland Park, I would approach other babies in prams, and making sure their mothers or nannies weren't looking, would prod the baby until it started crying. I didn't want to hurt them, just to make them cry – a couple of prods was generally all it took. Looking like a three-year-old I knew I had the perfect cover. Children are no fools.

My toys were wooden bricks and knights. As with music, there are infinite variations of games playable using basic ingredients. I had a Ladybird book about King Alfred the Great which taught me that I loved England. I also loved the Queen. She was young and beautiful like Mum – but seemed a lot kinder.

There was also an Italian ambassador who dated my mother. He gave me a clockwork train that went round its circle, and Tom received a large teddy. He took us into St James's Palace for tea in one of the staterooms. We watched the guards in their Busbies out of the window as they paraded below. He was nice and so was the next, also an Italian diplomat.

I sorely lacked male company and an ally, and was delighted to see these men when they came to our Kensington flat to take Mum out. But they never stayed for long, or came round more than twice. Mum was too adversarial. Dad had shot off like a bullet from a gun by the time I was one or two. No man could tolerate mater's raging storms, nor did.

In her defence, my mother suffered more than anyone from her madness which led to a life spent mostly alone without love or companionship, and thus I say she demands compassion. She couldn't help being how she was.

Dear reader, to be fair and to seek the truth as ever, let us attempt to find out what made her like this, for to understand is to forgive.

In childhood lie the clues.

My mum's mother, Cecilia Streeten, was born in 1911 into a wealthy Kent family.

Her father, Francis Streeten, was the Squire of Tonbridge and a decent and well-liked man by all accounts. He had made a fortune importing rubber. He was Kent gentry; or 'County' as my mother put it.

As children Granny and her brothers were brought up to the highest standards of upper-middle class wealth and privilege in a grand house with liveried servants: there were four of them waiting at table even for afternoon tea. Granny talked a bit like Celia Johnson in *Brief Encounter*: she rhymed 'cross' with 'horse'.

(Class note 1: the difference between the upper-middle class and the middle-class is that the former does a more convincing imitation of the upper class than does the latter; making it none the less fake for all that.

(Class note 2: Phil Daniels once said to me: 'It's really weird, Ed: whenever I'm with middle-class people they all start talking cockney at me!'

'My dear fellow, how infernally patronising that must be for you,' I said.

'Yes, it is a bit annoying,' he said.

Disaster struck with the Wall Street Crash of 1929, wiping billions off the value of global stocks and shares and making thousands bankrupt overnight – including my great-grandfather. Francis Streeten was now broke, and so were his children. The family lost everything they had, and Granny had just turned eighteen. She was now entering society as an elegant beauty with all the manners of a princess but not a penny to her name.

Meanwhile a man from Boston, New England, called Lincoln Brown (allegedly descended from John Brown the anti-slavery campaigner whose body 'lies a mouldering in the grave'), who spoke English with an accent more English than most Englishmen, came to Britain to seek his fortune.

Brown, with little to his name bar a modest allowance, had the plausible air of an affluent gentleman along with a measure of charm. As soon as he saw Granny he was bedazzled. She was gorgeous, charming and oozed opulence; and he pursued her.

As well as personifying wealth, privilege, beauty and charm, my grandmother had an irresistible sex-appeal which never left her. She could get any man to do exactly what she wanted, whilst at the same time making him feel that he was the masterful hero of the situation. She married many times, each husband richer than the previous. I adored her.

With no money of her own, Granny knew she needed to marry somebody solvent and Lincoln Brown seemed to fit the bill – and she wasn't about to confess to this apparently suitable suitor that a few months earlier she had become a pauper.

Dear reader, not about to admit they had none themselves they married for the wealth they mistakenly supposed the other to possess.

Soon apprised of their dismal folly and being quite unsuited in temperament, the marriage was a disaster. They produced a boy and two girls, my mother being the youngest, and stayed together 'for the sake of the children'. To Granny, unused to anything but affluence, now finding herself having to raise three children in the countryside to escape the Blitz, in a loveless marriage, with a ration book, no money and World War Two raging, it was a rude shock to find herself a member of the nouveau poor. It was an unhappy home. The parents had affairs and the children were left largely to their own devices.

Chloe, the elder sister, was the clever funny one. Mum, being dim and gullible and perfect 'victim material', was mercilessly bullied and teased by her brother and sister throughout her childhood. She never ceased to rise to the bait and was arguably their main entertainment. So when she became a mother herself, thus 'top dog', aged twenty two, it was natural for her to dish out the same torture to me as she had endured when she was little, because she knew no other way to behave, or climate in which to exist. This is my supposition: my father would call it psychobabble. But the fact is when someone is being bullied it takes over their consciousness, and normal development is impeded. Which explains her ability to be with a clearly miserable toddler and not feel compelled to try and cheer him up.

The prosecution will say, 'Who but a moron would inflict the same torture on their own children that they remember hating when it was being done to them when they were children?' The defence will say, it goes on all the time: the perpetrator can't help it. The prosecution will say the perpetrator must be insane. The defence will agree and rest their case.

My unaffectionate mother caused me no end of sorrow but let us dwell no further on't, dear reader. I've met many fans with far worse beginnings than I had: Tenpole Tudor was something of a magnet to people from dysfunctional backgrounds.

What is true to say is, if you raise a child with violence instead of affection, you are likely to breed a hooligan.

When I was two or three, Dad came round for the first time since leaving home, and seeing him framed in the doorway my heart leapt with joy. I ran to him and embraced his leg – I thought he was going to rescue me. We had a great day out in Kensington Gardens and then he dropped me back home.

But I was to be rescued, to an extent. Dad was living in 8 Woodlands Road, Barnes, with his lover Jacqueline, a beautiful French brunette single mum whom he would soon marry, and Anabelle, her daughter, who was a year younger than me.

Jacqueline's mother Rolande, who spoke little English, also lived with them and did the cooking and housework. Jacqueline was a secretary in the motor trade at Allan Taylor's, Wandsworth. Dad was unemployed; a background presence who didn't say much.

It was a normal enough family household. The telly was on when Jacqueline was there, and it was a peaceful atmosphere in comparison to my mother's. I lived with Dad and Jacqueline for the term times, and with my mother during the holidays until I was eight.

For one term I had to go to Anabelle's all-girl school as the grown-ups had omitted to enrol me anywhere, but I didn't care. Though detached and withdrawn, my sensors were aware I was in a safe zone at Dad and Jacqueline's. It was like being a guest in a friendly foster home. I loved its normality. The weeks of respite from the insanity at home were a blessed relief. Anabelle was a playmate and *The Beano* was delivered every Thursday; what luxury.

It was a French household: Jacqueline and Anabelle spoke in French to Rolande who couldn't speak English, as did Dad. So I heard the language a lot. I tried to speak French to Rolande, and she tried to speak English to me. She called me 'Edood'. We were the linguistic dunces of the family.

Rolande was kind and we got on all right. Her food was delicious but although I appreciated the good intention, I found it hard to eat the two bowls of porridge she served for breakfast 'to build me up' because I was so thin.

She made a different soup every day, proper 'pain-au-chocolat' and her French-fries were superb.

I knew my father's father, Wellesley Tudor Pole, was special in some way. But oddly, my grandfather seemed to be a banned topic and whenever I asked about him Dad would be evasive. Wellesley died when I was fourteen and I'd only met him twice. 'If you want to know about your grandfather, you'll find out about him yourself,' said Dad. Which actually lessened rather than piqued my interest: if he's too weird to talk about, I thought, then bollocks to him, I've got other things to worry about.

Jacqueline told me she was concerned because I never smiled. She said I didn't smile until I was eight. That, dear reader, was when the Beatles came along.

2

Beatles and Stones

In 1961, when I was six, my mother moved us to Tonbridge, Kent, land of our forebears. My mother's sister Chloe lived there. She was married with three children roughly the same ages as Tom and I, who would become our playmates. Mum now got on well enough with her sister so we had the beginnings of a social life and a semblance of normality.

Like Richmal Crompton's William Brown and the Outlaws, my cousins and I were independent. We were free to roam the surrounding countryside, climb trees, play in streams, steal apples and other traditional juvenile rural pursuits. With our pal Pogle, a friend from the town, it was easy to amuse ourselves.

We customised our bicycles with cow horn handlebars and distance was no limit – there was less fear of perverts in those days. We'd have sword fights with fence stakes in Elm Lane.

Always needing money for sweets we invented ways of getting it, some more inventive than others: we soon discovered knocking on people's doors collecting for 'The poor children' was too obviously fraudulent to work.

More successful was when I would accost elderly ladies walking along Elm Lane, a pedestrian route through fields fringed by elm trees. I'd emerge from behind a tree with a gun-shaped twig in my hand:

'Your money or your life!'

Being nine years old I knew I couldn't get into any serious trouble. I also worked out the best way to get the ladies to hand over their cash was to be unthreatening, somewhat inept, and cheerful. It was entirely calculated to the finest degree and the ruse often worked.

One hot summer's afternoon we divided into two groups for a 'thuggery' contest. I was paired with cousin Matt.

We both had black plastic Sekiden guns that fired dried peas, so for starters we shot peas into every open window we passed. On wasteland we smashed a window in a semi-collapsed derelict overgrown shed with its other windows already smashed, we stole some apples from trees, knocked on forty two doors and ran away; and other such low level 'crimes'. It was lighthearted entertainment but the reason me and Matt won the contest was because we kidnapped a baby. The others couldn't match that.

Along Elm Lane we passed a house with a sleeping baby in its pram by the front door. We crept up the drive and took the pram for a walk. Our hearts were hammering at the enormity of our crime as we pushed the baby in the pram ever further away from its home. But after about two minutes our nerve snapped and we wheeled it back sharpish. We weren't discovered and the baby slept throughout.

There were two prep schools near where we lived in Tonbridge: Hilden Grange and Yardley Court, the latter being superior and more expensive. We were living in class-conscious times and there was no question of us going to a state school even though Mum had almost no money. She constantly complained to me about the bills.

I enjoyed Hilden Grange, which was a fifteen-minute walk from home. They clad us in boiler suits and we were allowed to play by the stream and get muddy. It was a happy school and though I recall two older boys trying to bully me once I simply laughed, delighted by the attention. Mere schoolboys couldn't alarm me. Despite being stick-thin and no good at fighting I was never bullied at any school for some reason.

I got into trouble one day in the dining hall when the pea I'd flicked at a boy named Hill hit the headmaster's wife instead: Mrs Gracie.

Claiming a bad aim cut no ice with the authorities and I was duly sentenced to be caned by Colonel Easton the following day at 2 pm.

Filled with fear, I sweated anxiously through the night and the next morning, until the appointed time arrived and I had made my way to Colonel Easton's study door. I recalled the 'William' story where he is sent to the dentist and knocks so softly he is not heard. He later tells his mum there was 'no one in.'

That wouldn't work now.

'Come in!' said the door.

I entered the study, acting fearful and egging it a bit. The acting, being a distraction, fractionally took the edge off the actual fear I felt. Once again I explained I'd been aiming the pea at Hill and not at Mrs Gracie, and said I was sorry. Colonel Easton looked grim and told me to bend over. I did so, tensing myself for the first of the two strokes I'd been awarded...

Dear reader: he very lightly and quickly tapped my arse a couple of times with the cane, not hurting me at all. It was a moment of unbridled joy.

He smiled at me and told me not to do it again; I thanked him with all my heart, and walked out, my sense of justice entirely satisfied. I understood it had been a virtual caning and a symbolic chastisement – the punishment was in the waiting. It was a useful lesson in bravery: how to cope with fear and muster courage, and how things are seldom as bad as you fear they are going to be.

In 1963 Mum finally joined the modern world and bought a secondhand television set. Tom and I were now allowed to watch children's TV, *Deputy Dawg* being the initial favourite.

I saw the first *Doctor Who* episode, so naturally consider the real Doctor to be William Hartnell and his descendants a series of weedy popinjays, some weedier than others.

In the winter term of 1963, our class was to perform a version of Dickens' *A Christmas Carol* and I was cast as the ghost of Christmas past. A boy called Thompson was playing Scrooge.

I remember him asking me which Beatle I preferred, adding that he liked John the best. I said that I did too, without having the faintest idea what he was talking about. He told me about a forthcoming show on TV called *Top of the Pops.*

I was only days away from finding out about The Beatles and being swept away on the tidal wave of Beatlemania along with everybody else in the land. Suddenly, the nationwide talk was all about the BEATLES and their phenomenal success.

Beatlemania was totally exhilarating and I loved the band's catchy tunes and vocal harmonies. Thanks to their clean-cut image, Mum made no objection and she bought me their first EP 'Please Please Me', for Christmas when I had just turned nine. I was a dedicated Beatles fan and bought Beatles bubblegum which came with black-and-white 'Fab Four' photo cards to collect.

In those days I did like John Lennon the best. The onset of Beatlemania galvanised the nation, cheered everybody up and marked the end of post-war austerity. Thanks to Thompson's tip, *Top of the Pops* became the highlight of the week. I was fascinated by this type of game where groups or solo singers came on in turn to play their catchy songs, and how it was up to us, the viewers, to decide how successful the song would become by how many of us went and bought the record. I got it. The beautiful melodies made me happy. The pop song is a controlled environment where you're safe on the three-minute ride

'She Loves You (Yeah Yeah Yeah)', when it came out in 1963, caused a huge stir. I recall overhearing grown ups making much of the fact that the band weren't singing the word 'yes' correctly. The number one hit, when it came on at the end of *TOTP*, was always imbued with a magic, simply because it *was* number one, whether you liked it or not. I could tell why most of the songs were hits even if they weren't my cup of tea. I could see what it was about the tune that many found pleasing. To reach number one seemed no less a feat than making it to the top of Everest.

I loved hearing the pop records, and the joy of falling in love with a great one. I also found out the magic of a tune doesn't last forever. You can wear it out. It was the Beatles and the thrill of the pop tunes which shook me out of a semi-stupor and brought me to life.

Jacqueline, who was a good sport, and still only around thirty, shared our enthusiasm for pop music and the exploding swinging sixties scene. She took Anabelle and I to see the Beatles film, *A Hard Day's Night*, at Hammersmith Odeon in July 1964. I knew all the songs and immersed myself in the film to such an extent that when I walked out of the cinema into the blinding glare of the sunlight over Hammersmith flyover, I *was* a Beatle. Well, imagining I was a Beatle to such a degree there was no difference, in those few intense moments, from actually being one.

At the same time I was keenly aware that it was impossible for me to look like anything other than the nine-year-old boy I was. I told myself to be patient. Being old enough to look like a Beatle seemed a remote and distant future at the time but I remember reassuring myself that it would happen one day.

But back to Hilden Grange and the school play. Come the eve of the single performance of *A Christmas Carol* Thompson fell ill, and I stepped into the breach to play Scrooge. I knew most of the words already and in true showbiz tradition I saved the day and 'a star was born'.

All children have the capacity to immerse themselves in pretend characters and the deeper the immersion, the more effective the escape. Imagination was the fertile land upon which my playhouse sat and my head my only house unless it rained.

My performance as Scrooge caused a dramatic reaction and there was enthusiastic applause at the end.

As if by magic I had become a terrific fellow. Everyone – including Mum – was showering me with extravagant praise. Their eyes were shining and their smiles were genuine as I was lavished with hyperbole. I was shocked and thrilled by the extraordinary alteration in how people were now treating me.

On the spot I was offered the part of Chief Weasel in the forthcoming Tonbridge Amateur Dramatic Society's Christmas production of *Wind in the Willows* (featuring the brilliant David Goodale, aged fourteen, as Toad of Toad Hall).

That was when the idea of becoming an actor started to form. As I was acting an invented version of myself in the first place, it was just as easy to act anybody else. I would be an actor and people's eyes would shine when they met me. Thrilled with this unexpected success as Scrooge I even dared to hope, in vain, that Mum's new attitude towards me would become permanent.

The Pivotal Moment of My Life

A few months later the Rolling Stones emerged and I was changed forever. It was when I was at Jacqueline's that I first saw them on TV in 1964, playing 'It's All Over Now'. I was spellbound.

This was an epiphany, a revelation, like being struck by a lightning bolt, and any other cliché you care to mention. I was thrilled and seduced. Totally. For ever and ever. Straightaway I understood the band, and their rebellious stance. The sound of the song swept me away on the riptide of its rhythm to a kind of heaven. To this day it's one of my favourite records: the production and intermeshing guitar parts are astonishingly accomplished for ones so young and it's arguably the most definitively Stones-sounding record of all, despite it being written by Bobby Womack.

As for Mick Jagger, his style and his act thrilled me to the core. He was the most wonderful thing I'd ever seen. With their disdainful air their music gave me comfort. The Rolling Stones were perfectly realised and I knew they were on my side – which I somehow never felt about the Beatles. The Rolling Stones were the rebellious figureheads of a thrilling new and powerful movement. My undying loyalty pledged, they became my new family whether they liked it or not. I jumped onto the back of their wagon, like a stowaway, no less eagerly than a man in a fast-flowing river grabs an overhanging branch just before the waterfall sweeps him to his doom.

And that's when I became a bit of a bore for the rest of my life, like some people are about Tottenham Hotspur or Arsenal. From then on I could think and talk of nothing else but the Rolling Stones. They were the cavalry, come to rescue me. They were more dangerous than the Beatles, their hair was longer, they didn't wear suits and their winklepickers were winklier.

The Beatles had jolted me out of a semi trance-like state of disengagement, but the Rolling Stones electrified me, recharging my life. Unrequited love for my mother was the heartache on which my foundations were built, but now I could 'blot it out of the sky' of my mind with Rolling Stones music. By thinking about nothing but the band, all other thoughts were necessarily banished to the nethermost regions of subconscious. The Rolling Stones were my gateway drug to things that made you feel better than you did before. They could be slow and gentle, fast and rough and everything in between.

The band gave my heart a home and something to belong to that I could love: 'Rolling Stones' was running through me like 'Blackpool' runs through rock, and for all time. A man takes his salvation where he finds it.

I yearned for Mick and Keith to turn up at the front door to take me away. I would imagine it.

Mick: (estuary vowels) 'Hello Mrs Tudor Pole, can Edward come out to play?'

At Jacqueline's, the TV was always on and the Stones were always on it, whether it was on *Ready Steady Go* or *Top of the Pops*. They were in the charts, on the radio and all over the news. There was plenty of fuel to fan the flames of fanatical ardour.

Their manager Andrew Loog Oldham's ploy, later to be copied by Malcolm McLaren, of making the Stones the bad boy antidote to the Beatles, was paying off handsomely. Columns of outrage at their perceived depravity filled the newspapers. Such as being arrested for urinating against a garage wall (their request to use the WC having been refused). All the outrage made me stick up for them, and love them even more, of course. And it was always perfectly obvious to me that they weren't really baddies.

In return for my loyalty the group has worked its bollocks off to keep me entertained all my life. What blows my mind is that here I am, sixty years later, *still* listening to the latest Rolling Stones single on the radio! How is this possible?! That's what I call good service. Thank you very much, man, if any Rolling Stones are reading this book.

Fashion Note

When bell-bottoms came in I longed for a pair but not only did they not sell them in Tonbridge, Mum could not have afforded them even if she would have let me wear them – which she wouldn't.

However, one afternoon I worked out that if I cut a slit up the inside lower half of each trouser leg of my jeans, and sewed a slim triangle into the gaps I could make my own bell-bottoms. I found a needle and thread and scissors in the sewing basket and despite never having sewn before I didn't see how it could be that difficult and nor was it. In a couple of hours, the job was done and I was amazed by how well it worked. I felt sure my mother would be so impressed by the tailoring feat she would let me wear them.

She was impressed by my tailoring feat, and quite surprised, and she did let me wear them; but only for one day, before declaring 'You're not going out wearing bell bottoms!'

As for winklepickers, while we're on the subject of fashion: when I was thirteen, and on a week's holiday in a Bridport hotel with Dad, Jacqueline and Anabelle, I saw an actual pair of shiny, black, Cuban-heeled winklepickers in a shoe-shop window, in my size! It was the first time I'd ever seen a pair in real life. I begged my father to buy me them, a plea to which he was amenable, having none of the bourgeois sensibilities that made my mother hate them.

They were perfect in every way, with a seam down the front from the shin to the very shiny pointed toe. When it was time to go back to my Mum's at the end of the holiday, I vainly hoped that as the shoes were a gift from my father she would let me wear them.

When I became an adult, I bought myself a pair of winklepickers but I fear their value is more as a fetish item than tolerable footwear, except when worn by others. Many times have I put them on in the morning only for them to become too annoying to wear in real life for more than about ten minutes.

I became ten in December 1964, and in January 1965, on the day it came out, Jacqueline took me and Anabelle to a record shop in Putney to buy the second Stones album: *Rolling Stones No. 2*. Mick Jagger had told us about it in an interview with Cathy McGowan on *Ready Steady Go*.

I first listened to this heavy vinyl disc, with its red Decca label, sitting out of sight behind the sofa gazing at the cover, and reading Loog Oldham's notes on the back (which recommended mugging blind people to raise the money to buy the LP) while my father worked at his desk. He professed no objection to it.

This music was about a lot more than pop melody. It seemed more serious and meant for people older than me, which of course only added to its fascination. No Stones album has ever given away all its treasure on first listen, and I would play *No.2* many times, letting it wash over me as it introduced me to the rhythm and the blues. It is a terrific LP to this day.

3

Crime and Punishment

In 1964, in Tonbridge, a *Top of the Pops* seared into my memory was on the week when the DJ, almost incoherent with excitement, announced: 'Last week number twenty two, this week straight to number one! The Animals with "House of the Rising Sun!"'

I was blown away by the record and it was immediately clear to me why it was a hit. When the notes go a certain way something in me chimes with recognition and releases a feeling of pleasure. That's how I can tell if a song's any good or not.

I went up to my room, very excited, with a clear feeling that I too could write a pop song. This was before I had a guitar so I devised a derivative bit of doggerel to a basic tune, which I can still remember. (Sixty years later watching The Shadows' Farewell tour on TV I realised it was a ripoff of one of rhythm guitarist Chris Welch's songs).

We played at being in a group in my cousins' garden, with Steve on a tea chest drum kit, Pogle on his violin held like a guitar (in imitation of Paul McCartney) and me on lead vocals with the blue cardboard tube around which string is wound as a microphone. It was the sort of group Richmal Crompton's William and the Outlaws might have formed.

In the early sixties my brother and I would often see the rockers on motor bikes riding past the end of our road, followed half an hour later by Mods on scooters, on their way to the coast for a punch-up. I always preferred the look of the rockers. We called ourselves 'The Rockers'.

None of us could play an instrument, not even Pogle on his violin, and we only had one song. This game was only played a couple of times, the others being less in love with the rock and roll fantasy than I was.

I have spent my life trying to come up with three-minute records as effective as the ones I grew up with. A good pop record is a timeless piece of magic.

For Christmas Granny sent me a beginner's acoustic guitar, which came in a beige plastic soft case, with a set of pitch-pipes and a copy of Bert Weedon's *Play in a Day* book, a guitar manual I find impenetrable to this day. With beating heart I took it out of the case and gasped to be holding an actual guitar. I strummed the open strings which I thought sounded like the final chord of a song. So I pretended I had just played a song then twanged the open strings again to end it. It was a start.

Mum said she would pay for a teacher, and a matronly woman in a suit, a bit like Hattie Jacques, came round once a week to give me lessons. She showed me with pride a press cutting of a local group, the guitarist of whom she'd taught.

I would assiduously practise the exercises she gave me, and there was reward in seeing her pleasure as I progressed. Soon, I had learnt the chords C, G7 and Dm7, and how to play 'Bobby Shaftoe' and single-note tunes.

After five lessons my mother said she couldn't afford them any more and the teacher was dismissed. Because my learning abilities were underdeveloped, for the next few years I was stuck on what I'd been shown in those five weeks; and didn't progress at all.

Three years later inspiration came via a great family friend of my mother's since her childhood: Tony Snell. A dashing fellow, Tony was a Spitfire pilot in World War Two, had been shot down twice, and escaped from a firing squad. He wrote and sang amusing 1940s cabaret-type songs like 'The Elephant's Bottom' accompanying himself on electric piano or guitar which he played very well, in a pre-rock rock and roll dance-band style.

Tony came round one day, picked up my guitar and played a couple of songs for our amusement with verve and alacrity. Wow!

Play fast! Why didn't I think of that? When he'd gone I played Bobby Shaftoe at lightning speed for a change, instead of its hitherto plodding rhythm.

I still played the guitar every day, the perfect prop in my perma-fantasy daydream of performing in a group to a large crowd. I discovered things about the notes slowly but I could now strum the chords of A, B7, C, D, E, F and G and change them very quickly.

For reasons that were never made clear, I was taken out of Hilden Grange and sent away to a boarding-school at Penthorpe in Horsham, Surrey.

Dear reader, so dreadful was the school I can't bring myself to describe it. If I'd led a duller life we could make more of a meal of it; but we've had quite enough misery in Chapter One as it is, and I'm aiming to entertain. If you want unending horror, read about Fred West.

For two terms I prayed to God daily at chapel to be released from that hell. The desperate man leaves no stone unturned: the worse his life, the more fervently he turns to God, in case he's there. He was there. At the next school, full of happy boys, when a teacher asked our class to write out the Lord's Prayer from memory, I was the only one who knew it perfectly.

My mother had got a job as a junior teacher at Yardley Court, a family-run school led by Eric Bickmore, a kind and gentle man. My mother expressed her concerns to Bickmore about Penthorpe and his enquiries about the place chimed with my description of it. Mum, on £14 per week, could not afford the fees for Yardley Court so good old Bickmore solved all our problems by giving me a place at his school anyway, with a hefty discount. He was a true saviour, like Mr Brownlow in *Oliver Twist*.

Just as a good landlord makes for a good pub, a good headmaster makes for a good school. Yardley Court's atmosphere was essentially kind and gentle and the boys were treated with respect. Which didn't mean that we were spoiled or that the rod was spared, but being a civilised place, the punishments were entirely proportionate and not suddenly unleashed out of the blue for no reason at all, as at home. A child craves rational behaviour, and to find myself in an ordered universe was a godsend.

'Mr Eric' (Bickmore) ran the school with his two sons: 'Mr John' who had black hair and a fiery temper, and 'Mr Michael' a county cricket bowler and chief disciplinarian/flagellist.

The teachers were good: especially Mr Tutton, who in History would bring in the battle-plans he'd drawn on lining wallpaper for whichever battle he was teaching us about, and drape it over the blackboard. He then proceeded to re-enact it singlehandedly in front of us, giving a running commentary whilst charging across the room as if on horseback, being first one army, then the other, and vividly describing the actions and tactics of each. To watch this lanky fellow, usually the model of reticence and dignity, galloping around the room made me very happy, this was first-rate stuff. On summer afternoons we could smell the fresh mown grass through the open windows and I experienced happiness.

Mr Tutton also taught us English, and I liked writing essays. He would pin a choice of three topics for us on the classroom notice board. Once a boy complained that the titles were boring: e.g. 'A Walk in the Country', 'A Flight by Night'. Somewhat exasperated, Tutton added a further choice: 'Write about Nothing'. This was a challenge I enjoyed, never being deterred by deliberately difficult topics, conceived as punishments – like being told to write a five hundred-word essay on 'The Inside of a Ping-Pong Ball'.

Another extraordinary teacher was Mr Fisher, a florid-faced ex-army man, with a splendidly rumbustious method of teaching. He would hold a boy by the back of his collar and kick his arse, going round in a circle, whilst repeating what the boy had forgotten. He would barely hurt the transgressor, and we howled with laughter at this Punch and Judy-style buffoonery.

Fisher would hurl the blackboard rubber at you if you weren't concentrating. For talking in class, he would make you put a piece of chalk in your mouth, which rapidly dried up saliva and rendered you dumb. In Maths, if the question was 'What is minus three, minus two?' and any boy dared say: 'One', Fisher would pull three single hairs from the boy's head and ask him how many hairs he was minus.

'Minus three, sir.'

'Correct.' He then plucked out two more hairs.

'Ow! Ow!'

'Now how many hairs are you minus in total?'

'Minus five, sir,' the boy would say, with the chastened clarity of understanding. Nobody in that classroom would ever again confuse: '-3 -2' with '3 – 2'.

I loved Mr Fisher's roustabout, rollicking style, both grateful and surprised that this sort of thing was even allowed. I could tell he was sailing close to the wind with his outrageous antics but he was hilarious, it was art, and there was no malice in him. At mealtimes he piled his plate as high as they do in comics. At the beginning of the following term when I was told that Mr Fisher had 'left the school', I intuited immediately that he had been sacked and was most aggrieved. Some weedy day boy must have complained to his parents. OK, Mr Fisher's way was somewhat anarchic but he was most entertaining, a brilliant teacher, and you never forgot his lessons for the rest of your life. What more do you want? The one thing that kills teaching stone dead is a mediocre teacher with zero charisma who never makes the classroom laugh.

Another good lesson was from Mr Michael. I was surprised one day when the evening's prep (the boarder's term for homework) was simply to copy out a fairly short paragraph from a book.

'That's easy!' I said, whereupon Mr Michael raised an eyebrow and told me I was almost certain to make mistakes. I didn't see how I could!? I duly copied out the passage and wondered what he meant.

Later I was amazed to find I had scored a low mark. Every time I had put a full stop directly under an inverted comma, instead of in its own invisible column, as a typewriter forces you to do, or if a capital letter was not twice the height of a lower-case letter, or if the dot wasn't exactly over the eye, then I was penalised. The rigorous attention to these tiny details greatly impressed me; a lesson in the difference between first and second-rate.

Teaching Latin at Yardley Court was a fourth Bickmore, Mr Maurice, Eric's elderly brother, who in his prime in the 1930s had been a formidable and fearsome teacher, but by now was so ancient he could no longer control a classroom, so boys mucked about in his lessons. Schoolchildren will always exploit the weak teacher.

On one occasion the misbehaviour was overdone, and about ten of us were down for punishment. We were sentenced to be slippered after lessons by Mr Michael who, unlike Colonel Easton at Hilden Grange, seemed to relish corporal punishment, and not illogically, applied it as painfully as possible.

We all sat anxiously in the classroom at 5 pm to receive our chastisement. The first boy went forward and was ordered to stand about two thirds of the way across the room's width and bend over.

Mr Michael, armed with a black, size-12 gym-shoe, walked as far away from the boy as the room's spacious dimensions allowed, then turned round and began his run-up, like the county cricket standard fast bowler he was. Accelerating towards the bent boy, arm high, his sheer velocity greatly added to the force of the plimsoll which whacked the boy's arse with a noise like a pistol shot before Mr Michael crashed into the wall beyond the boy, the only brake to his momentum. Two whacks each was our sentence. When he had finished with the first boy he said, 'Who's next?'

My hand shot up like a distress flare: far better to get it over with now, I thought, than to become ever more scared and anxious by watching others being punished, and prolonging the wait.

I remember it being surprisingly painful, in a stinging way, but there was no better option than to take it bravely. After all, we had been out of order and the punishment was not unjust. Injustice is what really hurts.

I returned to my desk mightily relieved and watched the rest of the boys being slippered, now feeling perfectly relaxed, and even in quite a good mood. After a couple of minutes my arse simply felt very hot, as though I were sitting on a stove, not a particularly unpleasant sensation.

Later we wandered about as momentary objects of fascination to other boys, with the fleeting glamour of having undergone 'the whacks'. It was another lesson in bravery, the most useful asset in life.

I was always attracted to naughty types at school and sometimes hung out with a boy called Raggett. There was a Garden of Remembrance at the school to honour old boys killed in the two world wars, and a place we could go for a little reflective peace and quiet should we wish. One day in that garden Raggett and I, with our penknives, carved something onto one of the wooden benches, I can't remember what; presumably not our initials.

A couple of days later at morning assembly, Mr Eric announced that a bench in the Garden had been vandalised and that whoever was responsible must report to him and own up.

I felt bad about what we'd done and suggested to Raggett that we confess. He thought I was mad and said we should simply keep quiet. My conscience wouldn't allow it so I said to Raggett that I was going to own up anyway, but wouldn't mention him.

I mustered the courage to tell Mr Eric. His reaction was completely unpredictable. Instead of being angry he was clearly delighted that I had owned up and heartily congratulated me for so doing. He told me off for the carving crime, but far more did he praise me for honesty, and having the courage to admit it. I walked out of his study absolutely elated and empowered. Dear reader, this is teaching at its highest level.

After a term or two as a day boy Mr Eric suggested to my mother it would be a good idea if I were to become a boarder. This I was very happy to do, and so it was that term times became peaceful for me, unsullied by domestic violence.

In a school production of *1066 and All That*, I played the 'Common man' as I was the only boy in the school who could do a cockney accent. Mr Reiss the music teacher had previously had me singing the old cockney standard, 'My Old Dutch', at another concert ('We've been together now for forty years and it don't seem a day too much'). Actually Reiss later told me that Mr Eric had taken him aside and expressed disapproval at this vulgar choice of song, and of my 'mockney' performance.

Eric was an old-fashioned character, from a time when class differences in society were far more delineated. He was in the business of turning boys into gentlemen, and preparing them for public school. He didn't want us exposed to coarse entertainment. Even comics such as *The Beano* or *The Dandy* were forbidden, as they were considered oikish. Naturally I ignored this rule, as I do all rules that make no sense, as comics were top of my list of pleasures along with sweets.

The traditions at Yardley Court had hardly changed since the nineteenth century. The new cultural phenomenon of pop music now led by the Beatles and the Stones that would revolutionise society and make class differences massively less relevant had only just begun.

The majority of the boys were sports fans, especially of cricket: The *Daily Telegraph* and *Daily Express* were provided and you could ring an article with a pen adding your initials – then in the evening you could cut out the article to keep.

I ignored the sports pages, but anything about the Rolling Stones I would reserve. I had no competition for the prevalent Stones stories of drug-taking, police busts, and assorted outrages in 1967. It was common knowledge that I was a massive fan and I would sporadically jump about the classroom singing 'Paint it Black' – these impromptu performances were tolerated amiably enough by my classmates.

The only other boy in class who loved the Stones was Eddy Kirwan, a policeman's son and a day boy. He was my best friend and would bring in forbidden stuff like a *Beano* or a pack of Rolling Stones bubblegum cards, which, unlike the Beatles ones, were in colour.

Mr Eric had noticed, with some dismay, my reserving articles on the Rolling Stones and took me aside one evening to have a word. I told him I was a great fan of their music to which he replied that surely I could like the music without having to like them? I knew there was no way this traditional old chap from another era was ever going to get the Rolling Stones: their image at that time was calculated to be an affront to traditional values, just as the Sex Pistols' was in the seventies.

I understood and respected Eric Bickmore's ethos. His life had been spent educating boys to be decent and to play the game of life with a straight bat. I couldn't see anything wrong with any of that.

Later, I was panicked by Mr John telling me that I was to compete in the boxing tournament. I was stick-thin, unsporting, and had no experience of fighting. 'Please sir, I don't want to do it.' I said.

He swept my protests aside: 'Nonsense, it will be good for you! You are to fight MacGregor.'

'B-b-but...'

'Silence !'

MacGregor was not a particularly sporting type either: our fight was to be the opener, bottom of the bill. I had never donned a pair of boxing gloves before and had only fought with my younger brother Tom – which with my three-year advantage counted for nothing. Needless to say, I was nervous and scared before the match as the gym master tied up the laces of my gloves. Round one: 'ding ding!'

We faced each other, bobbing about as boxers do. He landed the first blow on my nose and it started bleeding. At that moment I discovered a vast wellspring of aggression within me. How dare he hit me!

And then I knew there was no way this boy was going to defeat me. My capacity for aggression felt limitless: a volcano's worth on tap. I went for him fearlessly, punching as hard as I possibly could: which wasn't very hard, handicapped as I was by lack of stamina and training. But I advanced and he retreated, and even though my nose was bleeding I knew I was winning. Afterwards I was much praised and congratulated by the masters and the schoolboys, a hero for an hour. I was proud of myself: it was an invaluable lesson of self-discovery.

I mention these lessons learned because not being taught anything useful at home they made a great impression on me. It is sad that today all or most of these examples of great teaching I've given would be banned.

Beware of seriousness, dear reader, it is a symptom of stupidity.

Aged thirteen I went to King Edward's School, Witley, in Surrey; a co-educational boarding school and a charitable foundation run by the City of London's Bridewell Institute, originally for orphans but now extended to people from broken homes or for those whose parents lived abroad. The fees were an affordable two hundred pounds per term.

Olympic Studios. Jimi Hendrix, Ringo Starr. Philip Pullman

By this time my mother had moved us from Tonbridge to 9 Byfeld Gardens in Barnes, South West London just around the corner from Olympic Studios where the Rolling Stones recorded a number of their albums, including *Beggars Banquet*. Alas, dear reader, they always recorded them in term time when I was at boarding school. Aagh. So near and yet so far. It was 1967.

Mum's friend Caradoc King and his friend Nick Pullman had both graduated from Oxford and she employed them to decorate the new house. Nick became the lodger. He had an acoustic guitar, quite long hair and seemed very cool to me. He was a serious man who never made jokes but was not unfriendly.

He played me Cream's first single, 'I Feel Free', telling me they were going to become huge. He also introduced me to The Incredible String Band's first LP and I became a big fan of them for a while. I was thirteen and fascinated by the hippy movement and its imagery: psychedelic Hendrix posters, beads, joss sticks, flowery shirts, long hair becoming ever longer: (I longed for long hair). Peace and Love seemed like a very good idea to me.

Nick was a writer, and wrote every day, with coloured inks, in very neat runic-looking handwriting, in large notebooks. When I came back from Kensington Market one evening in 1968 with a secondhand copy of the Rolling Stones' first album which for some reason I hadn't yet acquired, we listened to it together. Nick remarked on how rough and raw the band sounded but to me I didn't see how the songs could have been played any better. It did perhaps sound a bit old-fashioned in that hippy era of drugs, long hair and rambling guitar solos. But this was always a history record where the Stones showcased the black artists they loved. But now people were singing about LSD and wearing flowers in their hair. The Beatles' 'Hey Jude' was played a lot in the house. (Nick's girlfriend was called Jude.)

Nick's real name was Philip and after over a quarter century of unceasing toil and daily writing, Philip Pullman finally made the big time with *His Dark Materials, Book of Dust* and other acclaimed works. You can make it if you try.

Next to the Olympic Studios was a café with chairs outside where my mother sat one sunny day having coffee with a friend, she told me, when Jimi Hendrix emerged from the studio. As soon as he saw my beautiful mother he went over and flirted with her in the easy sexually confident way that rock stars have, complimenting her looks and inviting her to go for a drive with him. Mum was thrilled and delighted by this little encounter and told me he was gorgeous, although she turned down his offer.

Ringo

One day when I was about fourteen, I was near the end of our road and happened to see Ringo Starr walk into Olympic Studios. For about six seconds I was ten feet away from an actual Beatle. I was so electrified I had to go into the hardware shop next to the café to let my heart rate subside; I was hyperventilating with shock and excitement as I stared at packets of rawl-plugs and washers on the circular rack. To happen to see an actual Beatle was an unexpected and mind-bending event, the stuff of fantasy.

Looking at him in the flesh I could tell that Ringo was a nice chap, the only Beatle you'd want to be stranded with on a desert island. This was the first time that the pop world of my imagination collided with the real one.

4

Expelled

On my first night in the dormitory of King Edward's School, a lad called Freeman mocked my accent.

'Oh! Edward Tudor Pole! I say old boy!' he exclaimed, in a Terry-Thomas parody. 'OK, we'll call you Ted.'

Glad of the tip I modified my accent on the spot. I didn't want to talk posh. No one in bands talked posh that I'd ever heard, apart from Paul Jones of Manfred Mann, certainly not Mick Jagger.

It wasn't a typical public school, where you'd have the mickey taken out of you for talking like a yokel rather than a nob, but a pleasant enough place to be, surrounded by girls and countryside. It was a few notches down from Yardley Court's level of intellectual rigour but the country walks every day, to smoke cigarettes out of sight, inspired a great appreciation of nature.

Although I later wove an unrequited-love-with-Sandra-Philpott story into the explanation for my breakout it was most likely boredom and desire for adventure that prompted it. In the summer of 1969, I decided to run away from school. Me and my best friend Pete Whitaker started planning it in the woods, carefully working out the practical details. I could bicycle the forty eight miles home, and leaving after lunch on Saturday would give me the maximum time before my absence was discovered,

The irony was that whatever teenage blues prompted the idea, as soon as it became a committed plan of action they vanished. Galvanised and excited, I duly cycled the forty eight miles from Witley to Barnes in a few hours, and as I pushed the bike along the side of our house to the back I passed the open window and could hear my mother on the telephone saying: 'No, he isn't here.'

Whether I was casting around for some kind of sympathy I don't know, but it says a lot, either for the indomitable optimism of human nature, or for my stupidity, that I was taken aback by her fury at my action.

I was suspended for the remaining fortnight of term. The school sent me homework to do and said it was by no means certain I would be allowed to return at all, although I suspected it was an empty threat. The fact was through nobody's fault but my own I was in disgrace and in a worse situation than the one I fled.

Or so I thought until a few days later when the Rolling Stones announced their free concert in Hyde Park – not being away at school I would be able to attend: an extraordinary piece of good fortune.

I was doing a newspaper round at the time, and when I saw the headlines: 'Brian Jones Dead!' I went straight home in a state of shock to read all the papers before delivering them.

The Hyde Park concert became a tribute for Brian Jones, the show must go on. I went to the park the evening before on a number nine bus with a sleeping bag, and in the growing dark I picked a spot that was fairly near the stage. I could have got a lot closer but thought it best to keep a respectful distance from the Hells' Angels who were having a raucous jolly up at the front. I need not have worried but I was only fourteen. The only regret was that my brother Tom was not allowed to come with me.

The next day was a scorcher and I became ever more dehydrated as we sat through interminable blues bands twiddling away in the sun. The park was jammed by 10am. The only other group I remember without looking it up (which would be cheating) was Family with Roger Chapman on vocals.

Incidentally, forty five years later I was the compère at the Rhythm Festival with Roger Chapman on the bill and I met him backstage. I introduced myself and excitedly told him I'd seen him support the Rolling Stones at Hyde Park in 1969. His eyes were a lot less shiny than mine knowing full well I hadn't been to any of his other concerts in the intervening forty five years, but I digress.

'If you learnt bass,' I said to Pete one day at school as we walked to the woods for a smoke, 'we could form a band!' So Pete built himself a bass in woodwork. It was pear drop-shaped like Brian Jones's, and also painted white.

For the name of the group we came up with Denniss and the Lapels, a deliberately meaningless moniker. The band was mostly theoretical, a schoolboy fantasy. I knew little of music, mostly ejaculating very fast but meaningless fountains of notes untroubled by key or construction in a parody of blues guitarists. But I knew some chords and tried to write songs. Chris MacDonnell and his brother John, recent bad boy arrivals, played rhythm guitar and drums. Chris taught me what the blues was and how to play 'Blue Suede Shoes', for which I remain eternally grateful.

It was around that time, 1971, in the holidays, that Pete rang up one winter's afternoon and told me he knew where we could score some 'shit'.

'Where?' I whispered.

'Eel Pie Island,' he said.

I had heard about Eel Pie: a little isle on the Thames. The Stones had played there in the early 1960s. We knew there was a hippy commune on the island and the place had a groovy underground reputation.

It was dark when we walked across the curved footbridge and Pete led me to some waste ground towards a shed where a hippy was selling hash. We joined a short queue and, in as low a voice as my register would allow, I copied the bloke in front and asked for 'a quid deal man'.

It was Pakistani Black. We went halves on it but Pete had to get home so we didn't smoke it together. That night I waited until the house was asleep and decided, as it was my first time, to get extra high and smoke two joints in a row. Dear reader, I smoked them in the garden shed and it was horrible. I felt sick: I puked, I lay still, I sweated. It was hugely disappointing and the experience put me off smoking pot for the next couple of years.

Later I grew to like hash, but never Pakistani Black, which simply turns you into a cabbage. The whole point of drugs as with drink is to stimulate the mind, expand consciousness and enhance conversation. After a nice joint of Red Lebanese, say, or Gold Leb., or Nepalese Temple Ball, or Durban Poison, all courtesy of 'Mr Nice' Howard Marks's illegal import business, you felt you were on the very lip of enlightenment. Indeed sometimes you were, and stumbled upon elemental truths. Alas, the amount you needed to smoke in order to gain such insight was just enough to incur the unfortunate side-effect of obliterating it from your memory the following day.

Robbery

At school one Saturday afternoon, Pete and I went to the village shop, outside which was a cigarette machine – this area was out of bounds. That day a happy fault in the machine's mechanism gave us both the cigarettes and our money back, every time, until the column was empty. The yield was about eleven packets of ten Players No 6 and our criminal hearts hammered with excitement as we walked back to school promising each other not to tell anyone. I hid them in the neck of the soft guitar case under my bed.

Two days later somebody nicked them and I was furious. Knowing I was but the robber robbed, my moral indignation could hardly survive, but my irritation did.

Eleven years later in a London Underground station an amiable chap from school I didn't immediately recognise, Dave Torch, approached and introduced himself. He'd just flown back from a holiday in the sun and was feeling most unwell. He confessed it was he who had stolen my fags at school and it had been on his conscience ever since. As at the end of an Agatha Christie story, I was surprised it turned out to be Torch, the last one you would have suspected. I'd had him down as a good man. Dear reader, he is a good man. There and then he gave me his two hundred duty-free cigarettes by way of atonement which made me very happy and I ardently forgave him.

Debut Gig

One afternoon in the school hall there was a sort of variety show and I was allowed to perform a song on the guitar. I roped in Pete, Thompson and Wright to wear blue boiler suits and dance about behind me in a parody of Pan's People, while I played acoustic guitar and sang 'Clarke's Smile', my latest song.

After the spirited rendition there was great applause. Nick Miller from the year above shouted 'Bravo! Encore!' and instigated a standing ovation. The row was deafening. Not having an encore prepared I played a free form version of Richie Havens' 'Freedom'. I had stumbled on to the path of my future career.

Afterwards I was feted like a hero and showered with praise. And most wonderfully Sandra Philpott, the sexiest girl in the school, was giving me all the come-on a boy could want. We snogged behind the sheds and she told me she loved me. The ecstasy was almost more than this boy could bear.

That concert was my first experience of the extraordinary sexual attraction that playing guitar can lend a man. Music has magical properties that I can only begin to understand, but does that matter? You don't need to know how an engine works to drive the car.

I didn't learn much at the school except some history. Being constantly distracted by the girls, it was all Mills and Boon teenage crushes, snogging and trying to negotiate one-handed the unhooking mechanisms on bra straps.

By the time we reached 16, me and Pete were ready to leave school and the school thought so too. We were considered a subversive influence, although generally being pleasant and polite it was hard for them to pin anything specific on us. The call of the social revolution in the world outside became ever louder. I knew you didn't need qualifications to grow your hair, take drugs, play music, and drop out, as the papers we read, like *International Times*, *OZ*, and *Gandalf's Garden* were encouraging us to do.

Hendrix, Led Zeppelin, Taj Mahal, the Deviants, Taste, Black Sabbath, Soft Machine, Cream. We were dying to get out and join the revolution and do our bit to make the world a better place. Peace and love? Where do we sign? I'd lost my virginity to Beverley Harvest, a recent arrival, in the scout tent in the woods, and there was nothing further the school could offer me.

Pete and I were expelled after the plug was pulled on our Denniss and the Lapels' debut gig at the Leavers' Dance and we became drunk and belligerent. They'd already expelled the MacDonnell brothers, the drummer and the other guitarist, the week before so Nick Miller, a military drummer, was filling in. Our mistake was to play the worst songs first. We never got to play 'Body' with me doing my Mick Jagger act and singing 'Are wown yer bough dare' to a bass solo.

Next morning, whilst awaiting the sugar for my cornflakes at breakfast I was dragged out of the dining hall before it arrived. Pete and I were escorted to Witley station and put on the next train to Waterloo. Mary Watts, a form mate, wailed at the school gates.

5

Chiswick Poly

I was rescued by Jacqueline when I was about fourteen: she could see how unhappy I was at my mother's, and suggested I move in with them permanently at St Margarets, near Richmond. Dad agreed and had a loft conversion built atop the house for a bedroom. Living with them free from the daily insanity of being shouted at for no reason was an enormous relief.

Enrolled at Chiswick Polytechnic in Bath Road, Turnham Green, to take A-level English and Art, and a Drama course, I was thrilled when my father gave me, out of the blue, a Honda 50cc motorbike. He worked out it would soon pay for itself and be much cheaper than him paying my public transport costs. It saved him a fortune. To have transportation was such a boon, and no congestion, however bad, can prevent a Honda 50 from getting through it. The bike may not have gone above 40mph, but I made sure it seldom went much below it either, which became a skill; and whizzing along between the lanes of stationary traffic, going up Richmond Hill on a sunny afternoon, for instance, Pete and I would amuse ourselves by pausing alongside a smart car, and say to the driver: 'You ought to get one of these, mate!' and then zoom on.

OK, the Honda 50 didn't look very cool with its cream plastic shin guards, but I didn't care: wheels meant freedom. On a bike everywhere is reachable quickly. Chiswick Poly was ten minutes away. And in the evenings, I had transport to all parties, dances, and social events, with room on the pillion for a friend – all at a trifling cost. So, on a typical morning at breakfast, Jacqueline was smartly dressed for work, Anabelle was in school uniform, I was growing my hair, Rolande was making the porridge, and Radio 1 was on the radio – just like a normal family.

On the Honda in term time, I would turn left at the Hogarth Roundabout to the large house where Mary Moore ran the drama course. She was a Geordie who spoke like Glenda Jackson and was equally formidable

Mary Moore believed in the technique of breaking her pupils down and rebuilding them, only better. She was forty three, blonde, attractive, single, and with a will of steel. And she was passionate about drama and the theatre.

I was seventeen, unconstrained, freed of the shackles of petty authority, and hungry for fun. I was still wary of smoking dope after the Eel Pie score, so I got into pep pills, Blues and Dexedrine, and bought them at L'Auberge by Richmond Bridge. We just missed out on the sixties era of Purple Hearts. To take five Dexedrine pills on the way to college is to feel absolutely splendid all day. If Mary Moore wanted us to pretend to be a tree, man I'd be the best tree in the world! The trouble is, speed had the most unpleasant comedown and eventually the up wasn't worth the down. I would lie in bed exhausted, nerves jangling, and longing for sleep. The nearest thing I had to a tranquilliser was playing Anabelle's Leonard Cohen album over and over again. Quite soon I stopped the pep pills, I didn't want to become addicted. Hash, LSD and beer now became the drugs of choice.

We hung around in the Chiswick Poly common-room where there was a table-football table. You could smoke joints, listen to music and generally socialise. There would be regular dances of an evening where everybody drank loads of beer and danced like mad to all the records: Bachman Turner Overdrive, Slade, Sweet, Status Quo and Stones songs, like 'Jumping Jack Flash'. I used to love nothing better than this flamboyant gyratory free form dancing exercise, exploring shapes, endorphin-happy and drenched in sweat.

But then disco music was invented, and discotheques which were hard-nut places with a dress code, e.g. white socks and black loafers – and weren't for the likes of us long-haired students. Discos didn't play the Stones or the Who or Black Sabbath; they played disco music.

It wasn't until Gaz Mayall came to the rescue with his famous club 'Gaz's Rockin' Blues', that I found a place where I could freely dance again. In 1971 we were listening to his dad: John Mayall's Bluesbreakers. And you wouldn't have heard a John Mayall record played in a disco either.

LSD

Me and Pete's first acid trip was, aptly enough, on 5 November 1971. We had read so much about it we had to try it. I bought a tab of LSD off a hippy on the riverbank by Richmond Bridge.

'Have you taken it before?' asked the well-spoken chap with long hair.

'Yes, I have, a couple of times.'

He looked doubtful and then said he would sell me one, but only if I promised to take half of it with a friend, as it was 'very strong'. I was happy to comply with this. The Eel Pie score had taught me that when ingesting unknown drugs start with a minimal dose and work up. It's the same with trying to fly: start on the ground and fly upwards and only when you've mastered that do it from the top of a building.

Pete and I adopted a scientific approach: we knew the trip lasted about eight hours, so the obvious thing was to take it in the morning after a good breakfast, rather than late at night half-pissed. We even had a friend from school, a sweet chap called Tim Craig, who agreed to be our chaperone in case anything should go wrong. I can hardly conceive a more thankless task, and he deserved a medal. We took half the LSD pill each at 11am in the cabin of a shabby boat moored by the Richmond Bridge, belonging to some hospitable old character we had met.

The hippy wasn't kidding: the acid was extremely strong and I can only thank him for insisting we only had half each. Pete and I were sitting opposite each other on bench seats in the small cabin below, when suddenly all the proportions and angles changed. The flat deck beneath our feet became a forty five-degree slope so I was looking down at Pete, who seemed tiny at the bottom of the steep incline. If we swapped sides, it was like being a contestant on *The Chase* staring upwards, with Pete looming large above me; his hair all swirling paisley.

It is impossible to portray acid trips in words, unless you have the descriptive talent of a writer like Nabokov: many have been tempted but I won't even try. The 'acid bore' is one seventies cliche we won't be reviving in this book, thank you very much. But LSD was more extreme than any other drug I have taken, by miles. The acid-tripper needs to be mentally strong and not give in to panic. Things can disconcert you. Like the time at about five in the morning when, after an epic afternoon and night, tripping on Blue Microdot, and immersing ourselves in the *Who's Next* album, Chris MacDonnell and I were by now utterly exhausted and trying to get some sleep. We had to be at college at 10am. We bid each other goodnight and lay in our sleeping bags at our respective ends of the room.

Coming down off acid is not nice: you've had enough, you're longing for the trip to be over and desperate for sleep. To my slight surprise I could hear Chris having a wank. He was being fairly discreet but, yes, dear reader, at a steady even rate, he was at it. Well, fair enough I thought, it's not as if I can get to sleep either; although a wank was the very last thing I felt like doing in my jangled, decimated state. I wanted only sweet oblivion. But each to their own.

I tried to quieten the kaleidoscopically unscrambling, mustang-stampeding thoughts in my brain. The cascade of alphabetical symbols and swirling heraldry was starting to slide down the walls of my mind, like treacle, and abate; and still Chris kept on with his five-knuckle shuffle.

'My word,' I said to myself, 'he's been at it a long time.'

I was keeping my eyes tightly shut as the sun's rays started to emerge in the dawn and I was beginning to worry about Chris. He had been masturbating for so long, and with ever-increasing vigour – surely any man would have come by now? OK: full marks for dogged persistence and unquenchable appetite but his cock must be getting jolly sore by now, and I couldn't help wondering whether his mind was becoming deranged by anxiety and paranoia about his inability to climax. I dearly hoped he wouldn't give in to panic. After about an hour or two of this sort of conjecture, although it's impossible to judge time accurately on acid, I realised that what I had thought was Chris masturbating was simply a bit of nylon sleeping-bag rubbing against my ear as I shivered uncontrollably.

At Chiswick Poly I lasted the A-level course no longer than the first term: the English teacher was completely ineffectual and I cannot learn from someone dull. I was thrown off the course. In Art I would draw grotesque and derivative cartoons in the Ralph Steadman, Gerald Scarfe style but I also had to quit Art as it was part of the A-level package.

Happily, Mary Moore kept me on in her Drama course; Mary was a law unto herself. This worked out well as now I could take a part-time motorbike dispatch delivery job on the trusty Honda 50 to bring in money for all those teenage incidentals such as petrol, beer, fags and pot. In those days, hash was three pounds fifty a quarter ounce, 20 Players No.6 was twenty pence and the cheapest bottle of red wine was fifty pence. After you'd drunk half the bottle it didn't taste so bad. Money was also needed for rock festival tickets, and for tickets to see the Rolling Stones when they came to town.

The dispatch rider job was with a photographic studio: Panline, in tiny Pollen Street, off Maddox Street, off Regent's Street. All my ports of call were in the West End so I didn't feel the need for a bigger bike as the Honda 50 was often as fast as larger bikes in the heavy traffic. I was quite competitive with the other riders. There is an art to weaving in and out of traffic, and being on the bike morning, noon and night, for work and play, meant that I became adept. The job was part-time in term time and full-time in the holidays. My bosses at work knew I was doing a drama course and dubbed me:

'Ed the Ac-torr.'

In between the deliveries I would sit and drink coffee, smoking fags, reading the papers or chatting to Murray, the other delivery man who drove a tiny van. He was a posh, nice-but-dim type in his late thirties with a sun tan, a private income and a flat in Mayfair. The job gave him something to do in the day. He told me he was a keen naturist.

I prided myself in being very efficient and would get a kick when the bosses said, 'Blimey that was quick!' My rounds were regular and I enjoyed the friendly banter with the various staff and receptionists, and also got to know the streets of Soho and Fitzrovia intimately.

I would arrive at 8.30 at the start of a sunny day to see vignettes of early morning London life: shops opening, delivery vans parking, waiters wringing wet cloths into the gutter. This kind of familiarity breeds a sense of ownership. When I weaved around Trafalgar Square in the rush hour, a matador among the four-wheeled bulls, I knew it was my Trafalgar Square as much as it was anyone else's. I'm a Londoner.

The job was to deliver the package, come hell or high water. The mail must get through and if you entrust me with a mission, dear reader, I would sooner die than fail you. It's a question of honour.

On a summer's day lunch hour on the roof with a roll and a drink from the sandwich bar opposite, I would eat and look over London, then smoke a joint of Nepalese Temple Ball and relax for a bit.

One day when Keith Richards was due to appear at Marlborough Street Magistrates Court nearby on a drugs charge, I was there to witness his arrival. It was only twenty minutes before he came out again to be ushered by minders into a Mercedes-Benz whereupon a swarm of paparazzi descended on the car to take photos. I positioned the Honda behind the Mercedes and let my front wheel bang into the photographers' legs accidentally on purpose to get them out of the way, to help my man.

'Oi! Get out of the way! Get on the pavement! Oops, sorry mate! But if you stand in the road, what do you expect?!! Be fair.'

A Stones fan does what he can after all and I followed Keith Richards on the bike at a respectful distance, seeing him safely to Grosvenor Square before turning back...

One fine evening I got off with my first girlfriend at a Chiswick Poly dance. Celia Perry was a very pretty Putney girl on the Fashion course: I adored her and she often stayed the night. Dad and Jacqueline never said they minded and to have a lover was everything I wanted so I was very happy. Having gone to school in the area Celia knew everybody and soon, as her boyfriend, I knew everyone too, and so in turn did Chris and Pete.

There were parties all the time during which I liked to flirt with all the girls and then at the end of the evening whisk Celia home on the Honda, even more certain I was with the most attractive girl at the party. Celia was never the jealous type nor had cause to be. It was the freedom she gave me that tied me to her.

I was round her place one evening watching *Top of the Pops* and she was trying to cut my long pale hair to the style of Brian Connolly, lead singer of the Sweet.

Many events in my life have seemed like happy accidents of chance but are they all coincidences? Every single one? Some seem too neat to be accidental. Was it simply a coincidence that my first girlfriend, Celia Perry, just happened to be a future Mrs Sex Pistol? She was a future Mrs Matlock...

Tom Cooper, Tommy Cooper, and Paul Bradley

There were only about ten or twelve on the drama course at Chiswick Poly. Mary was always wanting more boys to join as it was a bit girl-heavy, making it harder for her to cast plays. There's only so many times you can put on *The House of Bernarda Alba*.

In my second year we were joined by Paul Bradley and Tom Cooper, who were both top chaps. Many years later Paul would find fame in *Eastenders* and *Holby City* while Tom Cooper just happened to be Tommy Cooper's son.

Tom was like a cuddly bear: a bloke with a heart of gold and the loveliest character. He would invite us to the family home in Chiswick and we got to know his mum and sister Vicky. There was a grand piano which Tom played like a dream, giving us recitals of Mantovani and stuff like that. He also loved a drink and would ply us with vodkas but I would be drunk after one, having very little tolerance for alcohol. He would also take us to his local pub and I got a nice little taste of his working-class local.

Above all, Tom was extremely funny: he would regularly have us in fits of laughter. He was a born comedian and possibly a genius. He felt he couldn't pursue a comedy career because of who his father was, although Tom's comedic style was very different from his father's.

Tom didn't want to trade on his father's name, he intended to make it in his own right. Thus, he took his mum's maiden name, called himself Thomas Henty and decided to be a straight actor instead of a comedian. This turned out to be a tragic mistake. Tom made very little headway as an actor and drank himself to death in his early thirties

One evening in his backstreet Chiswick local, Tom introduced me to his dad, who was sitting at the bar. I hadn't been clamouring to meet Tommy Cooper, thinking a famous chap like him would rather be left alone by strangers, but I could hardly refuse.

'Hey dad, meet Ed! He's on my drama course.'

The great man turned his head and I met his baleful gaze. Beyond 'hello' neither of us could think of anything whatsoever to say: he turned back to his drink and that was that.

Another time I saw Tommy Cooper, at the bar of another Chiswick pub, I said hello and he told me there was someone he'd like to introduce me to. It was the old trick of foisting me off onto another bloke who'd been pestering him, killing two birds with one stone as it were. I immediately saw through this ruse and told him in no uncertain terms I wasn't one of those types and wasn't about to bother him anyway! A bit later he got me to promise not to tell his wife that I had seen him in the pub. Now that's more like it.

I was with Celia when I saw the Rolling Stones for the second time at Wembley, in 1971. It is impossible to pick a best-ever Stones show, as ninety nine per cent of them feel like that at the time: but for sheer, jaw-dropping, athletic output on Jagger's part, that performance took some beating. The band had already done a matinee show when we saw them and the odd thing about matinees is that they give you more energy for the evening show rather than using it up. You would have to be blind not to be astonished and thrilled by Jagger's display of superhuman energy and fire. In my opinion he has never had enough recognition for his stagecraft: OK, I know he's had some but nowhere near enough. But then the English are very stingy with their praise, it's one of their worst characteristics.

The Stones were as tight as can be: they rocked the house to bits and I can still remember pivotal moments of Charlie Watts' cymbal work. Dear reader, they nailed it. It was the most ecstatic two hours of my life thus far. Afterwards the happy crowd slowly filed out, dazed and amazed, and when I had recovered sufficiently enough to be able to speak, I asked Celia what she thought of the show.

'It was OK,' she said.

It was as if I'd asked her how her day at the office had been.

On the drama course, from the outset and perhaps as part of the breaking-in process, Mary Moore had only ever given me trifling roles in our drama exercises and plays – bit parts.

I have never liked being sidelined and would sometimes add extra bits of surreal business of my own in the Vic and Bob style which me and Pete were doing at school while Vic and Bob were in short trousers. It was probably hugely irritating but I wasn't on a stage to be marginalised.

In the early days the drama course was a convenient holding-pen for me. After the restrictions of boarding school, I was running wild and free, teenage rampage all the way. The music scene, Celia, parties, and being off my head for as much of the time as possible was the sum of my activities. A great deal of my life has been spent in heading for the uplands of Anaesthesia.

It was the convention in those days. The trouble is, when people start telling you about how out of it they were, it's generally very boring, so I'll only share one example. At a Ducks Deluxe gig I met a girl who took me home with her. The baby in the bedroom rendered me impotent but her flat mates were friendly and had some very strong THC oil which I smoked with them. Later on, very high by now and grooving to the Santana record playing I gradually realised my chin was wedged in the right angle where the toilet door meets the floor, my body in a heap around me, and it wasn't Santana I could hear: it was the cistern refilling.

One afternoon, in a Chiswick Poly rag week, there was a 'folk afternoon' in the common room where, as well as a few featured artists, anyone could take turns to play. I went along and watched many skilled, finger-picking folk guitarists playing their wistful songs. I love folk music now, and I could take some of it then, but as the afternoon progressed it became ever more dreary, precious and boring. One gentle, slow, sensitive song after another.

Eventually I could stand it no longer, and towards the end of the afternoon I begged for a turn. On a borrowed acoustic guitar, I performed 'Blue Suede Shoes' with all the verve and vigour the song deserves and the place went delirious: I stole the show – well, of course, I did. It's a simple law of physics, or as Confucius said: 'If you play slow song after slow song for hours, and then man come play fast song, he will be king.' Elementary, my dear Watson.

At Plumpton Rock Festival, while still at school, my admiration for hippie culture faded somewhat. When I saw a central casting, archetypal hippy with long hair, beads and fringed jacket I went up to him and said, 'Peace, man!' Dear reader, he told me to fuck off! OK, I had short hair, but my heart was in the right place. Man, I was shocked.

Image-wise I naturally copied Keith Richards, who was more of a pirate than a hippy, which would do me.

Mescaline

At one festival I bought a mescaline pill, the only time I've ever seen or taken one.

It was a grey afternoon pouring with rain and I was somewhere in the middle of the mass of fans in front of the stage, huddled in a ball, quite dry under a clear plastic sheet. As the music played, I watched one of the many raindrops trickling down the outside of the plastic as it merged into another drop never to be seen again. I felt I'd learnt something about life and death and the circularity of nature. There were uncountable drops but if you followed one of them you had a sense of travel. These drops were absolute beauties: not only did they vibrate to the rhythm of the universe, they also moved in time to the music and perfectly reflected the interconnectedness of everything. It was as if a crumb of infinite wisdom had fallen to me from the high table of the ancients.

Seldom, I warrant, has a man in a field under a polythene sheet in the pouring rain been quite as content, fulfilled and philosophically satisfied as I was then.

Back at college, I was provided with another piece of insight. I always make a point of being friendly with anybody serving food, including our canteen ladies. They were kind and maternal towards me. One lunchtime when I was angry for some reason, one of them said to me, 'You know, Ed, when someone is angry, it usually means they are angry with themselves'. I knew she spoke the truth and loved her for that piece of wisdom.

Velvet Underground

Pete and I were still trying to keep our dream of Denniss and the Lapels going and we rehearsed in a Twickenham youth club one evening a week but our free form mode of musical expression was making no headway.

One day some of the kids from the youth club came to watch us, and were unimpressed.

'Do you know any T-Rex?' they said.

We didn't. Everyone likes a song they know and we didn't know any. As well as that, our drummer John MacDonnell was becoming increasingly fed up with our lack of progress.

After one rehearsal he said: 'And another thing: what sort of a name is Denniss and the Lapels anyway?! We should call ourselves something like...Red Hot Penis!'

John was ahead of his time: now why didn't I think of that?

Our schoolboy group slowly petered out but I played my guitar every day, and tried to make up songs. This routine continues to this day but, having learning difficulties, my technical progress has been slow compared to others. After twenty years on the guitar I became proficient, after thirty years I was a lot better, after forty years I was pretty good and after fifty years I became very good, which even in England is hardly a boast.

Neil, the polytechnic social secretary, hired the bands to play the college hall. Among others I saw Screaming Lord Sutch and the Crazy World of Arthur Brown. I was extremely impressed with how filthy and greasy Arthur Brown's long hair looked. I tried to imitate the look, took silt from the gutter and mixed it with water and worked that into my hair: quite useless. What would have worked was a liberal application of old engine oil, if I'd thought of it.

On one occasion Neil used up the entire college entertainment budget for the year on hiring the Velvet Underground for five hundred pounds. He put them on at Acton Town Hall which was a huge place and he assumed he'd make a killing on the ticket sales. There was some nice Nepalese Temple Ball around at the time, as well as some Red Lebanese.

I don't know if he'd smoked too much of it but Neil had forgotten to advertise the gig at all and come the night there were only the eleven of us Chiswick Poly common room cronies there, hugging the back wall of the vast hall where, about 100 yards away across the expanse of empty polished parquet floor, was the stage.

The Velvet Underground, whom I was mad about at the time, came on and started playing. Fuck this, I thought, I'm going down the front. It took a little bit of courage to walk the lonely walk, but what's the matter with everyone: this is Velvet Underground for heaven's sake! I went and stood by the stage. None of the others followed so for the whole gig it was just the Velvet Underground and me, with nobody else for yards around.

The band betrayed no emotion, said not a word, and doggedly ploughed through their contractual obligation. But they played all the songs I wanted to hear – 'Sister Ray', 'White Light/White Heat', 'Heroin' et al. It would have been better for everyone, of course, if the place had been packed, but it was quite funny to have them playing just for me.

Chiswick Poly Third Year 1974

At the end of the second and final year of the drama course Mary Moore helped me prepare some audition pieces with a view to getting me into a drama school. She applied to East15, the Rose Bruford Training College of Speech and Drama and the Drama Centre on my behalf. She thought I would stand a better chance of getting into one of those places than the more famous schools.

I was turned down by every single one but rather than bid me a regretful goodbye before casting me out into the world with no prospects Mary, with all the kindness of a Geordie heart, had other ideas.

'I've invented a third-year course, Ed,' she said, 'so you can stay on another year.'

And that was when everything improved. In this third year Mary took me seriously. She gave me leading parts in the plays, encouragement, and the opportunity to shine. And shine I did. Give me responsibility and I shall never let you down. Give me a leading role and I will give you a leading performance, give me your friendship and I will give you mine, treat me like a cunt and... you can see where I'm going with this.

It's not a chicken and egg situation: faith shown comes first, and is the catalyst for success. After a year of the only kind of treatment under which I shine, Mary Moore decided I should apply for RADA. We also applied to the London Academy of Music and Drama, LAMDA, and the Central School of Speech and Drama. I had to prepare a Shakespeare piece and a modern piece for my audition. For the Shakespeare Mary chose a *Richard II* speech, 'Of comfort no man speak'; for the modern piece I was a violent yobbo going mad from *The Sport of My Mad Mother* by Ann Jellicoe. In the event, I was turned down by Central but offered a place at LAMDA. There would be a delay before I heard back from RADA which was a problem: I wouldn't hear whether I'd got into RADA before the deadline for accepting the LAMDA offer expired.

My self-confidence may have grown but not by that much, and I wasn't going to gamble on being accepted at RADA. Especially as I'd had two more recalls after the initial audition which meant I must be a fairly borderline case.

At the last recall, it was just me and one other young man, with Hugh Cruttwell, the Principal, for a 'workshop'.

He had us do our Shakespeare pieces again so he could re-direct them. I went first: 'Of comfort no man speak.'

'Stop!' said Cruttwell.

He told me he couldn't bear the way I did it and said it was awful and mannered. He made me do it again in a completely different way, and then again in many other different ways.

Naturally I tried to oblige and do as he asked, jumping through the hoops he presented as best I could.

But when it was the other actor's turn to have his audition piece redirected, I couldn't understand why he kept doing the speech exactly the same way every time whatever Cruttwell said to steer it in a different direction. He was incapable of altering his interpretation by a single jot.

A bird in the hand being worth two in the bush, I accepted a place at LAMDA, and Dad, who was very pleased, filled out the forms for a council grant.

Thus it was, in September 1974, that I started at LAMDA. The main building was in the Cromwell Road, and the other rooms and annexes were dotted about the Earl's Court area so we had to walk through the streets to reach our classes. Nigel Planer was in my year and we were just starting to become friends when, two weeks into the term, I received a letter offering me a place at RADA.

I was chuffed to bits and Dad was utterly amazed. He couldn't believe it and didn't stop saying so. The extent of his amazement revealed the measure of his estimation and it started to piss me off. But there was no question of my refusing the RADA offer, so Dad duly coughed up the term's fees forfeit for LAMDA.

Bollocks to walking the streets of Earl's Court like some waif, when I could be at the beautifully-equipped premises of the Royal Academy! It had two theatres, a canteen, bar, a common room, and a range of studios and rehearsal rooms – and was meant to be the best.

RADA didn't begin until January so Mary Moore had me back to guest star in her Christmas production of the Ben Travers *Rookery Nook* farce.

I was the golden boy, the first of her pupils to win a place at RADA —and I basked in her approval.

PART TWO

6

The Royal Academy of Dramatic Art

In Burton Street, tucked away across the road from Euston Station, Caradoc King, trying to make it in the literary world, was squatting on the top floor of the end house of the terrace. He contacted me to say there was a room free in the house next door if I wanted it and I am eternally grateful for the tip. I was nearly twenty and had to leave home eventually: here was my opportunity. Needing no second bidding I bagged the first floor of 44 Burton Street by fitting a padlock to the door. There was no hot water or electricity, nothing but a sink in the back room with running water. But it had the great advantage of being a ten-minute walk from RADA.

Next door Caradoc, who had electricity, gave me a line from the adaptor in his kitchen out of the window and down into mine. All my electricity needs were drawn from a third of one of his plug sockets.

On the ground floor below me was Cledwyn, a Welshman who looked like Captain Haddock, with a Donovan-type denim cap. He liked a drink, and played up his Welshness with theatrical relish.

On warm days Cled would sit outside the house with a glass of sherry and, in his broad Welsh dialect, proposition every passing woman he fancied, inviting them indoors to go to bed with him. He told me he was often refused, but by no means always.

'If you don't ask, you don't get,' went his irrefutable logic. Cled addressed me as 'you middle class cunt', which as it wasn't meant nastily came across as affectionate and is actually much friendlier than someone being merely polite, when you can't tell whether they mean it or not.

The most vivid character on the street was 'Bookrunner Bill' who lived in the basement next door, and was a ringer for Bill Sykes. A huge and violent-looking man with a sweaty red face, he had a black mongrel dog, wore two overcoats and a hat, and a handkerchief around his neck. He carried a holdall filled with books, said he was a 'learned man', and quoted Bernard Shaw to me. When we were eventually evicted his basement was deemed a health hazard: every bit of floor and every surface was covered with cider bottles full of piss. But where else was he meant to go? He didn't have a toilet and being a learned man, he wasn't going to piss on the floor, was he?

Above me was Nik who was literally 'perfecting ways of making sealing wax': something in which he finally succeeded because, dear reader, you can buy 'Nikwax' at any leading store today.

Next door on the ground floor in what used to be a shop, lived Barry, a raggedy old junk dealer and hoarder whose place made Steptoe's seem tidy. I'd see him pushing an old trolley filled with scrap along the road to his lair.

In total contrast was Jack, a silver-haired old gentleman of about sixty five who was a bit like the drunk old buffer on *The Fast Show*. He had been a wealthy businessman: top job in the city, a wife and children and a house in Eaton Square, but he lost everything due to his alcoholism. Though he was a disgrace to his family and an outcast, he was granted an annuity. When his cheque arrived, he would stay at The Ritz for a week or two living in the style to which he was accustomed until the funds ran out. And then it was back to Burton Street and the carefree life he preferred.

In the mornings I walked to RADA across Tavistock Square and through Gordon Square, taking the horticultural route to Gower Street. John, a friendly retired policeman, was at the front desk to greet me. He never got over my once wearing two ties at the same time. Then up to the locker-room to change into T-shirts and tights for a movement class with June Kemp. This was essentially an aerobic workout to pop music and most invigorating. Then a voice class with Robert Palmer who looked like the kind of male model seen adorning the walls of old-fashioned barber shops. Robert was a sweetheart. His signature warm-up exercise was 'King Ha! King Ho!': I've never gone on stage without using it since.

'King...ha; King... Ho! KING-HA; KING... HO!'

Madame Fedro was in her late seventies and was an extraordinarily eccentric Polish lady who had once been a great star – as she never tired of reminding us. She would have us travel diagonally across the room in various ways and for the first couple of classes I couldn't help but weep with hysterical laughter: as if at a Norman Wisdom film – she seemed so batty and what we were doing seemed so bonkers. But there was method in her madness: in time I came to understand and appreciate Madame Fedro's immense value as a teacher. She taught me much about presence, poise and focus. She demonstrated how society figures moved in the eighteenth century (and the seventeenth come to that) the manner in which they sat down and arose from chairs, for instance, or how to perform a sweeping bow with a hat in the correct way for the period. I was receptive to her methods and she earned my respect: and you couldn't help but admire her outrageous style. She felt she was above the rules that applied to ordinary mortals. She would drive the wrong way up Gower Street and park bang outside the Academy on a triple yellow line in a bus lane.

'I don't care, my darling,' she would say, puffing her cigarette in its holder, and handing the car keys to John as if he was a doorman at the Dorchester. 'I am a great star; so relaaax!' She got away with it as she was simply telling the truth: it's a credit to Cruttwell's discrimination in perceiving her worth that he employed her when most others would not have.

Stage fighting with Henry Marshall was where I learned swordplay. I also learned how to handle various weapons, from a rapier to a dagger, from a double-handed broadsword or sabre to a pike, and how to stand and move, to lunge and parry, to cut and thrust, to maim and kill – but only pretending.

My fellow student Andy Wilde and I would, after classes, do real fencing with masks and foils too, for the fun of it – surely swordplay is in the DNA of every Englishman. Andy was the best actor I saw in my time there.

After classes we'd go to the RADA bar, run by a friendly couple called Peter and Peter. It was there I would meet Gary Whelan and Andrew Seear, friends from the term above mine. Gary Whelan was a second-generation Irish immigrant and raised on the mean streets of Islington. He told me he'd learned to fight at school when the other boys teased him because his family could only afford to give him bread and dripping sandwiches for lunch. He became the best fighter in the school. Gary could be spellbinding with jaw-dropping tales of outrageous exploits. How much was embellished in the interests of a good story hardly matters but it was a lot less embellished than many would have believed.

If we weren't rehearsing in the evening we'd go to the Marlborough Arms around the corner. Gary would get into fights there sometimes and it would be a Wild West-style pandemonium with tables overturned, chairs and fists flying, and Gary always coming out on top. He told me that in a fight you have to go instantly into a hundred percent all-out nuclear attack mode. He was a hellraiser in the old tradition. Is the breed extinct? I was standing at a bus stop late one night, having been out drinking with Gary, when I was arrested by the police and thrown into a cell. It was a case of mistaken identity as I was wearing his hat. I can't recall what it was he was meant to have done.

Andrew Seear was a Cambridge graduate capable of spinning stories with such virtuoso turns of phrase and rich vocabulary I would seek out his company for the sheer pleasure of hearing him talk – and he waxed ever more eloquent with every pint he drank. I prefer being in the company of people cleverer than me and was more than happy to let him do most of the talking. I earned my place at the table by being able to make him laugh, and getting my round in. A prodigious drinker, it was with Andrew I learned how to drink more than two pints of beer without becoming completely pissed.

Fate had led me to drama school, and I went with the flow,

enjoying every day and living in the absolute present, as a dog does.

I admired Laurence Olivier, John Gielgud and Ralph Richardson, the ageing theatrical knights who had made their reputations in the theatrical heyday of the thirties and forties. I liked the idea of being an actor: wearing a large hat and a cape and carrying a cane, and speaking in a booming voice. Albert Finney in *The Dresser* is my idea of a proper actor.

But RADA wasn't like that at all and those inclinations were ridiculed and quashed. Any signs of personal flamboyance were frowned upon and seen as a sign of lack of seriousness. When Michael McCallion, another voice teacher who actually hit me once, saw me walking down Gower Street wearing a fedora hat he was most cutting about it. Mind you, I can see it from his point of view: what right had I to be such a cocky little git?

We were meant to be serious, humble and to dress down. The dressing down thing is incredibly important to actors. Actors cannot bear to wear clothes with even the faintest hint of elegance. The only time you will ever see a well-dressed actor is when they're on stage or screen, but never in real life.

There was still a persistent notion in some circles that RADA was like a kind of finishing school for debutantes, and where everyone was posh. Now while it seems to be going back to that in terms of social class, it wasn't the case at all in 1975. There were all sorts of accents. One chap from a remote village in Yorkshire was dyslexic so he couldn't read, and had an accent as broad as bread. People were chosen for their signs of acting potential, irrespective of formal education.

Anton Lesser was in my term and from the outset it was clear that he would succeed. He was singleminded and the flame of his ambition burned bright. And he was a very polished actor. He once gave some of us a bollocking for larking around in a class, and told us he was there to work. It was a fair point and we were duly chastened. Dear reader, Anton Lesser is now one of our leading classical actors. He knew where he was going and he went there.

My approach to acting was to imagine that I was the person in the role so absolutely that I didn't need to do any acting: I could simply be.

Kevin McNally, a couple of terms above me, is an effortlessly brilliant actor, fully-formed even then – he was and is a lovely man, always very friendly and amusing in the common room, and he loved a spliff between classes along with Ciarán Hinds, who is also a very nice chap. Ciarán would sit on the sofa in the common room as high as a kite, smiling, benign and amiable to all.

Tim Spall, another gem and a Wandsworth boy, arrived in the term below me. Juliet Stevenson was there too. She elevates the art of acting into a high art form. And Imelda Staunton was always very nice to me. I didn't really get to know those girls well but I always appreciated their unfailing friendliness in the RADA bar when our paths did cross. I never forget an act of kindness. One element of what makes for a star is to be gracious and kind, which is why almost all the stars I've had dealings with have been both good people and easy to work with.

As at Chiswick Poly, attending the Royal Academy was to be in a carefree holding pen. There was nothing not to like, whether it was rehearsing a sabre fight with Ian Dixon, having a singing lesson with Mr Atkins, an improvisation class with Ben Bennison, or a Jacob's Club with David Shaw-Parker, it was all fun. And I would always do a solo guitar spot at the new intake parties pretending to be Keith Richards.

Early in the first term, in a class with singing-teacher Beth Boyd, she was testing our voices, having us sing a simple tune in turn. I went after Ian Dixon.

'You've got a good voice,' she said.

'Thanks!' I said, chuffed to bits.

Chuffed to bits, that is to say, in the nanosecond before realising she was referring to Dixon's voice not mine. The embarrassment was acute, I blushed crimson. Anger followed in shame's footsteps at both having my fantasy of being a singer exposed, and for it being so comprehensively shot down. The excruciating incident lasted about five seconds. Though to be fair to Ian Dixon, he did have a beautiful voice – as golden as his character.

Rolling Stones at Earl's Court

The Rolling Stones were playing at Earl's Court in 1976 and my brother Tom had blagged a job as an usher, the lucky sod. Meanwhile, my seat was on the back row of the stalls: I was about as far away from the stage as you could be.

I deliberately turned up dressed ultra-straight in a tweed jacket, and had no valuables with me. For the first ten minutes of the concert, I was creeping commando-style up to the front. My reasoning was that if I was challenged, I could play the dimwit and they probably wouldn't chuck me out. As I got very near the stage, chuckling audience members were actually helping me to get even nearer – as they pickpocketed me.

But I'd foreseen that might happen and had nothing of value on me beyond a bag of sweets, the loss of which, being a grown man, I could take.

The plan worked; I was now at the very front and it was a fabulous show. For a nanosecond me and Mick locked eyes. Jagger was giving me that same look he has on the cover of the *Black and Blue* album. That classic Stones look. Oh man, I was in heaven.

This was the tour when the stage opened up like a flower and Mick was doing his Little Lord Fauntleroy act. Everyone goes on about David Bowie's various personas; what about Mick's? He's given us many versions of Mick Jagger, and as in playing *Richard III*, there's more than one way to play the role. With Mick, each Jagger persona is so definitive in the moment it obliterates memories of other versions.

Ralph Richardson

We were all very excited when Sir Ralph Richardson, the great old theatrical superstar and knight of the realm, came to give us a talk in our Vanbrugh Theatre. There was a throne-like chair ready for him on stage next to a table upon which sat an empty glass and an empty jug. The theatre was packed with students eagerly waiting.

Ralph was introduced and lumbered on to much applause and sat down in the chair. He must have clocked immediately that the stage manager had forgotten to fill the jug with water but he didn't let on. He extracted maximum comic potential from the situation when he poured himself a glass of invisible water and mimed drinking. Everyone roared with laughter as he carried on talking, pretending not to notice. When he 'refilled' his glass and then poured it all over his head it brought the house down. And when the red-faced stage manager hurried onto the stage from the wings with some actual water, she got a standing ovation.

Ralph Richardson was a lovely, unpompous, funny man.

'Has anyone got a question?' he asked. My hand shot up.

'What is your name?'

'Tudor Pole, sir.'

'You've got a good voice. Tell me Tudor Pole, in your time at RADA has anyone tried to shoot you?' Much laughter.

'Not to the best of my knowledge,' I said, which also got a laugh. Whereupon Ralph Richardson leaned back in his grand chair, and with a perfect degree of studied theatricality gazed up into the heavens and in a slow tremulous voice, he said: 'Ah, times have changed.'

And this also brought the house down. I was most chuffed to have been Ralph Richardson's 'feed'. That wonderfully theatrical amusing type of grand actor was a dying breed, already being supplanted by the earnest types we have today – all jeans and T-shirts, left-wing, posh and dull.

Lindsay Kemp

It was in 1975 that I saw a show which made a colossal impression: Lindsay Kemp's *Flowers* at the Bloomsbury Theatre. Lindsay Kemp on stage was an extraordinary, glittering, shimmering creature; his bald head painted white, and with a mad mischievous glint in his eyes. It took him about two minutes to walk from the back of the stage to the front, in slow motion, five seconds per footstep, with bits of confetti or petals dropping from his hands outstretched in front of him as he quivered, like a man insane. I was riveted. I'd never seen anything like it.

The show is in a category of its own: an otherworldly collage of theatrical effects, lights and movement, tormented creatures in hell, and Mozart's *Requiem* playing as Jean Genet's story ends with the shattering impact of Kemp's gory death. But it was his appearance that totally blew my mind and I could not speak for about fifteen minutes afterwards, so poleaxed was I by Kemp's mesmeric theatrical potency. I would later imitate him.

And then we were evicted from Burton Street. It is most unpleasant to have one's home taken away. I had nowhere to go and no money to rent anywhere. My brother Tom was squatting with his friends in a damp, dank basement in Albany Street by Regent's Park. Less hardy folk would have considered it uninhabitable. I had no choice but to accept Mum's offer to rent the ex-lodger's room at her house in Mortlake, near the railway station.

I found out later that as soon as our end of Burton Street was evicted Johnny Rotten and Shane MacGowan, amongst others, moved in and squatted at the other end of Burton Street.

Tim Spall to the Rescue

On a late-night train journey from Waterloo to Mortlake I was accompanied by two RADA pals: Tim Spall and Hamish Reid who were getting off before me at Putney. I had been in a play that evening, and in my hurry to fit in a couple of pints at the Marlborough Arms before the last train back I'd not bothered to remove my stage make-up and I was looking pretty as well as being drunk.

Also in the compartment with us was an Australian man who was chatting to us. He was staring at me in an odd way. Tim and Hamish were sitting in between me and the man and they didn't get off at Putney as they said they would. They were worried about leaving me alone with this sinister Australian. I must have also had an intimation of danger, for when we got to Mortlake, I was first out of the door and through the barrier. Tim and Hamish delayed the Australian, who was desperate to catch me, for as long as they could, by waffling and blocking the exit as they 'searched' for their tickets. He elbowed them out of the way and ran into the night to find me. But I'd long since raced down the dark side road and was home in a flash. Poor old Tim and Hamish were now stuck in a lonely suburb, miles from home, the last train gone, and having to find a cab.

But they saved my life that night.

7

The Visitors

I left drama school in April 1977 when the punk rock scene was exploding. 'Look Ed, they're copying you!' said my RADA colleagues. The first time I heard the Sex Pistols was when Tessa Pollitt, soon-to-be bass player of The Slits, played me 'Anarchy in the UK' in her bedsit next to the Tabard pub in Turnham Green. I chuckled with the laughter of recognition. At last, another bad boy band to liven things up.

I immediately got what punk was about, and I also thought I could write songs that were just as good or better than the ones I was hearing. Had I not been making up songs for years?

Being at RADA is so intense and all-consuming there is no room for any life outside it. This is how it should be in the arts but it meant that I didn't go to a punk gig until 1977 – Generation X at the Marquee.

I had to gear myself up beforehand as I was feeling a little nervous and I wore a shiny grey jacket with half a twenty pound note pinned to my lapel, two ties and an inky old shirt. I needn't have worried as the vibe in the club was as friendly that night as it always and ever was.

'Sheena is a Punk Rocker' by The Ramones and The Modern Lovers' 'Roadrunner' were all over the radio and The Stranglers.

'Your Generation' by Generation X was a particular favourite and I hurled myself round to it in my room, along with 'Borstal Breakout' by Sham 69 whom I adored and 'In The City' by The Jam. I instinctively knew what the scene was about and understood the licence it gave us. I loved the violent rebel stance and hardly a day went by without a tale in the mainstream press of the latest bout of bad behaviour by the Sex Pistols. Walking with Pete one afternoon in a suburb, we read another shocking story about the Sex Pistols in the *Evening Standard*. 'You should be in that group, Ed!' he said, laughing.

After leaving RADA I went to a few theatre auditions without success. The punk movement was exploding across the land and a minor acting job in some provincial theatre, which it wasn't likely I would be offered anyway, seemed very small beer in comparison to the cultural revolution. It didn't take long to reach the logical conclusion: 'Sod acting for a lark, I want to be in a band.'

I replied to an ad in the back of the *Melody Maker* for 'Wild frontman wanted'. I had to pluck up some courage to actually dial the number and I put on a different voice, although I knew I was as punk as anyone, if that meant rebelling against petty authority.

The audition was in Chiswick and the band, called The Mirrors, was led by Mike Andrews, who wrote the fast, slick keyboard-driven songs. Apart from the drummer, Gary Long, who was the son of a Hereford butcher, it was a bunch of middle-class blokes. Gary was very charming and I was impressed by his flamboyant drumming style.

Mike was convinced The Mirrors would make it because they could play 'so much better than the other punk bands' – which, of course, was totally missing the point. I was the only 'punk' involved but I was delighted to be asked to join. I was over the moon to actually be in a proper group. Ever one for plunging in at the deep end, I wrote 'The Mirrors' on my acoustic guitar and pledged undying loyalty.

Their last singer had been fired and the band was already well-rehearsed so all I had to do was learn the songs and then we could start gigging.

It was October 1977 and Mike had now changed the name to The Visitors. I learned not to write on guitars. My first proper rehearsal was at two o'clock one afternoon, and in best RADA-trained fashion I turned up to the studio a quarter of an hour early for a vocal warm-up ready to begin on the dot of two. An hour later Jerry, the keyboard player, turned up but it wasn't until 3.30 that everyone was there and ready to play. So I learned that an hour, at least, must be added to the official start time before I needed to show up. This was hard to do as I've always hated being unpunctual.

I learnt about counting in fours, called bars, so as to come in at the right point – this may sound obvious but I still had little musical technique: when I sang my own songs I came in when I felt like it.

The first show was in late October 1977 in the foyer of the Unicorn Theatre in Great Newport Street, off the Charing Cross Road, on a Sunday. Mike had worked as a stage manager on the original production of *The Rocky Horror Show* in the King's Road, and was calling in a favour.

I was very excited at the prospect of performing. I was determined to make Mick Jagger look like he's standing still, and couldn't sleep a wink all night.

Come the gig I launched into the first song and gave it my all, going into a frenzy and jerking around like 'someone with Tourette's syndrome undergoing electroshock therapy' as a review later put it. The music dictates the physical moves, and this music was so fast you couldn't really dance to it, only twitch and flick.

Halfway through the second song I was seriously out of breath, and by the fourth song I wanted to die, and there were eleven more songs to go! Aaagh.

The hand of fate kindly intervened when one of the telephones on the tables behind us started to ring. I called for quiet and picked up the receiver. It was a man complaining about the noise: a gift I gleefully exploited to the full. Putting on my old-buffer voice, I sympathised with the caller, telling him he couldn't possibly hate the horrible racket any more than I did. We bemoaned the depravity of young people today and the crowd loved it. I replaced the receiver and on we played, now fully re-energised.

Having learned the hard way how fit a rock and roll frontman needs to be, I took up running the following day – a routine I kept up for twenty years.

Meanwhile, on tour in America, John Lydon quit the Sex Pistols – this was dismal news. I could understand the reasons, but it seemed far too soon.

As for The Visitors, a *Melody Maker* review by Chris Brazier of a Marquee gig said:

'All the musicians can play, Mike Andrews' guitar being clear-lined and fluid...the only technical doubt centring (sic) on the colourless and limited-range vocals of Eddie Tudor Pole. He acts the cretin, and plays up the disconcerting bug-eyed weirdness of his appearance.'

It was now March 1978 and this bit of negative press persuaded The Visitors I was a liability and therefore had to go. The unanimous verdict was delivered at a summit meeting and Gary Long said: 'Sorry, Ed, you're holding up our progress.'

I took it on the chin but it was a bleakly familiar feeling and depressing to take in that I wasn't wanted. I rode my bike back to Mortlake blank with delayed misery.

And then my brother saved me. Knowing how unhappy I was, living in my mother's house, Tom invited me to share the basement of his squat in Albany Street, a large house by Regent's Park opposite The Queen's Head & Artichoke pub. He and his girlfriend had the front basement room and despite it being a dark and extremely damp rear room, I was grateful for the kind offer – anywhere was preferable to where I was.

Diary: 2 May 1978[1]:

'I have been working on a basement room at 27 Albany St. NW1 converting it from a virtual slum, with slime, to reasonable accommodation. At last I am moving out of Mortlake and will once more be independent of maternal hassles.

I am looking forward to the move although there is only a cold tap on the floor above. But this only indicates how used to mod-cons I am getting.'

The first night I cuddled up close to my girlfriend Buttie on a bed made from two metal frames on milk-crates with a mattress on top.

1 Most of the Tenpole Tudor songs were written in that basement at 27 Albany Street (now no.17).

After about five days the electric fire, permanently on, began to make the room a bit warmer if not drier. Us humans are the most adaptable animals on the planet and even though it was grim I soon got used to living there.

This huge house of dilapidated grandeur alongside Regent's Park was romantic and perfectly-situated. I could play the guitar to my heart's content and without inhibition – the minimum conditions conducive to the writing of songs. On the rear wall, by the rickety old French windows which led to a sloping chute up to ground level undergrowth and a meagre light source, I daubed on the wall: 'WIN', as a memo and a guide.

If we had spent our dole money on drink and drugs, we could pick up dropped vegetables at the markets, buy potatoes and make a vegetable stew on a small electric stove. There was a kitchen room upstairs but it was never used except once when my girlfriend bought some supplies and cooked breakfast. Two years later when I next visited the room, the butter wrapping was still in its perfect cube shape on the sideboard though devoid of any butter: I think the ants ate it.

I would go to Sam's for meals, our local cafe in Cleveland Street near the Post Office Tower. Sam was a Kenyan who had worked with the Brits in Africa in the colonial era. He was as charming, eloquent and friendly as every other Kenyan I've met. Sam adored my brother and every time I went in, without fail, he'd say, 'How's Tom?'.

One Sunday morning I bought a nice pair of black brogues from a tramp in Sam's for ten pounds. He had two pairs in a suitcase: one black, one brown. When I tried to knock him down to eight quid he said, 'Oi, you know they're worth a tenner!' I knew he was right and paid up and I still have them to this day.

Off Cleveland Street was Warren Street, which was famous for its car-dealerships in those days. It was also where Boy George and Culture Club were squatting a few years hence. In fact, the first time I saw these dolled up New Romantics was at Sam's cafe: I thought they looked terrific but I was too shy to introduce myself – in my leather jacket and motorbike boots I felt at a distinct sartorial disadvantage.

Also on Warren Street was an old-fashioned dairy with blue tiles run by Miss Evans, an elderly white-haired Welsh lady who was always very friendly to us young punky-looking types. 'I am on your side!' she used to say. I occasionally used to see Kenneth Williams walking about, as he lived round the corner in a block of flats (now demolished) by The White House Hotel. One time I saw him with his cheeks puffed out, as if he were playing the trumpet and I wondered whether he was doing it as a disguise. Miss Evans told me he'd recently bought forty cartons of Long Life milk. We could only think that it was for bathing in, Cleopatra-style. You wouldn't want to drink the stuff.

For a while The Clash lived next door to us in Jasper Conran's house, who was embarking on his fashion design career. The band weren't there often as they were constantly working. One hot summer's afternoon I spotted the four of them in the next-door garden, through the foliage, on their own, talking in the sun, in front of the Corinthian pillars of the house. I was yet to meet them. It may not have been exactly punk, but where we lived was certainly fit for rock stars.

Somewhat at a loss around that time I clearly recall a conversation with myself which went:

'OK Ed, so what do you want to do?'

'I want to make music, I want to be a rock and roll singer.'

'So what do you need to do that?'

'An electric guitar for starters (all rockers have electric guitars).'

'What do you need to get that?'

'Money.'

'How can you get some money?'

'Get a job.'

So logic dictated that the first step towards making my dreams come true was to get another dispatch rider job, this time for Bureau De Change and with a motorbike included: a 200cc Honda.

Along with the currency I was ferrying around town, I tried to bring jollity to cheer up the workers trapped in their booths all day long. I felt sorry for them: they were confined whereas I was free as a bird. It wasn't all plain sailing though: one day, I narrowly avoided a collision with a poorly-driven limousine in Regent's Street and I lost my temper, cursing the driver roundly before roaring away. Minutes later, driving down Dean Street by the Jazz Pizza Express, a van shot out of a side road and my left knee acted as the brake as it smashed into the van. It was instant karma at work and a useful lesson to learn. If you are horrid to others horrid things happen to you. Dear reader, don't risk it.

The Bureau De Change were kind enough to give me a desk job in the Head Office basement while my knee healed. Under the supervision of Mr Patel, my job was to add up columns of figures and make them tally. It always took many attempts before they did but if they didn't there was no way of telling whether the error was mine or in the books. But for two weeks only I was very happy to be a bank clerk and chatting to the amiable Mr Patel.

In the Queen's Head & Artichoke over the road, having a pint with my leg bandaged, stretched out straight, I was getting solicitous enquiries from the other local squatters ('Poor old you!', 'Oh bad luck!' etc.) and then Steve Smith came in and told me he had a headache once, which made me roar with laughter and cheered me up no end. I spent the rest of the evening with him.

Regent's Park was our private night time playground and Pete and I would slip in through a gap in the railings after dark, especially on a full moon. We'd howl by the wolf enclosure by the Zoo, trying to commune with them, or stroll about in the open moonlight, high as kites and trying to work out the meaning of life.

From the top floor of our house, we could climb out of a hatch and walk over the rooftops down to the Marylebone Road, via a huge deserted Dunlop tyre factory which we could enter and explore: three floors of open warehouse space with junk and debris around. It looked exactly like the set of every gangster film you've ever seen in the final shootout. We didn't need money to live like princes. What greater privilege is there than freedom? Freedom from petty restraints and from people who think that telling other people what to do is acceptable. Freedom from the suburbs, from bills, from cramped accommodation. Freedom to play the guitar. Freedom to sing!

Hardly a day went by when I didn't thank the Lord for my good fortune in being granted such an estate. OK, there was no hot water but we could always boil a kettle and in those days you could hire a bathroom in Euston Station, a ten-minute walk away.

I had to have the electric fire permanently on all day, every day in the basement but we were yet to receive a bill. The glass was broken on the front of the electricity meter at the bottom of the steps, and someone before my time had jammed a fag butt under the disc to stop it rotating and clocking up the score. Only once did an inspector come round to read the meter. I heard the man announce his presence up at the front door and then saw his uniformed legs coming into view as he descended the basement steps – giving me just enough time to remove the cigarette end.

'I've come to read the meter, mate.'

'O hello, er...I am not sure where the meter is actually.'

'Don't worry about that, here it is...'Ere, do you know the glass on the front of your meter is broken?'

'Is it really?'

'You want to get that seen to, mate,' he said.

'I will!' I said.

He read the meter, I saw him out, and then replaced the butt. We never did get a bill.

Before the motorbike job I was signing on the dole which was £9 per week and on one occasion I was so penniless I was driven to walk from Regent's Park to Mortlake to request a pound from my mother. On the way, striding through Notting Hill, I was accosted by a tramp: 'Excuse me, mate, can you spare ten pence for a cup of tea?'

'Man, I have not even one pence! Otherwise I wouldn't be having to walk, as I am, all the way from Regent's Park to Mortlake, now would I?!'

His jaw dropped in amazement and I strode on. It was good to meet the beggar on more equal terms for a change, and without guilt.

Having absorbed my words the tramp caught up with me and not only apologised but offered me ten pence to help me out! I was almost overwhelmed by this kind gesture and heaped praise upon him. I continued my journey very much happier, my soul enriched. Whether you call it 'God' or 'Good' it does exist, dear reader.

By now I'd bought myself an electric guitar.

8
Sex Pistols

In June 1978 I got a message to call a chap called Chris: he'd been a fan of mine in The Visitors and had kept in contact – he could never understand why I'd been sacked from the group. I rang him from a phone box in Covent Garden and he told me the Sex Pistols were holding auditions for a singer the following day.

'You should go for it, Ed' he said. 'You'd be perfect.'

I had not spotted the tiny ad in the back of the *NME* and he gave me the instruction to turn up at The Duke of York's Theatre the following day at 11a.m. I stepped out of that telephone box jettisoned into a different reality: I felt dizzy, my mouth was dry and I had the sickening feeling I would get the job. I couldn't see how I could fail. Who else could top the furnace of my intensity? Who else could suggest such potential for violence? Who could possibly be better than me? My heart hammered with a level of excitement and adrenaline hitherto unknown.

Later that day, walking hand in hand down Cleveland Street with Buttie, I wondered what name I should call myself: 'Eddie' seemed overworked, what with Eddie Cochrane, and Eddie and the Hot Rods so for some reason I decided to call myself 'Ten' Tudor Pole. It seemed a suitably offbeat choice of name. Next day I turned up at the theatre at 11 o'clock wearing a vintage pair of tapered blue 1950s Swiss skiing trousers inherited from my stepmother Jacqueline.

I entered through the unmanned stage door and walked straight onto the stage, the most commanding position in the building. A few people, including Julien Temple, were milling about in the mostly empty auditorium. 'Are these the auditions for Hamlet?' I said, which got a big laugh.

('Well, it seems to be going OK so far,' I said to myself, ten seconds into my destiny.)

Julien Temple, Boogie and Roadent and a film crew were there, dotted about in the stalls. I walked down from the stage and joined the gaggle of other young hopefuls who had turned up. One lad from up North had come along dressed exactly like Johnny Rotten. I knew he wouldn't get it. They asked for my name: 'Ten Tudor Pole' I said, trying out the new moniker for the first time.

We were herded into a tiny office and given lyric sheets for the song we were to sing, and a demo of it was in rotation on a cassette player. It was called 'The Great Rock 'n' Roll Swindle' – not one of Steve Jones' finest moments as I'm sure he would agree: it is a leaden song, with a rotten chorus.

You do your best, though. There was a weeding-out process: we were each filmed singing the song on stage to a backing track. There was no sign of any Sex Pistols. Three or four of us were eventually told to come back the next day to do it again, this time with the band. It was made clear it wasn't an audition to be the new singer of the Sex Pistols as such; they said they simply wanted people to sing with the group for the film they were making.

The next day I came back and someone said, 'Ah, hello Ten. Go and sit in the stalls, Ten, and wait; as not everyone's here yet, Ten.'

Ten??!! TEN?? I HATED being called Ten. It sounded like the name of a cretin. It had to go: it fell at the very first fence. Being called 'Ten' was intolerable. Mental note to self: definitely get a better stage name!

When Sid Vicious and Nancy Spungen staggered and stumbled into the auditorium, they knew perfectly well the dramatic effect their entrance made, with all eyes turned on them. Sid looked pissed off and was plainly drugged. He sat down a few rows in front of us, while Nancy continued down the aisle to the stage. She climbed onto it and started doing a mock striptease, singing the trombone part of a tuneless strip tune. It was cringe-making: neither amusing nor remotely sexy. She too was obviously smacked up which generally renders people charmless, and when she got down to her bra and pants, she said in a whiny broad New York accent: 'The rest is resoived for Siddy boy.'

Steve Jones and Paul Cook turned up and, after the briefest of handshakes with them, I sat at the back trying to look nonchalant along with the others.

At one point, perhaps aware that everybody was staring at the back of his head, Sid turned round and mumbled fairly half-heartedly: 'Why don't you lot all fuck off.'

'Bollocks!' said a lad spiritedly, sitting behind me and thrilled to be in the same room as his hero. Energised to anger, Sid suddenly came alive and said, 'What! You dare say bollocks to me, you cunt?'

He arose from his slumped position and headed up the aisle straight towards the lad, clearly intent on violence.

I also stood up and looked on as Sid then started punching the boy who was forced to defend himself as best he could but without wanting to hurt Sid back. It was all over in a flurry: handbags at dawn, and before long they were sitting next to each other behind me, chatting away quite amiably.

I heard Sid say, 'Yeah, it's a good way to make friends with people, by having a fight with them.'

Sid Vicious, because he knew he wasn't in the band for his musical abilities, felt he had to behave badly to validate his position. Hardly a week would go by without a lurid press story of him fighting in a club and causing trouble.

And then it was my turn to be onstage with the remaining three-quarters of the Sex Pistols to perform 'The Great Rock 'n' Roll Swindle' song for the cameras. I was all bug-eyed, manic and crazed, and despite having no liking for the tune or the rhythm I had to pretend I did.

My antics made Steve and Paul laugh and in one of the takes I turned around and caught Sid about to kick me up the arse. In the headlights of my insane glare, he ran back to his spot like he'd been caught out in a game of Grandmother's footsteps. After that thrilling day I strolled home to Albany Street floating on a cloud. It was difficult to absorb. I had just been on stage with the blooming Sex Pistols, the most infamous group in the land! It was an impossible schoolboy fantasy come to life.

Ordering a pint in The Queen's Head & Artichoke I mentioned what I'd just done to someone at the bar: I had to tell someone. The Irish landlord overheard me and said he didn't believe a word, but I didn't care, I knew it was true. It was a magical unforgettable day in rock and roll fairytale land. Cheery with beer I went back to my squat for a smoke by the ever-radiant electric fire with a big smile on my face. And that I thought would be that.

Malcolm McLaren and Julien Temple were trying to make a film about the Sex Pistols without John Lydon, who had quit the band and wanted no part in it. Which is a bit like trying to make a film about the Rolling Stones without Mick Jagger, but Malcolm had plans to get round that; he always had plans. A week later Glitterbest made contact and said they wanted me to record a lead vocal onto a version of 'Rock Around the Clock' recorded by Steve and Paul.

I went to a small vocal overdub studio with Julien Temple and sang the song many times. Obviously, we wanted to punk it up, like Sid did in his rendition of 'My Way'. The trouble is, it is very hard to sing 'Rock Around the Clock' and not sound like Bill Haley, the squarest man in rock and roll, which is why I don't sing it live, but I just about managed it on the record. I added some bad language including the word cunt.

The record was once played over the closing titles of *Top of the Pops*, so I can claim to be the first, and last, man to sing 'cunt' on *TOTP*. Although to be fair, so broad was the accent and so exaggerated the vowels, it's very hard to identify. A Japanese girl came in to add screams and squeals which also helped to de-Haley-fy it.

Now I was going to be in the film, and had sung 'Rock Around the Clock' with the Sex Pistols. Once again I thought that would be it.

A few days after the audition Malcolm McLaren said to me, 'I want you to write a song called "Who Killed Bambi".' 'Who Killed Bambi' was the working title of the film he was making.

Russ Meyer, the cult American film director famous for featuring large-breasted women, had been Malcolm's first choice for director and some footage was shot, but when Meyer hired someone to kill a deer with an arrow, the crew walked out in protest and Meyer was fired.

I didn't know about any of this at the time; I didn't know anything. I was tagging along with events, a mere spectator, submitting entirely to the dictates of fate. As soon as I got home, I dutifully began strumming on my acoustic guitar trying to write the song. The only clue I had was the title, so I sang that:

'Who killed Bambi, Who killed Bambee!'

I took the commission seriously, thrilled to be recognised as a songwriter, but how did Malcolm know I could write songs? He seemed to assume I could, which, dear reader, gave me the power to do it.

It is faith shown that releases the talent, a prime example being when Chuck Berry was first offered a recording contract to record 'Maybelline' and 'Wee Wee Hours'. It was in the narrow gap after he'd signed the contract and before the first recording session that he went home and wrote 'Johnny B. Goode', his biggest hit. He was empowered, as was I, by the faith shown in his abilities.

Four hours later Malcolm came round to Albany Street to see how I was getting on. He liked the gimmicky way I sang 'Who killed Bam-booy' but didn't think much of the rest. He told me to keep working on it and he'd come back four hours later.

It was invigorating to be given such an onerous responsibility: Pete had jokingly said that I should join the Sex Pistols, and now I was writing a song for them! Spurred on with pride and excitement I strummed away trying this and trying that. For the verses I nicked the tune of 'One Man Went to Mow' but was at a total loss when it came to what the words could be.

Four hours later Malcolm came back. He liked a bit more of what I was doing but only a bit. He said he'd come round another four hours later. I went out for a meal. The third or fourth time he came round he brought Bernie Rhodes with him, manager of The Clash, who recorded me on a ghettoblaster singing a couple of versions of the song on guitar, such as it was, and then they left.

A day or two later Malcolm brought Vivienne Westwood round, his girlfriend and partner, to check me out. She was a serious and earnest woman quite devoid of any small talk, and we were both a bit shy. She didn't stay long; but told me most emphatically that punk was: 'To be original and create your own look' which remains my favourite definition. The delightful conundrum is that if you think you can define what punk is all about it proves you don't really understand it.

Malcolm's plan at this time, he said, was to feature me in the film singing 'Who Killed Bambi' in the subway as a busker. Vivienne wrote some verses for 'Who Killed Bambi', and with a bit of co-writing we came up with the final version of the lyrics. Most of them are hers. McLaren came up with the title, the verse tune is traditional, the chorus tune is mine. Becoming enthused with the song, and inclined to thinking big, it wasn't long before Malcolm decided to upgrade the 'Who Killed Bambi' musical accompaniment from a single guitar to a forty-piece orchestra. A meeting was set up with the classically-trained orchestral arranger Andrew Pryce Jackman.

I took my acoustic guitar to Andrew's studio and played him the song. In the chorus when it came to the fifth 'Who Killed Bambi' in a row, he said,

'Hang on, shouldn't it go to the "A" there?'

'Yes, of course,' I said: twigging instantly that he was right and it should, although it never had before. Thank you, Andrew. I went home, and Pryce Jackman set to writing the orchestral score. I thrummed with excitement, and smoked lots of joints to calm down a bit and slow my hammering heart. It may have been his idea to give 'Who Killed Bambi' a Mexican flavour, and he did an excellent job on the orchestration.

It was now full steam ahead: Malcolm planned to have the song recorded and filmed by the following week. On 8 January 1979,

I turned up at a studio in Wembley just as the Royal Philharmonic Orchestra, hired for the occasion, had finished recording the forty-piece backing track. I'd missed it.

No one had thought I might like to see the orchestra record my debut song, but I quickly had to pull that arrow of disappointment from my heart and forget about it. Time was money and it was now time for me to sing my part, to record 'Who Killed Bambi' into a microphone, for the Sex Pistols.

'Have you been in a recording studio before?' they asked.

'Oh yes,' I said, not exactly lying, as at RADA I'd played a policeman in a studio recording of a radio play we made one afternoon. But how hard could it be? 'Face the microphone and sing' ought to do the trick, I thought.

I could hardly believe what was happening. It was like a dream. When I was a boy, I used to imagine Mick and Keith coming to the front door to rescue me. This was on a par with that. But I dared not let my mind dwell on the bigger picture. Like a tennis player I had to stay in the immediate present.

Shown into the recording booth, I was given a pair of headphones and I started doing my Robert Palmer warm-up routines:

'King- ha! King- Ho!'

I sang a couple of versions and Malcolm said: 'Be more punk. You're singing too nicely.' We kept going and I was giving it plenty, but he didn't like what I was doing much, kept saying, 'Do it again, but be more punk!'

Nothing if not game to give him what he wanted I tried my utmost to be ever more vocally extreme, more nuts, more angry and more crazed with each take – assuming that was what he meant by 'more punk'.

Dear reader, I tried this and I tried that, I tried everything I could think of. Thirty times he said, 'No. Do it again.'

He worked me very hard. I was drenched in sweat, my voice was shredded, but he didn't let up. And nor did I. We did take after take after take.

Eventually, exhausted, on about the thirty ninth go, in a kind of desperation, I yelled: 'Who Killed BambaAAY, DaddaAAAYY!!'

which primal scream popped up from deep within. At which point Malcolm called it a day. I sensed I'd embarrassed him: the D-word making him uncomfortable. We spent the next hour going through all thirty nine takes choosing the craziest version of each line, phrase or word, and sticking them all together onto one track. It sounded completely bonkers. 'Jumping Jack Flash' it was not.

After all those takes, I was spent, but it was good to be driven that hard and to be made to go that far in. I like to be worked, to be jockeyed and forced to dig deep. Ever since then when recording, it is very annoying when I've done one or two takes of a song and hardly warmed up the engine, let alone begun, for people to say: 'Well done Ed, that's great. We've got it!!'

No mate, we haven't got it: we haven't even started. Why are people not greedier for greatness? Why don't they go for it? Why do they seem to assume it's not attainable?

When I said to Malcolm that I did not want to be called Ten Tudor Pole he agreed, 'I've changed it to Ten Pole Tudor! That's much better'.

'B-b-but I don't like that either!' I said, dismayed.

'That's too bad,' said Malcolm, 'we've just had ten thousand album sleeves printed up of the new Sex Pistols album, on which you are billed as Ten Pole Tudor.'

Dear reader, how could I complain? I took a rough mix of 'Bambi' back to Albany Street and played it to Tom. It is not a record that is trying to be liked, and bemused by its madness, Tom said:

'Well, it's not great, but it's not *too* bad.'

This was Tom being kind – in truth, I didn't know what to make of the record either.

The Filming of Who Killed Bambi

Originally Malcolm said that in the film I would be singing in an underground station. I was delighted when this busker idea was jettisoned in favour of having me sing the song in the foyer of a cinema as an usher; along with a host of classic 1950s British comedy film stars as my supporting cast.

Thus, on 10 January 1979, a few days after we'd made the record, we filmed the 'Who Killed Bambi' sequence in the foyer of the Rainbow Theatre in Finsbury Park, within which they had built a smaller fake cinema foyer for the set. I turned up on my motorbike at 9am and donned the burgundy-coloured nylon usher's jacket we had bought from kitchen staff outfitters: Denny's, in Soho the day before.

The set was teeming with film crew, props men, set designers, carpenters, lighting-men, hair and make-up, continuity-lady, extras, producers, McLaren, Steve Jones and Paul Cook, Temple, Boogie and Glitterbest's Sophie. There were some famous faces from cinema I recognised and my lovely co-star, the wonderful Irene Handl.

I was introduced to her as 'Ten Pole Tudor' and as quick as a flash she said, 'Hello Tadpole'.

Irene played an usherette and it was immediately apparent that she was a good sort. I was thrilled to be working with such a legendary star. She was a writer she told me, and that acting was more of a secondary pursuit. I fetched her a cup of tea.

In my role as a cinema employee, singing the song and utilising the props, I danced round the foyer with an old-fashioned upright hoover, which doubled as a microphone stand. I also served at the drinks and popcorn counter, all the while leaping around and miming to the playback of 'Who Killed Bambi'. The craziness of the rendition on the soundtrack engendered the crazy performance in the foyer and the hoover was my dance partner.

In take after take, for hour after hour, I simply reacted to the music, every time, and gave my crazed, over-the-top, absolute all. It was hilarious. I knew I was on it, and let everything rip. Everyone was laughing and everything seemed to be going splendidly: it felt special. Knowing that the whole day was based around me and my song brought out my best. There is always lots of hanging around whilst filming and at one point Irene said to me, ''Ere Tadpole, do you think they'd let me take this tray off? It's ever so heavy'.

Dear reader, she had been standing there for about half an hour with the heavy ice-cream and Kia-Ora tray around her shoulders.

I helped her take it off immediately. Being a professional she wasn't going to remove the prop until instructed and I realised that no one was looking after her. So after that I took care of her. There was never anything remotely resembling a gentlemanly vibe in the Glitterbest world.

Mary Millington the porn star turned up and we shook hands. She was in the scene where I serve a queue of famous British film faces going past the popcorn counter, like Liz Frazer and Julian Holloway from the *Carry On* films. Steve Jones later told me he got Mary Millington to fellate him, which is typical Steve: his powers of persuasion in that respect were extraordinary. With all the nonchalant swagger of a stevedore working the fairground dodgems, Steve Jones could seemingly get any girl to fellate him at the drop of a hat.

I was full of admiration and wonder at his sexual confidence, daring to hope these skills were somehow bestowed when one became a bona fide rock star. From all I had read about rock groups it seemed like they were. Mind you, Mary and Steve had a scene together in the stalls where they are meant to be being naughty, so they were somewhat thrown together, you could say. Steve Jones is definitely the 'sex' in the Sex Pistols.

At around teatime with everybody loving my performance, and knowing I was doing well, I was emboldened to ask Julien whether I was getting any money for all this fine work. He looked awkward and went and asked Malcolm the same question. Malcolm frowned and said, 'Give him one hundred pounds out of petty cash'.

That was my fee for the day and it was a good job I asked, otherwise I would have got nothing. I was delighted with the hundred pounds.

Many more times did I mime to the song, with the unflagging energy of youth. In one scene I had to throw hamburgers at the patrons, in another I had to look at the TV and say, responding to a news report, 'Sid Vicious has been arrested!' and 'Brazil'. Thirty years later a Glaswegian, out of nowhere, approached me on the street and said 'Hey Tenpole, say "Brazil!"'

At 7 pm, when Malcolm and Julien were satisfied they had all the footage we wanted, I was released and I roared back to Albany Street. Whilst lifting my Honda onto its stand by the railings outside my house, Phil Payne and Rob Rousers of a local Mod band the Low Numbers walked by.

'You'll never guess what I've just done!!' I babbled. 'Come and eat with me, I'm starving: and I'm paying! I'll tell you all about it.' I had ten tenners and it felt like a fortune.

We went to the Indian restaurant in Cleveland Street and as we sat down, I ordered a couple of bottles of wine. The staff looked a little sheepish and there was a certain tension in the air as the waiter informed me I'd have to pay in advance for the wine.

'Oh, I see. You don't think I can afford the wine. I assure you my good man, I most certainly can!'

I pulled the sheaf of brown banknotes from my pocket, peeled off a couple, and handed them over. He thanked me, looking embarrassed. Then I told the lads all about the most exciting day of my life so far, relishing every detail along with the delicious food.

And when it came to the bill the wine was on the house.

I soon got used to the name and began to like being called 'Tenpole' (though never Eddie).

The Great Rock 'n' Roll Swindle double album by the Sex Pistols, including my composition, was due for release soon. I heard from somebody at Glitterbest that Rob Dickins, at Warner Brothers publishing, wanted to see me. Communication was old-fashioned at the time: I would call the Glitterbest office from one of the Great Portland Street station telephone boxes every couple of days to see whether there was any news and there always was.

Rob Dickins had a reputation of being a cut above your average A&R man in that he actually went along to all the greasy clubs and pubs to check out the new groups in person, often with his mate Clive Langer. If he saw any genuine talent he was there before his competitors and first in line to sign them up. Rob Dickins was naturally proud that he had got to the Sex Pistols first and signed up their publishing rights to Warners.

I made an appointment to meet him and strode down Berners Street to the Warner Brothers offices, just round the corner from the 100 Club, feeling very important. I was shown up to his office and the first thing Rob Dickins said to me was: 'Tenpole, I am going to shower you with money!'

'That sounds nice,' I said, grinning like an idiot.

He offered me a publishing deal, (provided 'Who Killed Bambi' was included) with a six-thousand-pound advance. To me this was an absolute fortune, something like a lottery win. Dickins had seen a rough cut of the *Swindle* film and he loved the 'Who Killed Bambi' sequence. He said: 'That scene will make you a star, Tenpole, when the film comes out.' I said yes to the publishing contract.

One of Malcolm's great themes was how Sid Vicious was the true star of the Sex Pistols and how he was going to record Sid singing a whole album of Frank Sinatra songs. He was constantly bubbling with ideas and trying to work out the best way for the Pistols to carry on without John Lydon who was now in the process, along with Virgin Records, of taking McLaren to court.

The latest plan was to release 'Who Killed Bambi' and 'Silly Thing' as a double A-side – on Valentine's Day. Again, my heart was beating with excitement.

Although he never turned up to the band rehearsals, Malcolm used to come round to Albany Street. One time he brought Julien Temple, the most monosyllabic man I have ever met. Steve Jones and Vivienne Westwood may have had no small talk: Julien Temple had no talk. Not that he needed any with Malcolm around, who was all talk, and always highly entertaining.

There were some younger kids from the estate I'd befriended and with Malcolm we sometimes went to The Green Man pub by Great Portland Street tube station where he would keep us all enthralled with stories as he riffed with his imagination, becoming ever more inventive and hilarious as the night wore on, defining and exploring the possibilities of punk rock as he talked – with each idea more outrageous and hilarious than the one before.

Malcolm never drank pints; he would have first a rum, say, then a vodka, then a gin, then a whisky, with no apparent rhyme or reason. He didn't take drugs either, that I ever saw: his imagination was his entertainment.

On 10 December, 1978, reports of Sid Vicious being arrested in New York on suspicion of the murder of Nancy Spungen in a hotel room were all over the news. It was extremely shocking. I felt sorry for Sid but having seen Nancy Spungen at the audition, I wasn't surprised she'd driven somebody to kill her.

9

Steve Jones

Next door to Sam's cafe in Cleveland Street was a Christian youth club, 'The 3 Cs', run by a bloke called Jeremy, who was very straight and very nice.

Having made friends with Phil Payne, Rob Rousers and Del the drummer from The Low Numbers, they asked me to help them out on vocals for a gig they had at the club.

Because I had been onstage with the Sex Pistols I had respect from these boys. Phil wrote good songs and the band had enthusiasm, which are most of the ingredients you need. It was fun singing 'Police and Thieves' with them. Also on the bill was a young Ska band called The Invaders with Chris Foreman on guitar. They would go on to become Madness when Graham McPherson, aka Suggs, joined soon after.

One dank day in November, Steve Jones called round while I was out and left a note written on the back of a bit of fag-packet saying, 'Ring Steve Jones tonight 402 9897 8 o'clock.'

Journal 20 November 1978

'I'm going to join the Sex Pistols!!! Steve Jones and Paul Cook came round. They want me as the vocalist in their new group which will have a new name. Possibly The Swankers. I'm jolly thrilled. It's fab. This could be my break into stardom at long bloody last.'

I liked Steve although we were both shy and didn't really know what to say to each other. On the surface we had little in common except our love of music. I couldn't help but be awed to have the star guitarist of the most notorious group in the land, whom I read about every day in the papers, now in my basement talking about getting a band together. I was aware of my inferiority to Steve, not being working class, but at least my accommodation lent some punk credibility.

Thank heaven I wasn't living at my mother's.

Steve took me to 'Anwars', a vegetarian Indian restaurant off the Tottenham Court Road, and told me something of his story. He was gentle and kind and talked about Sweet, Slade, Roxy Music, T-Rex, Bowie, all the music we liked before punk. We both loved the swagger and groove of those flashy pop groups.

Another thing Steve and I had in common was being musicians: we were more into being on stage playing than being 'punks'. Steve was and always will be a rock and roll guitar supremo and he was ever insistent that we 'Give it plenty of bollocks'– his battle cry oft repeated. Paul Cook was friendly too but didn't say a lot – Sex Pistols don't do small talk.

We walked through Soho one sunny afternoon and Steve told us to 'Wait 'ere a minute' while he nipped into a 'Model Upstairs' doorway. Five or seven minutes later he emerged, doing up his flies. When I once visited a brass it took me infinitely longer to undress and then get dressed again than did the act itself. Steve, I realised, didn't bother taking his clothes off: now why didn't I think of that? Steve craved sex all the time; if children are sexually abused they can grow up to be highly sexualised. His stepfather was a nonce.

Me, Steve and Paul rehearsed at their small rehearsal room in Denmark Street, aka 'Tin Pan Alley', off the Charing Cross Road. This legendary music street was a location befitting their status and we had some terrific rehearsals: six in all, where we rocked the place to bits every time. Steve is such a great guitarist, and playing through an H&H amp, he sounded like three guitars at once which elevated me to the highest levels of endeavour. When McLaren said the band couldn't play their instruments it was a great line but quite untrue.

We began to work up a set and I was grateful to have gained

some basic musical knowledge from The Visitors. I certainly needed it now. When Steve said to come in after two and a half bars, I knew what he meant. I hurled myself around the room as I sang. We also had a long-haired chap called Andy Allen (ex-Lightning Raiders and later to be in The Professionals) on bass and it was around this time a paragraph appeared in the *NME* with Steve saying the new singer was 'better than Rotten'.

There is anxiety as well as a thrill when you read about yourself in the papers. You need a certain reckless frame of mind and to be ready for anything. In the control room of my consciousness I was but an observer to unfolding developments, and as curious as the next man to know what happens next.

Meanwhile in England at 'SHAM'S LAST STAND' at The Rainbow were my old mates The Low Numbers, bottom of the bill, and they had asked me to sing 'Respectable' with them. What? Sing a Rolling Stones song to a packed-out Rainbow Theatre? Er... yes please.

By now Sham 69 had unwittingly become a magnet for ultra right-wing skinhead factions like the National Front. Their gigs became flashpoints for violence and the situation had got beyond the band's control. When every show ends with the police being called you know it's time to pack it in – hence the farewell show. Sham 69 are not in the least violent or racist and Jimmy Pursey is more of a flower-power type of bloke if anything, even Pierrot-like.

The atmosphere before the gig in the now-demolished Sir George Robey pub across the road, packed with skinheads, was ominous. They were out to 'Get Pursey' and said so. They were intent on some kind of revenge, for what I never knew.

Dear reader, they hated me on sight: my very presence was as a red rag to a bull. Coins were thrown very hard which hurt, and you can't see them coming... Ow! But I am fearless on stage, and throwing myself into the performance I became a rapidly-moving target and it was over in a flash.

When Sham hit the stage the crowd started 'Seig heil-ing'. There was an observation gantry high up at the back from where I watched the mob below driving Pursey to tears: he implored them in vain to embrace the principles of peace and good vibes but soon the band had no option but to beat a hasty retreat. The fire curtain came down in a trice and prevented the stage-invading mob of thugs from penetrating backstage. They didn't get Pursey.

On 3 February, 1979 it was all over the papers, SID VICIOUS DEAD! While Sid was on bail in New York, Sid's mother (a junkie herself) had given him a mercy-killing heroin overdose. That's what I believed did happen. It was arguably the kind thing to do and certainly kinder than sprinkling a little heroin on the fairy-cake she gave him as an eighth birthday treat.

It was all very shocking although there was a grim sense of inevitability about it. The press will always lionise a fragile star who looks like they are going to die young. That's why, for a while, Pete Doherty was never out of the papers with lurid stories of his drug-taking and general excess. When it eventually became clear he had an iron constitution and wasn't about to die any time soon the papers dropped him like a hot brick.

Exit Malcolm

And then came another bombshell and it was all over for Malcolm McLaren. Lydon and Richard Branson successfully sued him for mismanagement of funds: i.e. spending the lads' royalty money on making the film. Malcolm saw it as reinvesting but that was how they got him. He certainly wasn't stealing the money for himself. Above all Malcolm McLaren was an artist and The Sex Pistols was his palette. He was ousted and prevented from having any further dealings with the band.

When Malcolm was a student, he and some pals dressed up as Father Christmas. They went into a large toy shop and handed out toys from the shelves to all the children in the store.

'Look Mummy! Santa's given me a Scalextric set!' Chaos ensued. That's McLaren in a nutshell. For something to be punk there has to be humour in the mix on some level or another. If it's all serious, it's not punk. If it's all serious it's rubbish anyway.

Being forbidden from having anything more to do with the Sex Pistols or Glitterbest was a massive loss to Malcolm, like Van Gogh having his paints and canvas nicked. It hit him hard.

We had in common unhappy childhoods and a lack of maternal affection. Soon afterwards a feverish Malcolm came round with his latest plan: that I go with him to Paris and be filmed singing whilst having sex with fifteen-year-old girls. What?! For a start, I said, having sex and singing don't go together as each requires one's full attention. Anyway, I pointed out I wouldn't be able to get the horn under such conditions.

'Oh, don't worry about that, we can sort *that* out!' he said airily, swatting the objection away like a fly.

'B-b-but, I don't want to be a Porn Star, I want to get a band together!'

'We've DONE rock and roll, Tenpole. That's old hat!', he said. I told him that whilst he may have 'done rock and roll', I had not.

Malcolm said: 'Sex is the laughter of genius', and went to Paris without me. The last time I saw Malcolm, a quarter of a century later, shortly before he died of cancer, he took me to lunch in Charlotte Street telling me how he'd just blagged five hundred thousand dollars from a Hollywood studio for his idea for a film about Coco Chanel, by playing off Elton John, hot from his *Lion King* songwriting success, against the Disney Studios in a bidding war. The upshot being they gave Malcolm half a million dollars for the rights to the idea: the 'intellectual property'. That's genius. He'd done nothing but talk. And the musical was never even made. This was another example of Malcolm's extraordinary skill in extracting huge sums of money from large corporations. He cackled with the same old impish glee as he told the story. He was my mentor for a while and taught me a lot. He was a maverick, a Fagin, and I was one of his willing urchins.

Steve Jones popped round occasionally with his friend Helen the dwarf girl. He was doing the odd dab of heroin now and it was clear the band idea wasn't happening anytime soon.

Sounds, April 79

'Ten Pole Tudor is a possible front for the band', said Jones, ''Cos 'es great to look at and 'e's really funny, but he just can't cut it on his voice alone. I dunno, I might even take up singing myself.'

I knew I had to form a band of my own but was unsure as to how to go about it and then someone suggested I ask Gary Long from The Visitors to play drums. That group had now faded out and he was looking for a band.

Here I was in the charts, with 'Who Killed Bambi' having shot straight into the Top Ten but it was less of a thrill than you might imagine as anything with 'Sex Pistols' on it would have been a hit anyway. Whilst blagging my way into the pop charts was a punk thing to do I suppose, I could take no credit for the success.

But I was tickled to read on the sleeve that 'Who Killed Bambi' was by the 'Sex Pistols' for, as I was the only person on that record apart from the Royal Philharmonic Orchestra, who were a session group, that made me, by definition, on this occasion, not only a Sex Pistol but all of them!

10

Tenpole Tudor

The full-page Sex Pistols adverts in the music papers for 'Who Killed Bambi' said: 'Introducing Ten Pole Tudor. Direct descendent of Henry VIII who spills the beans on the assassins of innocence.' I had said to Malcolm I was descended from Henry VIII which, while not being entirely accurate, seemed like a good line at the time. He loved it.

(Actually, I am descended from Richard III's older brother, George, Duke of Clarence, who, if he hadn't been slain already by their eldest brother Edward IV, would certainly have been killed when the Tudors came to power, having a superior claim to the throne. The Poles and the Tudors were sworn enemies. I'm proud to be a Pole but it's less impressive when you consider I share this lineage with hundreds of thousands of others. The 'Tudor' was added by my great grandfather).

I was delighted when Jeremy, the nice man who ran the 3 Cs club, offered to learn the bass to three of my songs, and demo them with his mate on drums. Bernie Rhodes let us use his rehearsal rooms, near the Roundhouse in Chalk Farm. I bashed out the chords on electric guitar along to basic drums and bass, and then overdubbed the vocals and was pleasantly surprised by the result, especially how good the vocal harmonies sounded.

Being in the charts made it easy for me to get my foot in the door at record companies – a phone call was all it took. I played the songs to EMI, and to Simon Draper at Virgin records, who talked of a ten-album deal with a twenty thousand pounds advance.

In those days the music business still didn't really understand the punk thing, and with enough blag and bravado you could get a record deal, it seemed, with apparent ease. However, the phrase: 'Talk is cheap' is nowhere truer than in show business.

I met up with Gary Long, played him the demo tapes, and he agreed to be the drummer. Suddenly, I had half a band already.

With the six thousand pounds advance from the publishing deal with Warner Brothers, I could afford to pay for things like adverts for 'Bass player wanted' in the *Melody Maker*, a telephone line, a new amplifier, another guitar, strings, leads etc. I could afford rehearsal-room hire and meals in The Spaghetti House, Goodge Street. I could buy rounds of drinks in the pub. The cash helped greatly to ease it all along.

At the Notre Dame Hall, Leicester Square I joined the Low Numbers on stage again to sing 'Respectable'. They were bottom of the bill supporting The Clash, who were doing two 'secret' shows. I was over the moon to be in the same building with, let alone appearing on the same stage as, The Clash.

Also on the bill were The Mo-dettes, an all-girl group featuring June Miles-Kingston on drums who were great. I told June I was getting a band together and asked if she knew of a guitarist. 'Yes. My bruvver Bob Kingston!' she said without hesitation, and wrote his number on my fag packet. Later on, to the Clash, down the front, I was in the pogo-ing throng, going wild and drenched in sweat – surfing on the waves of unbridled abandon and exhilaration along with everybody else.

Needing somewhere to rehearse and to audition musicians, Gary and I checked out Halligan's Rehearsal rooms, at 103 Holloway Road just past The Castle pub. Tony Halligan, the Irishman who ran the place, showed us the basement where there was a neon-lit room with microphones, a PA system, a drum kit and a tatty carpet. Not too smart: perfect for rock and roll.

'Are you pro or semi-pro?' Tony asked.

I remembered noticing these distinctions in the 'Musicians wanted' columns of the *Melody Maker* when I was at school.

'We hope to turn professional one day!' I said cheerfully.

Me and Gary giggled and Tony cackled amiably along.

And so it was that Halligan's became our base camp. Next door was The Hope Dining Rooms with the old-fashioned style of two rows of bench-seat tables, its decor unchanged since 1905. We were served the most delicious meals by Tina, the lovely Greek matriarch who looked after us.

One thing I knew for sure, I didn't want any middle-class people in the band. Some folk are genetically incapable of having a rock and roll bone in their body: like John Cleese for instance. The same applied to all middle-class people as far as I was concerned. I wanted no bourgeois types from good homes called Simon who'd had soft and easy lives. No, I wanted the classic, slightly sinister, hard-nut look, very similar to the Rolling Stones in fact.

Two days later at Halligans Bob Kingston swaggered into the room. We loved him on the spot. Funny, cocky, good-looking, charismatic, a classic rocker's quiff and the best voice I've ever heard. He was perfect.

Bob's guitar-playing was rudimentary but good enough for our type of power-chord songs. We knew we wanted him and with me also on guitar at rehearsals we sounded good together. Best of all Bob Kingston could harmonise effortlessly in his fine, rich baritone voice.

Diary
29 July 1979
I now have a band! Dick is the bass player.
We saw him before and called him back. He's a good player for sure and seems friendly and easy-going, let's go Bob Dick and Gary!

Dick Coppen, renamed Crippen, looked like a builder from Reigate, and was a perfect fit. He was keen to join, he could sing and he had a van, which swung it in his favour.

'You won't have any problems with me, mate,' said Dick.

We rehearsed pretty much every day. The evenings were for drinks and jollities. At the outset I laid down three rules: no being late for rehearsals, no being drunk on stage or drinking in rehearsals, and no one was to bring their girlfriends on tour with us. I had read enough rock and roll history to know that steady girlfriends and bands on the road is a disastrous mix. Girls picked up along the way are a different matter, of course. The band agreed to these terms. When it came to what to call the band, Gary said, 'let's use your name, Ten Pole Tudor'. This became Tenpole Tudor. Thank you, Malcolm.

When not at rehearsals at Halligans or in The Castle pub, I was at home writing songs for the band. It is a lot easier to make up a song when you know there's a band ready and waiting to learn it: it gives you the motivation to work it up until it's great. The songs started to come in fairly quick succession and we needed enough for a forty-five-minute gig at the least.

I was absolutely focused, thinking and caring about nothing else but the band. The band was my mission in life and I was determined we would succeed. Naked ambition burned within like a permanent fire and I was woefully negligent of my girlfriend at the time, with literally no room for her in my mind. Being too much of a moral coward to call it a day, I later withdrew from our affair shabbily which weighs still upon my conscience. I hope to be forgiven one day but doubt I ever shall. But I won't be going into great detail about my love life in this book.

Diary

24 August 1979

I'm very happy to be working with these three blokes because I like them all so much. Bob the guitarist is perfect for the group; he has greased-back hair and looks a real rocker. He's a good player, can sing, and I bet he'll be a good performer. I hope I can be a good frontman. All of us can sing. Dick is really good; a very experienced trouper and an asset. I believe in this group so much. In one way the whole exercise is futile as I can't see it being that much fun when we've made it but it's such an addiction. The ups are so high, the lows so low; but it's so fucking exciting.

After their recent prominent support slots to the Clash and Sham 69, the Low Numbers were interviewed in *Sounds*. Rob 'Rousers' said:

'Give Tenpole Tudor a mention. You know he jammed with us at Notre Dame? Well I see 'im as saviour of England, 'onest. If I was his manager I'd promote him as that.'

The love and respect had always been mutual and naturally we asked The Low Numbers to support Tenpole Tudor at our debut gig at the Moonlight Club, West Hampstead, 5 September, 1979.

It went down well enough for the venue to offer us another gig the following month. Twelve days later Nancy from Warner Brothers Publishing rang to offer us several dates supporting The Undertones on their October UK tour, if we wanted to, starting at Leicester on 7 October. Of course, we wanted to.

Though things were happening very fast, it didn't seem so at the time. I was very impatient: an hour seeming like a week. The day before our first Undertones support slot at Leicester De Montfort Hall, I was walking down Gower Street towards Denmark Street, when Feargal Sharkey and another Undertone walked out of a small hotel onto the pavement just in front of me. My heart gave a leap when I saw it was them, but I was too shy to stop and say hello. I'll meet them all tomorrow, I thought. When I mentioned this the next day, after we'd been introduced, they laughed and told me I should have said hello. They were all friendly and funny.

I had heard their music on the radio: hits such as 'Teenage Kicks', 'My Perfect Cousin', 'Jimmy Jimmy' etc. I liked the songs well enough but they didn't sound that powerful on vinyl so I felt sure we were going to blow them off the stage with our explosive show.

De Montfort Hall holds two thousand standing, and seems vast from the stage. It was sold out. We went on and bashed away, me hurling myself about and Gary playing more fills and rolls than an actual beat. Our frenetic style failed to make a connection with the audience, and our inexperience was sorely exposed.

The Undertones came on, and two thousand people went crazy. It was the most powerful, irresistible rock and roll pop music I'd ever seen performed. The O'Neill brothers' guitars perfectly meshed: one played a chord, the other a riff. The harmonies were true, bass and drums steady, and Feargal Sharkey drenched in sweat, shirt off, was singing his heart out, giving his all. Like many of the best bands, the Undertones made it look easy.

I was ecstatic, watching them from the wings, soaking up the atmosphere, observing and learning; and high as a kite with post-show adrenaline and Rider beer (we were thrilled to find we merited a case of beer of our own backstage).

Despite being brought up in the 1960s and having a healthy appetite for drugs and drink, I never got drunk or high before going onstage. I would have a slow pint of bitter but never a joint. On stage you need to be utterly present: the more focused you are the more interesting it is to watch. Later, job done, you can get happily drunk, and soak up the beer along with the praise.

At the same time as we were supporting the Undertones, I was on another Sex Pistols single, 'The Great Rock 'n' Roll Swindle' with 'Rock Around the Clock' as the B-side, which had just shot into the top twenty.

At our third show at the Moonlight club, it was busier than before and Jones and Cook were there. Gary yielded the drum stool to Paul Cook as they came on stage at the end and played both those songs with us.

At the first two Moonlight shows a fan called Lee kept shouting for us to play 'The Great Rock 'n' Roll Swindle'. Rather than explain that it's a rotten song to sing (and that I hate it) I told him, 'We don't do that one 'cos it's a Sex Pistols song, and not a Tenpole Tudor one, see?'. It seemed logical to me. So, at this Moonlight show Lee was beside himself with excitement. When it came to that song, I got Lee up to sing it himself. This got me off having to do it, made him look good, made me look good for letting him, and what's more he knew all the words and I didn't. By now the club was going wild and I danced about, stage-left, grinning from ear to ear.

Steve Jones was giving it plenty of bollocks on electric guitar and seeing Lee at the mic singing his heart out, word-perfect, made me happy. The thing about punk was that it was an anti-star system. Punk was for everybody, including its fun.

Two days later Dick drove us to Aberystwyth University for the first date proper of the Undertones tour. We were in very good form that night and this time the crowd responded: even the Undertones, watching from the wings, urged us to do an encore. What we lacked in musical finesse we made up for in spectacle.

Crude though we were, the three-part harmonies, our secret weapon, elevated the noise into music. The question in those days was how much melody dare we put into the songs before it stopped being 'punk'?

Years later when I toured with Stiff Little Fingers, Jake Burns told me he faced the same dilemma, he said he used to shout the vocals to disguise the melody. These days Jake sings the songs much more tunefully.

The Undertones tour took in Cardiff, Liverpool, Birmingham, Loughborough, Portsmouth, Bournemouth and Bracknell before ending up at the Rainbow on 30 October, 1979. What I loved most was meeting everybody after the show. To be surrounded by friendly people who want to talk to you is fun. I was meeting fellow punk rock adventurers everywhere, our pleasure at the encounters entirely mutual.

The Hope and Anchor in Upper Street was a venue rich in punk history. Though small, it had a great atmosphere. Everyone had played there so naturally we wanted to as well.

I was being perfectly truthful when I rang Julia, the American girl who booked the bands for The Hope and Anchor, and told her how great Tenpole Tudor were. But less so when I introduced myself as 'Bob Whitaker' their manager. The first time I rang she wasn't enthusiastic,

'I've heard no buzz about that band,' she said.

But I was polite and persistent and rang her at regular intervals until she relented and gave us a date: 13 December, 1979. Of course, when she actually saw the group she loved us and told me so on the telephone the next day.

'But where were you?' she asked. 'I was there, Julia,' I said. 'I am medium height, medium build, brown hair, leather jacket... I couldn't see you either!'

After that she would book us often and I had to become increasingly inventive in my stories about why we still hadn't met after umpteen gigs there. She eventually discovered the deception when I told the story in a press interview but I think she forgave me and was good enough to enjoy the joke. So, the 'Bob Whitaker' character was our first manager.

Pages from old Rolling Stones fan magazines from 1964/65 lined the walls down the steps to the cellar where we played. We always went down a storm at the Hope and Anchor and once there were so many people trying to get in, the police were called.

Rob Dickins had started a small record label and offered us a one-off single deal. Gary Long and I had a very productive afternoon and wrote 'Real Fun' which we decided would be the A-side while 'What's in a Word', the song I had originally written for the Sex Pistols, would be on the reverse.

Steve Jones regularly came to our Moonlight Club gigs and joined us on stage at the end to play a couple of numbers. Once he came onstage a song too early. He wasn't at all put out when I told him, and calmly sat on my AC30 until we were ready for him.

I had bought a tenor saxophone from the brass instrument shop that used to be on Cambridge Circus, and after a couple of lessons I was impressed by my progress; after a couple of weeks I felt I was getting quite good. My line at the time, with all the arrogance of youth, was : 'The hardest thing about playing the saxophone is being able to afford one in the first place!'

I was less impressed when, two years later, I was no better on the instrument than I was after the first fortnight. It takes a lifetime of dedication to come anywhere near to mastering a musical instrument but when you are starting out there is nothing like blind faith and burning optimism to get you going.

The Pretenders were on a UK tour and we had another lucky break when UB40, their support act, couldn't make the Cambridge Corn Exchange gig on 29 February, 1980, and we were called as replacements.

Journal 1 March 1980
Yesterday had one of the best days so far this year supporting The Pretenders at the Corn Exchange; a wonderful old building. Our dressing room was the boiler room! Kicked a ball around with Pete (Farndon) and Martin (Chambers) then went with Dick to find some fags. Bumped into Chrissie and had a brief word. We did a great gig and not only did the audience shout for more but the road crew and The Pretenders wouldn't let us leave the stage until we did an encore. The show is really coming together now. I'm more controlled and focused instead of going mad from the start. It's really working now. Bollocks to our depressing single reviews. And afterwards we had laughs and drinks in their dressingroom. They're so friendly, I love them. Even Chrissie proposed to me, it being 29 February and I kissed her (chastely!). There was even talk of supporting them in the USA. What a night!... Coming down is the problem.

When we first met them, guitarist Jim Honeyman-Scott did his Hereford yokel parody, 'Oi've got a noice new Fender-Gibson!' he said in exaggerated rural dialect, hunchbacked and with a limp, to make us laugh. The Pretenders had been touring hard: they had a hit single, 'Brass in Pocket' and were number one in the LP charts on both sides of the Atlantic. They were friendly. Musicians on tour, I've always found, seem all too pleased to meet other bands when their paths do cross.

A week earlier our debut single, 'Real Fun', had been released (22 February, 1980). A thousand copies were printed and it would reach number ninety three in the charts. The reviews were not exactly glowing. Danny Baker wrote:

'Basic bombast and ground floor heavy metal result in an eleven-year-old's idea of how to copy Cook and Jones.'

Which was so accurate I could hardly take offence.

That same day we supported The Ramones at the Electric Ballroom. Their song 'Sheena is a Punk Rocker' was pretty much the first 'punk' record we'd heard in the UK on the radio three years earlier. At the venue The Ramones were road-weary, immobile and monosyllabic. 'Hi' in their dressing room when I said hello from the open doorway was the sum of our conversation.

Later, shortly before they went on stage, I was amazed to see them all tucking into a large Indian takeaway. Which explains why Joey Ramone didn't move about much on stage.

The Ramones were wonderful. As soon as one song ended, the drummer yelled '1-2-3-4!' and the next one began: you couldn't fit a Rizla paper sideways in between the songs. The cumulative effect of this relentless, tuneful, onslaught sent the audience crazy, including me.

When we weren't rehearsing or gigging I was on the telephone as Bob Whitaker, Tenpole Tudor manager, booking rehearsals, talking to promoters, hiring the PA, and calling record companies. Or running round Regent's Park for stage-fitness training. Above all, we wanted a record deal.

In March 1980 we supported The Pretenders at The Hammersmith Palais no less, a two thousand capacity ballroom. It was a triumph and at the end of the night, having said goodbye to everyone, Chrissie, alone in the corridor, called after me and said, 'Is that it?' in a certain kind of loaded way and set my heart pounding. I said no, trying to be cool, and went to the van.

Dick Crippen was hard-working, willing and able but it was too much to expect him to drive the van on top of everything else. Jos Ingham, Gary's old schoolfriend from Hereford, became our roadie and did all the driving. A good-natured chap, what he lacked in brainpower he made up for by being loyal and true. We also liked the tiger tail he wore which dangled from his belt.

Heroin

Chrissie Hynde had a room in photographer Peter Warner's large flat in Marylebone. One night Chrissie, Pete Farndon and Warner came to see our show at The Greyhound in Fulham Palace Road where we often played. It was a triumph and I was invited back to the flat with them afterwards. Drinks were poured and everything was jolly.

Very discreetly, Pete Farndon said in my ear, 'I say old chap, would you care for a little line of heroin?'

As if post-show euphoria and hanging out with friendly rock stars was not intoxicating enough for a young rocker, I said, 'Yes' and followed him to the kitchen where he chopped me a tiny line to sniff. I blossomed like a tree in spring to a whole new level of high, soaring in the blooming pharmaceutical rush.

I instantly understood what all the fuss was about and how easily heroin could enslave you, but you don't become addicted after one dose. Heroin addiction is a decision not an accident. One reason Mick Jagger or I didn't become junkies is because it removes your charisma: fatal for a frontman.

Pete Farndon soon after became a junkie. The last time I saw him was a couple of years later, at a secret Rolling Stones gig at the 100 Club. He was now in the vice-like grip of full-blown addiction and had been kicked out of the band. His hair was long and curly, he looked like a Californian beach bum, and he wasn't making much sense, but he was still the lovely friendly chap I remembered.

Chrissie lived on the other side of the park from me and I would stroll over and have tea. She was now becoming massively famous and would share wry observations about the effects of stardom, and how she was trying to adjust to it all.

Our moments were few and far between as The Pretenders were constantly touring. In one snatched hour we had Irish coffee in a secluded upstairs bar in Chinatown before she had to go and record the spoken overdub on the outro of their forthcoming single, 'Talk of the Town' ('Maybe tomorrow, maybe some day'). One time when she had a couple of days off in London mid-tour she asked me very nicely whether I would mind doing her laundry. What would *you* say if Chrissie Hynde asked you to do her laundry?

I did it in the launderette in Cleveland Street a few doors down from Sam's Cafe. The sexy American beauty had me in her thrall but I understood how touring precludes the frame of mind where it's possible to think about doing the laundry. It would be ungallant of me to reveal what her favourite perfume was, but I was impelled to buy her a bottle as a present, from a perfumier's in Chinatown, where the smallest bottle cost about three hundred pounds in today's money. I was in love.

Meanwhile, Tenpole Tudor were busy playing all over London. We were regularly getting repeat bookings as the word spread about our exhilarating live performances. My father, who wrote to me regularly, told me he'd overheard a couple of lads on the bus saying that the two best live bands around were 'Tenpole Tudor and Adam and The Ants'. Our ethos was that we were for everyone, including the reprobates, delinquents, village idiots and outcasts: no one was excluded. We often put poverty-stricken youth onto the guest list. Not everyone can afford seventy five pence. The whole point of a gig is that it be full. The good thing about punk is that the oikish dimwit normally at the bottom of any social pecking order now had somewhere they felt they could belong.

We played another show at The Rainbow, this time with The Undertones. But mostly we kept going round London venues like Dingwalls, The Hope and Anchor, The Moonlight Club, The Greyhound, The Marquee, and The Bridge House in Canning Town, with a few out of town, like Darlington and The Retford Porterhouse. All these concerts cemented our live reputation and brought us together as a band.

We weren't the first group to think of ourselves as the Four Musketeers and won't be the last: 'All for one, and one for all!' I decided to hire seventeenth century musketeer costumes from Berman and Nathans, the theatrical costumers, for a photo session and drove to the Cambridgeshire countryside for the shoot, where some excellent photographs were taken. The great thing about historical costume is that you not only look fabulous, but they never become any more out of date than they already are. If you're going to be old-fashioned, be more old-fashioned than anybody else.

At long last *The Great Rock 'n' Roll Swindle* film was released on 15 May, 1980. My 'Who Killed Bambi' sequence went down very well in the cinemas and at our first gig at The Nashville following the film's release, instead of the usual cohort of fifty loyal fans, the place was rammed.

We played our first song, said, 'Thank you very much, goodnight', left the stage then came back on for a storming forty five-minute encore. Near the end of the show Chrissie Hynde appeared at the front of the crowd and threw her handkerchief on stage at my feet. Dear reader, it doesn't get much better than that. It was clear that we had turned a corner.

Robert Plant came to a Dingwalls show to check us out and was most encouraging to me backstage. Ray Davies had also seen the show and, very much brokered by Chrissie Hynde, he offered us an afternoon session at his 24-track studio, Konk, in Muswell Hill with him 'producing'. I had written a song called 'Anticipation', with a nice sax rhythm part, that we recorded. ('Anticipation's better than when you've got it.') Ray said that as it was just a demo we should simply bash it out and save all the painstaking detail for the actual record.

It was great to work with Ray Davies whose Kinks records me and Tom had bought and loved. 'See My Friend' is my favourite. The demo sounded great with the saxophone part taking it to a higher level. I played it proudly to Chrissie Hynde the following day.

Our next gig was at The Thomas Á Becket in South London and also jammed. The dressing room was upstairs and there were lots of criminal-looking types milling about as security guards. But the stage was set, with the sax in its stand by my microphone at the front.

We descended the stairs and mounted the stage and I instantly saw that my sax was missing. Some swine in this heaving South London crowd had nicked it in plain view of everyone but it was clear no one was going to reveal the culprit despite all my expostulations and impassioned appeals. They relished my indignation, grinning from ear to ear and I realised I had to forget it and get on with the show.

My anger lent its energy and we went down a storm – I was delighted Chrissie Hynde and Ray Davies were there to witness our triumph.

A couple of days later, they unexpectedly paid me a visit at my squat. They had been visiting Chrissie's friend Jasper Conran next door. She and Ray descended the steps to my basement but the place was too squalid for rock stars and they stayed barely a minute.

It was soon afterwards that Chrissie told me as gently as she could that she and Ray now had a thing going and that I could see her no more. I said I understood, and of course I did: Ray Davies clearly outranks Eddie Tenpole in any game of Top Trumps – facts, dear reader, have to be faced.

The next day I was walking along Store Street after dark when, ambushed by grief, which welled like a volcano, I burst into tears and sobbed like a child into the trunk of a tree.

At my shoulder, I heard a man's voice saying with concern, 'Are you alright? What's the matter?' I tried to answer his question in some detail, despite my sobs rendering all words completely indecipherable. He gave me a few 'Cheer-up-old-chaps' before I was able to recover, thank him and wend my way back to Albany Street. I went to my room, and wrote the song:

'I Wish' (I was with her again).

A concert is not so much about playing each song well as the accumulative effect of all of them. A straight run-through helps the band find the most dynamic set order. 'OK chaps, imagine it's a gig: no teabreaks or chats or stopping until we've finished,' I would say, 'One-two-three-four!'. .and off we went. One day, we were having a nonstop run-through when, after about twenty minutes, water slowly started seeping into the room under the thick soundproof doors.

'Don't get distracted by that! It's only water. Keep going!' I urged, not remotely interested as to why water was coming in.

The band kept going until the water was an inch deep and rising up to the level of the electric plug sockets.

'If you don't want to get wet feet, then stand on your amps, but don't stop!' I yelled.

The band played on, but by now the water level was above the plug sockets. Dear reader, I was merely sticking to the plan: surely the whole point of making a plan is that you stick to it?

At this point Gary upped his sticks, stood up and said I was mad, and the others followed him up the stairs out of this paddling pool of a rehearsal room. Considering we were all lucky not to have been electrocuted by this time, I had to concede that Gary had a point.

Freak rainfall in the Holloway Road had caused the flood. We went next door to the Hope Dining Rooms to be mothered by Tina the Greek lady and fed delicious food. She made the best tea in London and was very kind.

11

Stiff Records

There was nothing in my life except Tenpole Tudor – and my vaulting ambition. We were on the up and up and we could feel it. The second time we played The Marquee there was a queue down Wardour Street. The Marquee was the hottest venue of them all. In the dressing room after the show Gary and I were as wet as if we had been swimming.

Alan Black, an A&R man from Polydor, agreed to pay for us to record three songs at Free Range Sound Studios in Covent Garden, in the basement below Charles Fox, the theatrical make-up shop – which seemed fitting.

Dick had always shown an aptitude and fascination with the techniques of recording so he was appointed 'producer'. We recorded 'Three Bells in a Row', (inspired by the amount of money Gary and Bob used to put into the fruit machine at The Castle pub), 'There Are Boys', a Bo Diddley pastiche with Jagger-esque vocals, plus a much better version of 'Judy Annual'.

There was a delectable beauty working on reception who, it transpired, was the girlfriend of a famous rock star who was violent and abusive she told me and was easily persuaded to come to my place one afternoon. I'll not reveal the name of her boyfriend but her love was sweet as honey.

On the third and final day in Free Range, having mixed the tracks, we strolled back to mine for the 'home test'. If it sounds good on the home system you know it is good. We were optimistic but we couldn't believe how great the songs sounded. As good as anybody's. It was a hot summer's night and after last orders in the

Queen's Head & Artichoke we went into Regent's Park through the gap in the fence, with my portable cassette-player, and walked around playing the songs over and over again until dawn, glowing with pride at our achievement.

A week after the Free Range sessions we played The Bridge House, Canning Town and this too was packed. Gary Bushell the music journalist was there to see us, and he put us on the front cover of *Sounds*. Dave Robinson, the Stiff Records boss, seeing the cover picture and learning Tenpole Tudor were unsigned, came to our Richmond show at Brolly's, one of a four-date tour supporting Spizz Energi.

After the early soundcheck a young punky girl introduced herself, wanting to make sure she could get in. 'But, of course!' I said. This was Sarah Newton, a Yorkshire girl with black spiky hair, who was cheeky and funny. She had 'The Nolans' painted on the back of her black leather jacket which I thought was genius. I took Sarah and her pal to a burger bar and fed the penniless punks and she made me laugh. She was only fourteen and definitely not groupie material. She was having trouble at home. It turned out we shared a birthday: 6 December. She aroused my protective instincts, like a kid sister.

Dave Robinson came to see us again the following week, this time at Dingwalls, in Camden Town. There were several other record companies there too. Onstage, when I happened to mention rockabilly music, a glass was thrown at me cutting my head. Some idiot now being manhandled out of the building had mistakenly thought I was mocking the genre, which I would never do.

This was just before we played a straight version of Otis Redding's 'My Girl'. Oblivious to the pain, I gave a heartfelt rendition as the blood flowed down my face, relishing how dramatic it must look. After the finale we retreated to the tiny dressing room – followed by Dave Robinson.

In his earlier days he had been a roadie for the likes of Jimi Hendrix, and understood rock and roll practicalities. Dave tended my cut, washing it at the tiny sink and told me I would live. Of all the other record company people there, Robinson was the only one who came to check I was OK. I took this as a sign that we should go with Stiff Records.

We met up the following day in a pub, and Dave said that he was putting together The Son of Stiff tour. It would be three months long and cover the UK, Europe, Canada and the USA. There would be five bands on the bill playing thirty-minute sets in a rotating order. Stiff had a tradition of this type of tour modelled on the touring revues of the 1960s, where you could see several decent acts in one show. He wanted to know whether we would like to be on the tour.

Carrots don't come more tempting than a three-month northern-hemisphere world tour; this was my every dream come true.

'Where do we sign?' we said in unison.

When we asked him about an advance, Dave said to itemise the cost of what we needed and to let him know the amount. Walking into his office the next day to give him our estimate, it was like talking to someone else entirely and all the charm had disappeared. Not for the last time we heard him say, 'Just because you sell a few records doesn't make you an artist.' In the end Stiff advanced us fifteen thousand pounds.

Bob Whitaker now made way for a new manager: we gave Gary's mate Jos the role, reasoning that we would have a greater level of control over him. A handsome lad, he got off with Dave Robinson's secretary and we hoped this would also give us a bit of inside leverage.

The snag to the Stiff deal was that we only had a fortnight to record an album before the tour began. Though we were totally unprepared we had to start work immediately at The Workhouse, a 24-track studio on the Old Kent Road. The Workhouse was owned by Manfred Mann.

Alan Winstanley and Bob Andrews were the producers and our inexperience showed. Gary in particular had to concentrate hard to be precise with his drum patterns. The initial backing tracks did not impress Dave Robinson when he came to listen to them, but when the vocals were added the tracks came alive.

My voice was rather shot by the end after spending a couple of days doing all my singing parts. The whole thing was hurried and, frustratingly, with the tour imminent, we couldn't oversee any mixes.

'You will make it sound good?' we said nervously.

'Leave it to us!' said Bob Andrews cheerily as we bade them goodbye. He was very straight.

The following day there was a full technical rehearsal at Shepperton Film Studios with all the bands for the three-month tour. It would be years before I had a day off.

Aged three with my father in Kensington Gardens.

My mother, Shirley. (Photo: Tony Snell)

My father, David Tudor-Pole.

My grandfather, Wellesley Tudor Pole.

In the woods at school. My first group, Denniss and the Lapels.
L-R Pete Whitaker, Chris MacDonnell. ETP, John MacDonnell.

First photo of Tenpole Tudor. L-R Gary Long, ETP, Bob Kingston, Dick Crippen, 1979.

Tenpole Tudor in the Holloway Road, 1980. (Photo: Virginia Turbett)

Sue and Sarah.

Sue Berry and ETP, 1982.

ETP and Bob Kingston in Amsterdam. (Photo: Maarten Corbijn)

ETP at Dingwalls with the Hayrick Band, 1983.

John Michell. (Photo: David Speed)

Dick Crippen.

Sean Poe.

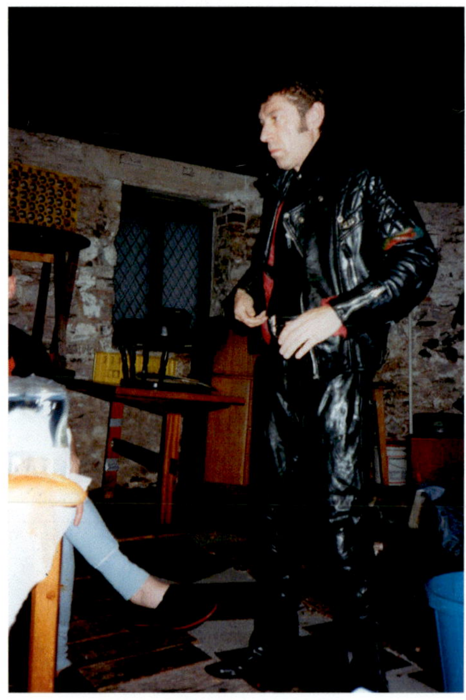

Mick O'Donnell prepares.

Death of Rock and Roll Show.

Tenpole Tudor Mk II. L-R Mick O'Donnell, Sean Poe, ETP, Paul Martin, Matt Fisher, 1986.

Me and my brother Tom.

Backstage at The Haymarket, 1988.

Backstage at The Haymarket in *The Admirable Crichton*, 1988.
L-R Steven Pacey, ETP, Martin Clunes.

ETP in *Walker* (1987, dir. Alex Cox) starring Ed Harris, filmed in Nicaragua, playing Mr Doubleday, a war artist. (Photo: Richard Edson)

The Crystal Maze, 1992.

Ed happy on stage, Lets Rock, UK tour 2022. (Photo: Martin Shaw Photography)

'Hello everybody!', Lets Rock, UK tour 2022. (Photo: Martin Shaw Photography)

ETP on stage in 2024. (Photo: Andy Muscroft)

12

The Son of Stiff Tour

There were five bands on the 'Son of Stiff' tour. The Equators were a black reggae/ska band from Birmingham. Any Trouble were a tasteful, tuneful soft-rock outfit with skilled musicians, fronted by Clive Gregson who was slightly reminiscent of Elvis Costello – or was it just the glasses? Joe 'King' Carrasco and the Crowns were a Tex-Mex outfit from the USA who did a great version of 'Wooly Bully' while Dirty Looks were a slick three-piece from New York; and Tenpole Tudor.

We travelled in a coach which soon became like home. You could either be sociable and sit at table seats chatting, or sit alone and gaze out of the window. There was no shortage of entertaining company.

As well as the musicians, we were joined by B P Fallon, the Irishman who used to be a publicist for Led Zeppelin. He had plenty of stories to tell, as did Johnny Green, who joined the tour for a while. I recognised him from Clash gigs I'd been to: he was the tall bloke with big glasses you saw on stage checking the mics before the band came on, and hovering in the wings to repel stage invasions. I liked Johnny. He would always say 'Hello Ed, are you rockin'?' and I would later borrow the phrase for *The Crystal Maze*, imitation being the sincerest form of flattery. A journalist and a film crew joined us for the first leg. It was usually fairly chilled on the coach with the musicians husbanding their energy for the evening's full-on extravaganza.

It seemed like the best job in the world. It was certainly a life of luxury: there were people being paid to cook for us, to herd us to concert halls and to check us into the hotel. Tony the tour manager would hand us room keys and all we had to do was carry our bags up to the room.

I shared with Dick. He was the philosopher of the band and game for discussions about the meaning of life, my favourite subject, and had a dry sense of humour. Dick and I were both up for the full sex-and-drugs-and-rock-and-roll experience – the others, having girlfriends, were more circumspect. Tony would sit at the front from where he addressed us all with a microphone. He had been in the band Christie who had a hit with 'Yellow River' so that was sung a fair few times on the coach, to tease him.

The Equators chain-smoked puff all day and all night, claiming in best reggae musician tradition that it was essential for their minds and for the music. I might have a joint in the morning and contemplate the show towards which we drove, but nothing after lunch.

The show comes before all else. If I am employed, I need to give my best. The aim was to deliver a top performance every single night, and as showtime approaches the focus gradually zooms in.

'King... ha; King... Ho! KING-HA; KING... HO!'

If I wasn't having fun on stage I tried to look as though I was. But as it's so much easier when you need to look like you're having fun to be actually having fun, I mostly did that.

The drink after the show is the performer's reward and I'd either chat to the fans or watch the other bands. There was never a shortage of friendly people to talk to. It was odd at first only playing for thirty minutes but it raised the standard of songs, and was a workload that could be sustained over the days, weeks and months ahead – we played fifty nine concerts in total.

Some nights we would be on first, some nights last, and all slots in between. We found the most advantageous place on the bill was to be third or fourth band on because, by the time the fifth group went on, the audience was starting to tire.

On day one, at 11am, 1 October, 1980, a camera crew filmed me getting on to the tube train at Warren Street station heading to the rendezvous for the start of the Son of Stiff Tour. Dave Robinson warned me that I would finish the tour a different man from the one who began it. That was fine by me. I had nothing to lose.

The friendly coach driver had a seventies footballer's hairstyle and a bright red tracksuit. He looked straight out of a *Carry On* film, and was up for a laugh. A very excited coachload of musicians was driven up the M1 to the first gig at Leeds University – Tenpole Tudor were topping the bill, and I was very happy to see Sarah Newton there. She'd brought her friend Sue, who had dyed blonde spiky hair. They were the most entertaining and gregarious company and I fell in love with all their patter, their cocky, self-assurance and Yorkshire-isms (Ay oop chalk). I adopted them and they would follow much of the tour and sometimes Tony allowed them to travel on the coach with us. Sarah had run away from home as her father was violent. Sarah liked a drink, as did Sue, who was older and came from the rough part of Sheffield.

Halfway through Joe King Carrasco and the Crowns' set at Leeds, Joe, their multi-talented frontman, jumped off the stage whilst playing his guitar. He worked his way through the crowd followed by a roadie unspooling his guitar lead to the microphone at the back of the hall by the sound desk, to resume his singing.

It was a good stunt, simple and effective. On the first night he wore his trademark crown and someone immediately nicked it off his head! Well, what did he expect? This is England, which has a long tradition of people seizing crowns. Joe was shocked and dismayed but it was hard not to laugh. The crown was never seen again: the tour would be a learning process for all.

The Equators usually went down well with their reggae/ska beats and spirited delivery, fronted by their young star, Rocky, nineteen, who always wore a baseball cap. Some nights Any Trouble would have a large gaggle of rapt student girls sitting cross-legged on the floor giving Clive Gregson's sensitive songs the attention they deserved. In rougher places Any Trouble weren't always treated with such respect, like at Ayr Pavilion in Scotland, where the crowd hurled missiles at them.

At Ayr it seemed like they had only come to see us. Tenpole Tudor, our punk rock rebel credentials intact, who delivered a wild show every night, often had it a lot easier than Any Trouble, certainly in the UK.

It was somewhere in Scotland that I was taken to a police station for questioning.

'Some parents have reported a missing daughter believed to be following the Stiff tour', said the Superintendent to me in his office.

He wasn't referring to Sarah. The girl in question was fifteen and I said truthfully that I had no interest in sex with underage girls and that it's far more fun to make love with a woman who has had some experience. He smiled, said he was a man of the world, and told me to 'be careful'.

After the Ayr show it was interesting chatting with the locals. They felt aggrieved by life, they told me, and were up for the 'punk revolution'. I was delighted to have a role in life which made these people want to talk to me in the first place. All I had to do, mainly, was to listen to them. Our conversations made us both feel connected and involved in the 'scene' – I loved hearing the different local accents as we travelled around the land.

It is very difficult to describe a rock concert more than once and make it interesting. There are only so many ways you can say 'the audience went wild', 'we rocked the house' etc. No wonder Mick Jagger gave back the advance for his memoirs. The successful show is where the audience and band become one: it's a visceral exercise which bypasses the intellect. The most tiring thing about a world tour is the first three days when you feel exhausted, but then the second wind kicks in and you feel as though you could do it forever, and this is when the band starts hitting heights that are impossible at a one-off concert, however many rehearsals you have.

Magical powers are gained by playing music; being in a band lends you a sexual allure that wasn't there before – which was one of the reasons for getting into it in the first place and I eagerly took full advantage of these new powers. It was blissfully easy to persuade girls to come back to the hotel and I loved them truly, every one, and kissed them most sincerely. Which may have been a mistake: these girls weren't looking for love, they were looking to be fucked.

If I got off with someone, Dick might stay on at the hotel bar with the road crew, or lie in bed pretending to be asleep or, far more likely, actually be asleep.

There was a lovely girl, a friend of B P Fallon, who rode on the coach for a few days and she and Dick had got together. One afternoon at the hotel Dick went down to the restaurant while she stayed to have a shower. It was lovely when I managed to have a bit of sex with her while Dick was gone. Mind you, when he returned she was back with him again as if nothing had happened. I met her on the street thirty nine years later and there were very happy hugs: she hadn't changed a bit.

One night in Newcastle a lovely Scottish girl was in my bed and we were getting cosy when, rather abruptly, she got up and went to the bathroom. Quite soon I found in the bed a small pellet of shit, like a rabbit's, that she'd obviously let out by mistake. I didn't want her to be embarrassed at all, so I flicked it towards Dick's sleeping form before she returned, and didn't allude to it. We made love, sweet and tender, but she didn't want to sleep. That day was the sixteenth show in eighteen days and I was dog-tired. She was very nice and will reappear later in this story. Actually, I may as well tell you now: bollocks to later.

Tenpole Tudor were in Edinburgh, we were in the charts and very unusually had a matinee show for the younger Tenpole Tudor fans who wouldn't be allowed into the evening show. It was a club right next door to a large theatre where Cliff Richard was performing on his sellout tour.

We arrived at Edinburgh early and a pretty young Parisian girl presented herself to me. She was dressed in leather, more chic than street, more French than punk. A sucker for a honey trap, I accepted her overtures and instantly she was 'my girlfriend'. That's how easy it was to pick up lovers when you're in a famous band. A couple of hours before the evening show, we found a connecting door to the adjoining theatre and suddenly found ourselves at the back of the upper circle watching Cliff Richard. Cliff wasn't a punk rocker's natural choice but my negative preconceptions were soon supplanted by slack-jawed astonishment and admiration. Cliff was a superb performer in every way and we watched for about twenty five minutes before it was time to get ready for the evening show.

Back in the dressing room, shortly before we were due on stage, a Scottish girl with a large dog steamed into the dressing room like a force of nature. She'd had a few drinks. Blow me down if it wasn't the lovely pellet girl although now looking a lot wilder than before with hair in dreadlocks. I was very pleased to see her again and my heart sank for I was stuck with the French girl and already beginning to tire of her. After the show, like some pre-booked gigolo, I told her with sincere regret that I was taken for the night. She vigorously protested, but me and the French girl eluded her somehow and got back to the hotel: it would have been too mean to expel the mademoiselle for no other crime than being less interesting than the lassie. But it was bleak in bed listening to the raging and screaming in the street outside – the lassie became increasingly demented and ended up being carted off by the police.

For a long while, life on the tour was 'an eternal round of delights' but as the weeks turned into months, with shows almost nightly, I would sometimes feel exhausted and worry that I wouldn't have the strength for that evening's show.

I would have an hour's siesta when we reached the hotel, then wake up at 5 pm feeling even worse; groggy and awash with another wave of anxiety. Sheffield, Loughborough, Liverpool, Colwyn Bay, Belfast, Dublin, Glasgow, Newcastle, on we rolled.

I learned that to go on stage too surly, or to be genuinely angry and aggressive, makes the audience uneasy. Yes, anger is an energy of punk but the bunch of lads who've turned up from Colwyn Bay, for example, are there to have some fun, and they don't want it to get heavy.

At breakfast at the Holiday Inn, Plymouth, 28 October, 1980, a journalist, Mike Nichols, joined my table and was being friendly. I don't like talking at breakfast: I am an Englishman. But being naive I decided to be polite. Soon, Nichols started asking about my father and prying into my background.

I told him that I didn't come from wealth and privilege – quite the opposite – saying that my father spent much of his life unemployed and there was never any money. Dear reader, I know now that I should have been more circumspect: Nichols printed the conversation about my father in full as the centrepiece of the interview I didn't know I was having, in the *Record Mirror*. Dad went nuts, of course.

At one show the chaps from Motorhead came along. We knew Lemmy because he was often to be seen propping up the bar at a gig or playing on the fruit machines. He was approachable and you would say, 'Hello Lemmy, are you alright?' and he would say 'How are you doing' but without the conversation generally going much further. I liked that he was equally friendly to everyone and I tried to be the same. Bernie Rhodes once said to me accusingly, 'You're just like Joe Strummer: you want to be friends with everyone!'

It was the time of the Irish Troubles and in Belfast we stayed at the Europa Hotel, the most bombed hotel in Europe. With barbed-wire barricades, it was essentially a fortress where you had to go through a military checkpoint to get in. It didn't make for a great atmosphere but at the concert we were warmly received and I felt a lot safer after that. The show I was most nervous about was Glasgow. I had heard many stories about how someone with my accent wouldn't survive five minutes in a Glasgow bar. Dear reader, that's bollocks, but I didn't know it then. Never trust the man who tells you to be frightened.

The way to be safe in any territory is to be open-hearted. The Scots are a great people but you cannot fob them off with English politeness. You have to give something of your heart and prove yourself in some way before they will befriend you and give the same back.

As so often happens in life, just when everything is going swimmingly and all is right with the world, something comes along to spoil it. No matter how much money you have and however insulated from life's problems you think you are, you can never escape fate. If you try to by sitting at home all day, the ceiling will fall upon your head. Some years ago, I remember bumping into

Mick Jones at a time when he was making films rather than music, and he said, 'There's always anxiety when you're in a band'. He's right.

Winstanley and Andrews had mixed our hastily recorded album and the Stiff art department had designed the sleeve. The cover was a photograph of the band from a Stiff photo session where the photographer had got us all stoned; not a great look. But that concern paled into nothing when we heard the record which was truly dreadful. With a very trebly sound, thin guitars with no bollocks at all and weedy vocals it was AWFUL. The thought of that rubbish being our debut album was too much to bear. After many frantic calls to Dave Robinson voicing our concerns, he agreed that we could polish it up and redo the vocals when the tour was over – and if I could design a better album sleeve, I was welcome to try. I would later discover that, instead of destroying these initial two thousand duff versions, Dave Robinson sold them in Europe. The result of this was that Europe, not unfairly, thought Tenpole were rubbish.

Robinson was always a man who would rather make ten pounds now than a thousand pounds later. I didn't know that he'd done that, so ignorance was bliss, but never again would I allow our music to be mixed and produced without being present. If everyone else's standards were as high as mine this wouldn't be necessary. For Andrews, a throwback to the pub rock era with whom I had nothing in common, my music was an afternoon's work: to me it was my whole life and heart and soul and journey so far!

On the thirtieth show of the tour, on its thirty third day, we played Slough at a rough old place with a violent atmosphere. Someone offered me, and I took, a line of cocaine. The drug was less prevalent than it went on to be, and that was the first time I tried it. It gave me a massive lift and lent wings to the performance. I blazed and had the dead fish killer look of Mick Jagger on the cover of *Black and Blue*. The drug turned me into Superman. I was King, nay Emperor, of the world. I chewed up and spat out the show with the haughty disdain and flashy panache of a matador.

I couldn't wait to take some more the following night at Queen Elizabeth College in London but it wasn't as good. It never works when you try to recreate the previous night's performance, and I vowed never to take it again before a show. Cocaine is an overrated and rotten drug: you feel OK for fifteen minutes and then it's downhill. It kills your sense of humour and habitual use turns you into an idiot.

One evening, after one of the London concerts, I was sitting with Sarah in the darkened coach parked outside the venue, having a joint, when she noticed her mum and dad walking in the car park. They had driven down from Sheffield to look for their errant daughter. I felt a bit sorry for them and urged her to go and say hello.

'No way!' said Sarah, staring at them wandering round like lost sheep and far from home.

Sarah was a vivid character on the tour, and often joined us all on stage for the big finale. She was roaring drunk a lot of the time and would alarm people. 'Oi Ed! Sarah's off her face again. Can you please come and control her!' She listened to me because she knew that I cared about her. At the last British date of the Son of Stiff tour on 4 November, 1980 at The Music Machine, the police, acting on her parents' tipoff, were waiting to pounce and Sarah was arrested in the wings as she came off stage.

The show was the last one on the UK leg of the tour and, despite being under a mile away from home, I was pleased to go with everyone else to a warm hotel in Bayswater. My basement would have been even colder and damper than usual. And I'd become accustomed to having hot water at the turn of a tap.

European Leg

The next day, 5 November, 1980, we drove to Sheerness to catch the overnight ferry to Holland to begin the European leg. It was a very rough crossing: we were hit by a force eight gale and everyone else was seasick. The boat lurched and lifted and tilted. There was vomit everywhere and people groaned in their bunks. Me and Phil Barnes, the bass player in Any Trouble, were the only people unaffected. I felt like Captain Ahab or King Lear and, lashed by rain on deck in the wind, and holding on tight, I ranted at the storm like a madman. Such was the force of the wind it took both of us to heave the metal door open to get back inside. I strongly advised Rocky not to go out there but he wanted to see for himself. We helped him open the door and he poked his head gingerly outside. His baseball cap was instantly whipped off his head by the gale, and shot to a quarter of a mile away in under a second before disappearing. Never has a cap travelled so far and so fast away from the head upon which it sat. Rocky thought better of going out on deck.

The first gig in Holland was horrible. The cocaine comedown was making me feel flat, tired and tense. I would rather have been curled up on my Granny's lap being read *Peter Rabbit* than on stage giving my very life away.

The show at Arnhem, the second night, was also a case of grin and bear it, but after that I was back on form and wiser. Moral of the story being: if you have to take cocaine on tour, wait until the last night.

We had a new coach driver for Europe, and he could never find the venue; it would always take at least an hour of driving around the locality before he found the hall where we were playing. When after a couple of weeks I asked him if, just for once, he could drive us directly to the venue for a change, he suddenly went mad and chased me round the coach: a game of catch he could never win. Groningen, Arnhem, Eindhoven, Amsterdam, Deinze, Herenthout, on we went.

The irony of being on tour is you play a lot less music than when you're not on tour. In this case for only half an hour a day. So, for the European leg I put an acoustic guitar on the coach in the luggage rack with which, in theory, I could write songs. With room-sharing, there was little opportunity for the solitude required for the songwriting process, so I would lock myself in the coach toilet cubicle. We needed a hit record to justify being given a recording contract, and I reminded myself we were not on holiday.

Our first single on Stiff, 'Three Bells in a Row', may have got to number one in the Skinhead sub-chart but it wasn't threatening the top twenty.

I tried to analyse what it was that made a hit record. What would The Rolling Stones do? For a start, find a great rhythm that people can dance to.

OK, what rhythms do the best songs have? Canned Heat's 'On the Road Again' sprang to mind, which is similar to 'Spirit in the Sky' by Norman Greenbaum. It's a boogie riff. Canned Heat taught me to love the boogie, people. OK, we'll have that one, I thought, like a shopper walking along a designer rail of rhythms.

Necessity being the mother of invention, I persuaded myself that the poky little toilet on the coach was a soundproof place. I locked myself in with the guitar, and played that boogie rhythm in B for hours, trying to make it hypnotic. I was hearing the accompaniment in my head but to anyone listening it would simply have sounded like someone strumming a blues in B. I had no other ideas for it, there were no words. I always found lyric-writing problematic. What was a man meant to sing about: the Vietnam war? Whereas Bob Dylan always sounded like he knew a thing or two, I didn't know anything and I knew it. Not that I told anyone. But even if I did have some lyrics I was too shy to be overheard singing in the khazi.

I hope I thanked the Lord for my daily girl; I certainly looked forward to her. Self-confidence is all. Having sex freely and often is very good for body and soul, and most beneficial to the mind also. When you're getting plenty it's not in your thoughts all the time, and you are freed to think of other matters. Being imbued with these new powers that came with the job was intoxicating and the lonely sex-starved boy was now consigned to history. Give us this day our daily girl.

On the 13 November, 1980 we played Hamburg and it was a thrill to see The Star Club where the Beatles used to play. I brought a girl back to the hotel as usual. The next day Dick told me he reckoned she was dodgy. I'd thought she looked like Marilyn Monroe in the low light.

Next, we went to Berlin: this was still in the Iron Curtain era. We had to go through an East German border crossing. A couple of armed soldiers came onto the coach. I had taped my lump of hash under a seat on which I wasn't sitting but we weren't given hassle and they waved us through. The view became extremely grim; everything was drab and miserable, and in poor repair. There were no posters advertising anything, because there was nothing to buy.

Anyone who thinks communism is a good thing is either a moron or someone who relishes human misery. We were glad to reach West Berlin, an island of affluence and smart shops, but that didn't seem quite right either, given the context. After Berlin at Le Palais in Paris the next day there were loads of French skinheads chanting what sounded like 'Wisdom! wisdom!' as we came onstage. I later found out they were saying 'West Ham, West Ham!'. I tore up a French flag that I'd found lying around backstage on stage in front of them. It wasn't meant as a political gesture, it just seemed to be, in the two seconds I spent considering it, like a wonderfully melodramatic, anarchic thing to do. As the roughest element in the crowd was chanting the name of an English Football Club, I neither feared nor had any reprisals. But I knew the promoter was lying when he said how much he would like to have us back again.

Later on, I was chatting to some lingering fans, one of whom took my fancy. I told her that she was mine and to go and sit in the coach and wait for me as I had to retrieve my bag from the dressing room. Everyone else had gone by now, and bag in hand I let myself out of the building through an exit door off the auditorium.

I saw the outer metal security grid was down and turned to go back, but the double doors had swung shut behind me. Dear reader, I was trapped like a caged animal. There was nobody left inside the building to heed my banging, so I rattled the grid and shouted 'Au secours! Au secours!'

A Frenchman came along the dark empty street outside, hissing at me to be quiet as people were trying to sleep! His lack of empathy amazed me: perhaps he had been to the show. He certainly conformed to the stereotype of the rude Parisian. I was eventually rescued and apologised profusely to the girl still awaiting me on the coach.

I tried to make it up to her and explained what had happened, and from then on I gave her my best. Later, when I came, it didn't feel right. It was a bit painful.

The next day on the coach en route to Lyons, there was no getting away from it: I had VD. I felt terrible for the girl, as I had no way of contacting her. All I knew is that she came from Marseilles. I told the tour manager Tony and he arranged for me to visit a doctor in Lyons.

At the doctor's, in schoolboy French, I explained that I had 'un mal dans mon cock'. He gave me some antibiotic pills and an address down the road where I was to go for an injection of penicillin.

It was more like a garage than a medical establishment. A brutal-looking workman in green overalls told me to lie face down on the workbench while he injected my buttock with the largest syringe I have ever seen. I was doing some penance for my promiscuity. Now I would have to be celibate until I got the all-clear in London before we left for America (medical note: it was NSU, non-specific urethritis, a basic but not very serious venereal disease, usually easily cured by penicillin).

The next day we were in Milan. Italy had a much better vibe than France. Beautiful architecture surrounded us. But I was very shocked to hear that in the queue outside to get into the amphitheatre, someone had been stabbed to death. When I mentioned it later to the promoter, he shrugged his shoulders and told me not to worry about it. He wasn't in the least bit concerned and said it happens all the time.

Much later, after the show, Phil Barnes and I were extremely hungry and ventured into Milan to find something to eat. We approached a restaurant with an ancient-looking facade. The proprietor told us, alas, it was too late and they were soon to close. Seeing a few diners inside at tables, I implored and entreated and said we only wanted some pasta and a bottle of wine. He relented and, joy of joys, we were admitted. It turned out it was an actors' restaurant and most of the other clientele looked as though they had been on stage that evening as well. We ate a splendid meal with plenty of wine, with no pressure at all upon us to leave. It was a heavenly oasis of civilisation in the greasy world of rock and roll. Viva Italia!

When we arrived in Lisbon there was more of a sense of being properly abroad; a Mediterranean balm was still detectable in the air despite it being 24 November. The local drug dealer sold us some marijuana but warned us it was extremely strong. He said *not* to smoke it before going on stage.

The Equators, who were on after us that night, promptly ignored this advice and had a few spliffs before going on as usual. They became so high so quickly they couldn't play properly. They played extra fast but with no one playing in time with anyone else. The drummer was speeding up and slowing down like a nutter and you could see pure panic in his eyes. I was out front weeping with laughter at their plight. It's one of the funniest things I have ever seen. The moral of the story being: 'Perform the show sober and focused, and save the party till you've earned it.'

The day after the two shows in Portugal we had to be in Madrid, the last show of the European leg, a three hundred and fifty three mile journey. We drove for hours and hours but we still didn't arrive at the venue until 8 pm, when half the audience was already seated. A bag of cocaine was awaiting the crew to help them set up all the equipment double-quick in full view of four thousand impatient people.

Everybody agreed, including us, that Tenpole Tudor should go on first. The crowd was getting ugly. Without time for a soundcheck, me, Bob, Dick and Gary took to the stage and I went up to the microphone:

'OH YEAH, BAY BARE!!' Bang: the whole place went nuts.

The release of pent-up energy from the crowd was extraordinary as they went crazy and we stoked it to make it even hotter. How hot can we get it I wondered? Rock and roll wants what the arsonist wants: to set the place ablaze. And that was the final show of our European leg of the Son of Stiff Tour.

The next day, back in London in a freezing cold even damper basement, huddled in front of the two-bar electric fire, I had the weekend off and the VD clinic to look forward to. I was given a sore knob again from the process which ascertained I was all clear (I could have told them that!). Dear reader, it is the most terrible thing for a man to have anything wrong with his old bill.

The horrific postscript to this story occurred thirty seven years later in Leeds, supporting The Damned. I'd played my set and was front-of-house, in the circle, chatting to fans, when a German bloke approached me like an old friend.

'Hello Ed! You remember me?! Hans!'

I have long since learned that it is always better to say yes to this question. He reminded me that we had met on the Stiff tour in Hamburg. When he said Hamburg the VD incident came to mind and I mentioned it to him.

'I know, I know, I remember!' he said (...what?) 'I know this girl; she gave it to you on purpose! Ha ha! She thought you were getting too big for your boots, Ha ha ha!'

'Whaaaat??!!'

I was shocked, appalled and much saddened by the pitifully mean spirit this story revealed.

Canada and the USA

Our first show, having crossed the Atlantic, was in Toronto. It was deep winter and twenty degrees below outside but as it was such a dry crisp cold it was remarkably tolerable and the tour jacket was doing its thermal trick in the freezing night.

There was an old hotel next to the venue which had operated until recently as a brothel. There were enough rooms for everyone to have their own. The rooms reeked of sex and I loved it, it seemed perfect for rock and roll. We played OK at Toronto but I was looking forward to making our debut in America the next day in Detroit City on my birthday, 6 December, 1980

All the coach journeys were hours longer now in the vast expanse that is North America. We were suddenly in a very alien land where nothing was familiar except from the movies. Detroit was icy cold and snowy and looked forbidding; completely run-down and depressed; a grim vista of metal, stone and brick.

Despite it being my birthday, Tenpole Tudor were awful. Americans know about music, especially ones from Detroit City, home of Motown Records, and our crude efforts went for nothing.

This depressed me greatly and on the long drive to Chicago the next day I thought long and hard about the next concert. I swapped around a few songs in the set order. By the time we went on stage that night, at a modest-sized club in the Windy City, having been thinking about it all day, I was laser-focused. We were superb and made a genuine connection with a North American audience for the first time.

I left the stage like a racehorse having just crossed the finishing line at the Grand National; all sweat, foam and heavy breathing. I was ahead of the others and first into the dressing room as usual, being unencumbered by a guitar. There was a woman there with a microphone aimed at me.

'John Lennon has just been shot dead. Would you like to say anything?'

Well, dear reader, this was impossible to compute; I was annoyed by her very presence in our dressing room in the first place, and my instant response to the news, it not yet having been thirty seconds since the white heat of our final song, was: 'Good riddance to the boring old cunt!' When what I wanted to say was 'Fuck off out of my dressing room!'

Dear reader, this wasn't me talking. You have to leave the singer alone for ten minutes to let him come down a little from the frenzied persona of a psychotic angel taken to extremities. It is only fair to all parties. Being a double Sagittarius and born in the year of the horse, the equine analogy is apt. In an ideal world I would have all the stable hands, grooms and trainers that a Derby favourite horse commands on raceday, to keep me calm and shepherd me to the starting gate, onto the field of action, shielded from any distraction, then back again afterwards to the stable to be towelled down and restored to docility having won. The Beatles were my first musical love and I always liked John Lennon the best so, of course, I didn't mean what I said.

Very soon the tragic news of John's awful demise sunk in: it was unutterably depressing. I looked out of the window at Chicago's vast skyscrapers and felt very small indeed. Though we were in the English-speaking world, the USA can feel far more foreign than Italy, Spain or Greece. The sense of vastness was humbling – and anything could happen in America; people had guns and they used them.

Late one night Bob ordered us some pizzas to be delivered to the hotel. We were all hungry so he ordered large ones. Dear reader, in America 'large' is the size of a lorry wheel. We gorged ourselves on the first one, almost finishing it, and the remainder we stored on the luggage rack in the coach. This cold pizza snack, available to all who wanted any, lasted until the end of the tour.

Every day saw the same routine: eight or nine hours on the coach looking at the unexciting scenery of north east America, with no day off. Toronto, Detroit, Chicago, Cleveland, Buffalo, Albany, Boston, Hartford, Philadelphia, Washington DC, Long Island and two nights at The Ritz Club, New York.

When I walked into the Boston venue the manager asked whether I was Ed Tudor Pole. When I said I was, he told me I had a message from 'The John Lennon Preservation Society'. My heart jumped into my mouth.

'What message?' I asked.

'That was the message,' he said cryptically.

The Chicago woman reporter had published my remarks made in the dressing room as though they were serious and I felt a mixture of fear and annoyance at the cheek of Americans interfering in what an Englishman says about another English band. (Although The Beatles are more of an Irish band if you think about it). This was the second time I had been sold down the river by a journalist, and it wouldn't be the last.

The show that night in Boston was horrible. I darted about the stage as erratically as I could in full bullet-dodging mode. Suddenly the tour didn't seem quite as much fun anymore by a long chalk. I felt a very long way from home indeed, sunk in thought, and huddled into my window seat, hat low, scarf high, as we ate up the miles and the hours towards Hartford, Connecticut, to a venue called Stage West, on 12 December, 1980.

We were on early that night and after a couple of songs I suddenly noticed a girl standing near the stage in the half-empty auditorium. She was very straightly dressed, and looking at me. Dear reader, the bolt of electricity that shot between us generated six scissor-kick leaps in a row instead of the usual three.

I found her after our set and we were inseparable. She was intelligent, classy, beautiful and shy and I wrapped her in my fond embrace. We were inseparable that is, until noon the next day when the coach was due to depart for Philadelphia. That morning we'd strolled about a street market, hand in hand, as lovers do and there was a two-for-the-price-of-one deal on some trousers: I bought them so we could have a pair each. All too soon we had to part and that was the nadir of the tour, dear reader, it was the rock bottom. I wept on the coach as it drove me away from my new love blossoming large, whom I would never see again. If I'd lived in Hartford we would probably have got married. How my heart did ache.

The last three nights of the tour were spent in a dingy New York hotel. From my bed I could see the edge of a skyscraper in the ice-cold blue sky out of a small window. I was knackered, and trying to summon up some strength for the final shows. I even opted out of a day trip to see the Niagara Falls; Bob and Gary went. At the end of the tour, the normally reliable tour manager on the US leg walked off with my passport in his case. Luckily, he remembered in the nick of time. Which was a relief, as Madness, our label mates, had invited us to support them for two nights of Christmas shows at the Hammersmith Odeon, 22 and 23 December, 1980

– the day after we got back from New York. It would be a sprint finish to Christmas after a year of unceasing toil.

'Come on men, once more unto the breach!'

I first went to the Hammersmith Odeon in 1964 to see The Beatles' film *A Hard Day's Night*, and many live concerts there since, so it was a big deal for Tenpole Tudor to be playing that famous venue.

Madness were now phenomenally successful and hardly ever out of the charts. The place was packed with fourteen- and fifteen-year-old mods and skinheads. We played while those flint-hearted little hard nuts sat there with their arms crossed, staring at us with eyes like pebbles. When we finished a song there was not a shred of applause, nor any reaction at all – just gum-chewing silence. This was the acme of passive aggression, and was so extreme we found it rather funny.

I could hardly blame the fans; they were only there for Madness and didn't know who we were, but I was damned if our very last show of the whole year was going to be such a damp squib. The next day I fished out some old seventies live albums and recorded the applause in between the songs onto a cassette tape. That night at the Odeon, after our opening song, I held the cassette-tape of applause to the microphone. Even that bunch of hard nuts cracked a smile and the last show went much better.

Utterly shattered and hollowed out by fatigue I went home to my deep-frozen squat and tried to sleep.

13

Top of the Pops

It wasn't the touring that got Keith Richards into smack, it was the post-tour blues, that dreadful time afterwards when, suddenly deprived of the daily release of energy, the roar of the crowd and the exultant joy it brings, you plummet into a spiral of gloom and misery.

It was a dreadful comedown after the Stiff tour and I was to learn that the post-tour blues last as long as the tour that precedes it. What goes up comes down and it was a miserable winter back in the cold basement.

In January, somebody tipped me off about a large sale of ex-hire theatrical costumes being held in Covent Garden. When I saw the historical clobber, piled high on trestle tables, I was happy as a boy in a sweet shop. There were Doublets and Hose galore; Tudor clothes! And then I spotted a Herald's tabard, embroidered with the royal coat of arms, lions, leopards and fleur-de-lys – the very symbols of our land. It was all going cheap and I bought lots of stuff. We had already dressed up as musketeers, but weren't they French? Thus, we adopted the English coat of arms as our logo and, lo, our historical theme developed.

At the first rehearsal after the tour, I showed the band the boogie idea in B that I had been playing on the bus throughout the European and American legs of the tour. They couldn't quite get the boogie rhythm I wanted. The nearest they got was what you hear on the record, which would do I thought, but what should it be about? We had no words.

The 'Grand Old Duke of York' came to mind, the one who had ten thousand men, which led us towards battle themes. Bob sang a great harmony as we 'fol-de-rolled' our way through, in lieu of lyrics. It sounded good.

After rehearsals we went as usual to The Castle, the one with the inspirational fruit machine that gave us the song 'Three Bells in a Row'. This time it gave us the opening line of 'Swords of 1000 Men': 'Deep in the Castle and back from the war'.

And lo, the words flowed out from my pen in about twenty minutes. We recorded it at Basing Street studios in Notting Hill to add to our debut album.

After almost three months of feeling depressed, the unstinting monotony of its gloom simply added to its burden. If my mood didn't change soon I felt I would go mad. So, in desperation I asked Jos to go and score me some heroin, having no idea where to get any, and recalling how nice the line was that Pete Farndon gave me.

Jos obligingly scored me a 'five quid deal' (enough for about three or four small lines) and brought it round. He was more experienced with drugs than I was and chopped me out a very tiny line which he said would be enough; and it was. At last, and all of a sudden, everything was all right. Dear reader, I felt like Father Christmas. Feeling fab, and happy again, in every way, I went over to the pub. I bought a pint and sat down next to the pub bore whom I usually avoided – an ex-military type who told interminable and dull army tales. This time I indulged him most happily, lending him my ear whilst picking at a pork pie and pickle.

I finished the rest of the drug the next day and the high was already less intense. I certainly wasn't about to buy any more; it was too dangerously nice and too obvious a trap to fall into. But that small self-medicating amount jolted me out of the three-month depression and I felt a lot better. Heroin is the drug of self-pity and despair, an evil substance that destroys everything eventually. But trying anything once won't do you any harm, knowledge is power.

My brother Tom heroically and once again came to the rescue. He and his girlfriend had been offered a council flat in Lissenden Mansions, in Kentish Town. Tom, who loves being the bearer of good news, was as happy to inform me as I was to hear it, that I could now move up in the world and take over the first-floor, which they had restored and redecorated to a high degree.

Overnight I was in heaven. In the tall room was a large marble fireplace and bay windows with a balcony overlooking the corner of Regent's Park. The contrast from the basement was extreme; this was a happy room filled with light, a room fit for a king. I went from cold to warm, from damp to dry, from night to day. I was ecstatic.

Endless firewood was available from builders' skips, and I became adept at creating a blazing fire within five minutes of arriving home. I didn't get a telly until years later. I would stare at the flames for hours seeing how they flickered.

There may have been no running hot water but, in seventeenth century terms, it was the dog's bollocks, and I had an electric kettle. The Queen's Head and Artichoke was across the road for a pint, a pork pie and pickle, or crisps or peanuts, which was the general extent of pub grub in those days. That is, if you discount the time when they raffled a roast chicken: if a pale dead chicken crammed into the newly-invented microwave oven and cooked for sixty minutes can be called 'roast'.

To the local clientele I was pretty much ignored and filed under 'one of them squatters across the road', but as I was always courteous, and disported myself with the modesty that is only right and proper for a newcomer, after two or three years I began to be accepted and got to know some of the local characters.

George, another squatter on the floor above me, was a gentle chap from Liverpool, an old-school socialist type who loved Dylan and Bruce Springsteen, and refused to countenance any of the New Wave and punk bands who had taken over the music press. We would sometimes share a joint and inevitably the conversation would turn to The Beatles, which was always fine by me.

While at drama school I often wondered how to get the man in the street back into the theatres, to make it less elitist and more inclusive as it used to be. I harboured dreams of connecting the forces of rock and roll to theatre.

I had stayed in touch with Malcolm McKay, my tutor from RADA, and we would meet in Lamb's Conduit Street, talking up the idea of a punk musical. This was before I discovered that, as Benjamin Disraeli observed before me, there are two separate societies in Britain that run in parallel, seldom meeting and which have no interest at all in each other. Theatre is predominantly for the middle-classes to enjoy, and the live music scene is for the other eighty percent of us. To put it another way, the theatregoer doesn't want to see Cradle of Filth in a greasy music club any more than a skinhead wants to see the latest Alan Ayckbourn play in Shaftesbury Avenue.

Bob, Dick and Gary all instinctively understood that when playing a gig we occupied a theatrical space, and that the deaf as well as the blind should be catered for. We tried to make our shows as entertaining as possible. At The Marquee Club once, a brass bed was wheeled on stage in the dark between bands, with me in it. The lights come on, I do my sleepyhead waking up routine, notice the audience, come alive and say:

'Good morning, everybody! You're all up very early! Shall we play some rock and roll?... I can't hear you!'

Tenpole springs out of bed, the roadies remove it, the band comes on, plug in the guitars, and '1-2-3-4' BANG, they're off. The punks transform themselves into a delirious, heaving mass, writhing and leaping like salmon swimming upstream.

When I say 'punks' I mean all the various people who were joining and participating in this still comparatively new movement of misfits, delinquents, dispossessed young groovers, and longhaired people who've just had a haircut. Anyone and everyone could be filed under 'punk'. There was no uniform then.

Rossini's *William Tell Overture* was our intro music, and sometimes I would declaim the St Crispin's speech from Shakespeare's *Henry V* to begin: 'Once more unto the breach, dear friends!'

As the original press advert for 'Who Killed Bambi' had said, 'Introducing Ten Pole Tudor, direct descendent of Henry VIII', people were now jokingly saying that I was 'the rightful king of England'. Which greatly tickled me who rebutted it, and greatly tickled them who insisted upon it.

'You're the rightful King!'

'No, I'm not!'

'Yes, you are!'

One of our most elaborate stunts was when I brought the electric stove from Albany Street to The Marquee wearing a tall white chef's hat from Denny's with 'Punk Chef' written on it. I then fried up a rasher of bacon and egg on stage whilst chatting to the crowd who had queued along Wardour Street to get in.

'Who wants some bacon and egg?' I asked. Everybody did.

It was hardly Jesus feeding the five thousand as only one bloke got the grub but by then the band was on, the stove was off: '1-2-3-4!' and on with the show. The frontman must have mastery over the audience and direct the action. It is most empowering.

Our concerts were an escape from the horrors of real life rather than a reflection of it. If, for instance, you were singing Joy Division songs every night it would be very difficult not to feel like committing suicide eventually, whoever you are. My instinct has always been to escape the horrors of life, to uplift and entertain – like the Rolling Stones have always done. The point of playing music in public is to entertain. Our tunes are simple and melodic and my pantomime yobbo frontman act gives the crowd permission to shed their own restraint. I loved that our gigs attracted the sort of rough-looking types that I used to fear as a teenager – now those once-feared skinheads were my supporters. We liked each other, and over the years I always found the rougher the crowd the better the show. Being frontman connected me to people of this land I would otherwise never have met.

Sometimes the start of a show was like dropping a match into a lake of petrol. The sublimation of violence in the enactment of these shows lanced and released an inner boil of rage within me, but without anybody getting hurt. We let rip with the joy of prisoners released. There was no safer environment than in the mêlée down the front, where no one could touch you (it wasn't called a 'mosh pit' in those days, a term I dislike).

'Hate' and 'Destroy' may have been the banners under which punk marched but in actual fact it was all peace and love, in deeds not words, and rather cosy. At the end of the night everyone goes home feeling happily spent. We never had fights at our shows. Trouble only occurs, whether in the classroom or the concert hall, when people are bored. No one was bored at a Tenpole Tudor show. You better believe it, baby.

We kept busy. We had the album to finish and a lengthy UK tour planned for April, May and June to promote it, not to mention a single release. I'd done the artwork for the LP cover one evening when still living in the basement. When it came to colouring the lions in yellow, my yellow felt-tip pen ran out of yellow before I'd finished, which is why the top left-hand lion on the LP sleeve stayed white. The record was called *Eddie, Old Bob, Dick and Gary* as in 'They let any old Tom, Dick and Harry into the party'.

Peter Warner, a photographer and Chrissie Hynde's landlord, agreed to shoot the band photo. We couldn't think of what to wear and twentieth-century fashion trends not being our strong point, we did it naked – well, from the waist up. We greased ourselves in oil so we looked as though we had just come off stage. Any vaguely homoerotic undertones could only be to the good. Dave Robinson, who hated anything remotely sexual, disliked it intensely, and only grudgingly agreed to have it reproduced (as small as possible) on the back cover.

Mind you, he saved himself a thousand quid or more by using one of our musketeer photos as the cover for 'Swords of a Thousand Men' – the obvious choice for the single.

Mick Jagger

I took the best three musketeer photographs to Stiff one morning for Dave Robinson to make the final choice for the single cover. There was never much of a welcome at the cheerless Stiff office. The vibe was dour, the staff all had their heads down, looking busy, and people seemed wary of Dave Robinson. He chose one of the photographs and then I left.

As it was lunchtime I went to a cafe at the Tottenham Court Road end of Warren Street; the cafe where we'd written the first two verses of 'Real Fun'.

I bought an *Evening Standard* to read with the sausage, egg and chips, and saw in the entertainment section that Mick Jagger was going to be interviewed on Capital Radio at 3 pm. Funnily enough, the actual Capital Radio building was just over the Euston Road from where I was sitting, less than a minute away. And my watch showed 2.45 pm.

Now, dear reader, I have explained about my learning difficulties, and I am sure most of you would have been quicker off the mark than I to realise that 2.45 pm, i.e. now, was just about the time, probably, that Mick would arrive for his 3 pm interview (unless it was pre-recorded) and as the penny dropped my desire to check it out accelerated so fast I could feel the G-force.

I paid my bill and crossed the Euston Road and there in the sunlight outside the Capital Radio entrance I saw a gaggle of about fifteen people holding Rolling Stones albums and autograph books. My surmise was correct and my heart had barely enough time to jump into my mouth when, blow me down, Mick Jagger appeared. He was on his own and walking towards us. He wore sunglasses but it was him alright. He paused to sign a few record sleeves. All I had for him to sign was a Tenpole Tudor musketeer photograph.

'Alright, that's enuff,' said Mick, getting impatient.

'Please Mick,' I entreated, 'just sign the musketeers!'

He took my A4 photo and signed the back of it while I told him, quite sincerely, he was still the greatest.

'Ta,' he said, before disappearing into the building.

Now there are many times in this tale when thrills are mentioned, and how thrilling they were, but this one took the thrill biscuit.

I was punched by a feeling of elation capable of making me vault the entire Euston Road in one bound and I swear I nearly did. My head swam and my heart did hammer. Fuck me... Mick Jagger.

It seemed impossible. Ten minutes ago, I was a simple rocker eating egg and chips. Now I have stood next to the greatest performer who ever lived while he signed the back of a picture of *my* band – which, if it were not for the Rolling Stones in the first place, would never have existed! What are the chances!

How could I not see Mick Jagger's signed endorsement, albeit unwitting, on a Tenpole Tudor photo, albeit on the back, as anything other than a major sign, an omen, that success would be ours? And what sort of person given this scenario could possibly say they didn't believe in signs? ('Nah mate, that's just a coincidence.')

We had a three-month UK tour planned, starting in April, to promote the album and single, so apart from a few London dates, we were not gigging in early 1981. However much you rehearse, a one-off gig is only warming up the engine; for only by playing every night does a band reach its peak performance.

I admit to making excuses but both Bob and I were below par at the Imperial College London on 6 March, 1981 where we were comprehensively blown off stage by the support band 'The Adicts', from Ipswich, who were (and still are) sensational. We decided to get another guitarist to fill out our sound.

Munch was a shadowy figure who worked at Halligans and volunteered for the post. He seemed to be able to play OK, and being a humble sort of chap, he wouldn't be upsetting any apple carts. He also had a wonky eye so would not threaten Bob's matinee-idol, guitar-hero status, and because we found no one else we liked, he got the job. He was no trouble and amiable enough, and he couldn't believe his luck, I'm sure.

It was after a show in Liverpool that we were told that 'Swords of 1000 Men' had climbed to number thirty seven in the charts.

Liverpool was very rundown in those days. Our hotel was separated from a deserted street of boarded-up terraced houses by an expanse of weeds and rubble waste ground. I wandered about on it the next morning in my leather jacket, feeling like an early Beatle on the cover of the 'Twist and Shout' EP, and turning over the news in my head.

Aged nine, I'd felt like a Beatle walking out of the Hammersmith Odeon having seen A *Hard Day's Night*, and I felt like a Beatle now; but this was in real life in a group of my own who were in the actual pop charts. It was hard to believe: my fantasy world was becoming real. The next week the record climbed higher and before long Jos came up to my floor to tell me: 'We've got the Pops!' meaning *Top of the Pops*.

There was a sense of inevitability about the news. I'd dared not hope but could feel it coming. Even so it was still quite shocking.

I felt a bit as if the nurse had just poked her head around the door and said, 'The dentist will see you now', with a sick feeling in the stomach as you steel yourself to be brave. This was a landmark moment. Up to then I could have said to myself, 'well, if it all ends tomorrow it's been a blast and no harm done' and that would be that. But going on *Top of the Pops* is the point of no return: it changes everything forever. 'Bring it on!' I said.

Top of the Pops

The sun shone as we arrived, bright and early, at the BBC Studios in White City, brimming with excitement at 10am on 29 April, 1981. I decided to wear my sixteenth century Tudor trousers and heraldic painted leather jacket.

We were shown into a dressing room for hours of hanging around. Each act in turn had a lighting rehearsal and then a dress rehearsal in the afternoon. Until very recently the bands could hang out in the bar to more happily pass the time, but thanks to our label-mates, Madness, who had become so drunk and badly behaved the last time they were on the show, the bar was now off limits to all bands.

Everyone is excited and it's all too easy to spunk away your energy during the day. Jimmy Savile was the presenter. He introduced himself, shook our hands and congratulated us; I was thrilled to meet the bloke I had first seen in 1964 on black and white telly. When it came out that he was so evil I was furious he had conned us into liking him. But moving swiftly on...

Walking past Dexys Midnight Runners' dressing room I saw Kevin Rowland giving one of his band members a haircut, creating a zany semblance of calm amidst the excitement. This impressed me. The leader's job is to serve his band. I would make tea for my band at rehearsals, but haircuts are a cut above.

Sheena Easton bravely chose to sing her vocal live on the show; we just mimed along to playback like everybody else did. You pretend it's a live show and the small studio audience plays along; it is a fairly technical exercise but knowing you are on *Top of the Pops* is a thrill.

After a long day Jos drove us all home and I went over the road for a nightcap in the Queen's Head & Artichoke and the jovial Irish landlord said, 'Well hello dare; have you made it into the top twenty yet? Ho, ho!'

'Yes, we have actually,' I said, quite calmly. He paused.

'Get away wid ye!'

'Well,' I said, inwardly squirming with delight and trying to be as offhand as possible, 'you don't have to take my word for it: just watch *Top of the Pops* next Thursday. May I have a pint of bitter, please.'

Dear reader, that was a delicious minute of my life.

We watched the broadcast of our *Top of the Pops* TV debut at the Stiff offices and when I awoke the next day I lay in bed and thought, 'You are now famous' which was technically true as the *TOTP* viewing figures ran into many millions but even so, it was hard to believe. I decided to test the degree of how famous I had become. Wearing the same jacket I'd worn on the show, I walked along Warren Street past the car showrooms and cafes. As I crossed Tottenham Court Road, a bloke in a van called out to me: ''Ere mate! Are you the geezer off *Top of the Pops*?!' I said that I was, and gave him a wave; and suddenly felt unnecessarily conspicuous, realising this was different from the fantasy game I'd played in my head since I was nine. This was real life.

I went swiftly back to Albany Street to await Jos and the band. We had a gig in Scarborough that evening. Come showtime, we went onstage to be faced with an empty dance floor, with those who were there sitting at the very back. Like at The Velvet Underground at Acton Town Hall.

Now, you expect this when you start out, and I've faced an empty auditorium many times, but bloody hell, dear reader, we'd just been on *Top of the Pops*. Surely that was sufficient to promote us into being one of those bands where everyone's down the front before they come on? Irritated, I picked up the microphone stand and strode down the length of the hall placing it three feet in front of the people sitting on the red plastic bench against the back wall. It was a case of Mohammed going to the mountain. At least the audience was now right in front of me.

'I wanna see the whites of your eyes!'I said.

In defence of the good people of Scarborough, we had never played there before and none of those at the gig had bought the single. The reason for this, which I found out years later, was that it was every twelve-year-old boy in the land, all three hundred and fifty thousand of them, who'd bought 'Swords of 1000 Men' and made it a hit, and no one else whomsoever. Our prepubescent fans couldn't attend the gigs as they were all tucked up in bed – this was a great weight off my mind when I eventually found out. But you have to shrug these things off. When you're on the road every day is a new day, and the next night was Glasgow.

You don't approach a Glasgow show half-cocked and nor did we. That fabulous night was yet another confirmation of the truth of the adage that 'a bad show is always followed by a good one'. A good one? They went ballistic at Glasgow, and so did we. We ripped it up and ate it whole. The passion of the Scots is a truly wonderful thing and we upped the ante as high as it would go. Again, the Glaswegians lifted us to new heights, primordial and glorious. Paisley was great as well, the tour now up and running. Three days later in Sheffield we found out that 'Swords' had jumped up to number twenty two.

Our life was spent in the van; it was our home, our ship, our security, driving us all over the kingdom to the next gig while we listened to our song being played on Radio 1 at regular intervals.

Being part circus-horse by nature I love the ordered life on tour with a performance every night. It tickled me to be making a living by singing and dancing; the two things I was apparently no good at when at drama school. Coming off stage drenched in sweat having given my all, like an athlete, is to feel satisfied and alive. It is a wonderful thing to inhabit and relish the physical, animal side of yourself. We read the music papers – *Melody Maker, NME, Sounds* – and if there was ever a week when we weren't mentioned I would be a bit put out, but it hardly ever happened.

There was a mattress on top of the gear in the back so I could lie down, and sleep when I wanted, husbanding my energy for the evening. Sometimes, I had no voice at all in the mornings, and could only talk in a whispered croak, but somehow, I would always be able to sing at the show. And if my voice was hoarse, I would simply sound more like Rod Stewart for whom singing like he's got a sore throat made him a global superstar. I have no sympathy with singers who cancel, or indeed any performers who cancel. Sing with whatever voice you have, and if it has a rasp to it then sing with your soul.

After our first Canterbury show on the Monday, at the Art College, we found out we were at number ten. And before the second Canterbury show, on the Friday, at the University, we had been on *TOTP* a second time. Yeovil-Plymouth-Torquay-Barnstaple-Birmingham-Brighton, the tour went on. In Plymouth we were told we had risen to number six.

This was pleasing but no longer surprising. By now we thought we were as good as any of our competitors and felt we had every right to be in the charts. It was Adam and the Ants, Kim Wilde, Shakin' Stevens, Madness, Stray Cats and Tenpole Tudor.

The Yorkshire girls, Sarah and Sue, now good friends, often came to shows on this tour. They had recently formed a group of their own: Debar. They may have played a gig or two in Sheffield but no more than that. Both girls could write songs, especially Sue who had a great voice and sense of melody. I borrowed some of their musical ideas, I do admit. That they were total beginners and could hardly play was no bar to their enthusiasm and talent. And when in Torquay the bottom-of-the-bill support band dropped out and I suggested that Debar played, the girls, though unprepared, agreed – and ever more eagerly with every tin of beer they drank. Their guitarist was a docile Sheffield lad who drove them about and had very little say in matters.

I watched from the balcony as their chaotic cacophony began. Dear reader, it was so bad it was brilliant. Sarah banging every drum and cymbal at her disposal as hard as possible, with Sue singing melodically over drums and guitar noise as if she was at Las Vegas. I was in hysterics; tears ran down my face – one of the funniest things I've ever seen: pure anarchic heaven.

And Sarah, who perhaps shouldn't have had those final tins, had taken great offence at some heckler's remarks and was challenging him to a fight right there and then, standing up amidst her drums and waving her sticks at him. That was the best thing about the ethos of that era: for a few years there was a time when anyone could get up and have a go...punk rock!

Oxford-Bath-Manchester-Wolverhampton-Newport-Shropshire, and then Loughborough where we played a show with The Exploited, who had just sprung up and were at the vanguard of the so-called 'second wave' of punk, when the look became more of a uniform with Mohican hair, multi-studded leather jackets and multi-holed D.M. boots. This new cult was harder, more confrontationally, uncompromisingly PUNK; and with a new way of playing it. You could say that The Exploited invented the template of what is known as 'punk music' as at every punk festival you go to that's the style they're playing.

If a music formula could be patented like Coca-Cola they would be nearly as rich as Paul McCartney. The fact that me and Steve Jones hated it is neither here nor there. Credit where it's due.

One very hot day, me, Bob, Dick and Gary were having a break from rehearsals in a small church garden off the Holloway Road, and got chatting to a couple of fifteen-year-old boys. We asked them what music they liked.

'Madness,' they said.

'What about Tenpole Tudor?' I asked, not revealing our identity.

'Not as much, no,' said one.

I was curious as to why he didn't like Tenpole Tudor, for market research purposes.

When pressed the lad eventually said, 'Because they sound old-fashioned'. I thanked him, happy to be enlightened at last. Shortly after we stormed the charts, we bumped into The Clash and Bernie Rhodes at some dive or another, and always friendly, they shook our hands and congratulated us on our chart success, Joe and Mick freely admitting their envy. The Clash were yet to have a hit single at this time. I could see they were surprised. The entire music business was surprised. No one saw it coming except every eleven, twelve and thirteen-year-old schoolboy in the land. We ended that tour with two Marquees in a row; two packed-out triumphs.

Musikladen Incident

The day after the two Marquee shows we flew to Bremen in Germany to mime to Swords on *Musikladen*, their equivalent of our *TOTP*. We made friends with Kim Wilde and her band who were on the plane with us and I enjoyed chatting to her brother Ricky, the main songwriter, guitarist and my fellow budding hit-writer, about our craft.

Robert Palmer was also on the show. At the beginning of his song, he didn't get the microphone out of his jacket pocket in time for the first line, making it obvious to the viewer that it was a mime. He smiled it off in a self-deprecatory manner that was nicely done.

Pat Boone was on as well, that anodyne purveyor of white-man versions of songs like 'Tutti Frutti'. I didn't meet him but Bob did. He said Boone was so perma-tanned that, after they shook hands, he checked his palms to make sure they hadn't turned orange.

Like *TOTP* (although with a jollier atmosphere) The Musikladen show took all day to film after which we were taken to 'Jimmys', being a cosy club where the hosts took all their acts, conveniently within walking distance of our hotel.

It was all very pleasant: Dick Crippen was deep in conversation with Robert Palmer, I was chatting to Ricky Wilde, and Bob was being charming to Kim. We had all been given cocaine, now the ubiquitous drug in rock circles. As I have said it is not a drug I have ever grown to like, but not for the want of trying.

Far more times than necessary I have accepted the offer of a line of cocaine when experience told me not to, to give it yet one more last chance to reveal some hitherto hidden charm; which I could never find. My theory is that because cocaine is part of rock and roll folklore there's a lot of peer pressure to pretend to like it.

At Jimmy's bar it was now 4am and I was tired of talking, had drunk enough vodkas-and-orange, and smoked enough complimentary Rothmans for one night, danke very much, and decided to slip off back to the hotel. I have been very much helped over the years by some inner voice which tells me: 'OK mate, you've had enough now go to bed' like a valet/ guardian angel to help me home.

It was only a short walk back and when I arrived the building was dark. I knocked on the wooden border of the glass door, not at all confident the rusty little stub of a doorbell button was working, and listened. All remained quiet. I banged the door louder and more impatiently and took it in my stride when, with a sudden crash, the whole pane of glass gave way. It shattered and smashed, and clattered and fell, and tinkled onto the steps below.

My reaction as I carefully stepped through the jagged hole wasn't so much regret for the damage done as relief to have got into the hotel at last. I'm a believer in sticking to a mission through thick and thin, and right now my sole aim was to go to bed. Walking up three steps to the inner door I was intensely annoyed to find it was also locked.

I shouted for attention, this second door being a far stronger one. If it had been another glass fronted door, the logical thing to do would have been to smash that one too and climb through. As I had already broken the first door, the breaking of the second one would merely be another door to be taken into consideration, your honour. And are not obstacles to be overcome? What surprised me was what heavy sleepers the people of Bremen were. Everything was so eerily quiet. I peered in through the second door and could make out white-clothed tables which made me realise that, bless my soul, it wasn't my hotel at all but a restaurant!

Discretion being the better part of valour I knew the best plan now was to go, fairly briskly, back to the safety of the club and we'd say no more about it. I set forth along the road and fifteen seconds later three siren-blaring police cars surrounded me. Armed men tumbled out shouting at me in German.

'Ich knicker spreche Deutsch!' I expostulated.

I went quietly, they shoved me in a car and took me to the police station where, thankfully, the Kommandant spoke English. Dear reader, there was nothing wrong with the hearing of the good people of Bremen, and nor do they sleep abnormally deeply. I was arrested within five minutes of breaking the door.

I began by explaining to the chief that I was in Germany to do *Musikladen* and… I got no further than that. Like many of our own bobbies he was a good sort and an ardent music fan. He was impressed that I was appearing on that esteemed TV show *Musikladen* no less and clearly a bit starstruck. He couldn't have been more helpful, and I gave him a Tenpole Tudor badge. The hotel key-fob told him where I was staying and I said he needed to talk to our tour manager, whose job it was to sort out broken doors: it certainly wasn't mine. I was simply the lead singer of a group with a full enough plate as it was. I said if he would be kind enough to give me a lift to the hotel I could get him a T-shirt as well. He drove me there himself. As soon as the irate tour manager appeared in the lobby I realised my continued presence would only exacerbate his anger, so I left them to it and went to bed at long last. Mission accomplished.

The next day, most foully hungover and poisoned by vodka, I related this tale to the others on the way to the airport as we drove past the restaurant I had mistaken for the hotel. Such is German efficiency the glass door had already been reglazed and everything looked quite normal. They'd have accused me of making it up were it not for the corroboration of the tour manager.

Gary and Bob also told me how Dick, in the club at five in the morning, having been deep in conversation with Robert Palmer all night, had asked him, 'By the way, what do you do?' He hadn't realised it was Robert Palmer, he simply liked the guy. I think Palmer was a bit miffed.

Crystal Palace

The following Saturday, making a big end-of-tour finale, we played our first open-air show – a one-day event at Crystal Palace with Ultravox, Madness, Phil Lynott and Hazel O'Connor, among others.

For some reason I had been against doing it, fearing that we would make little impact on hippies lying about on the grass. My fears were groundless and thank goodness I was overruled by 3:1.

Melody Maker feature 13 June, 1981 by Colin Irwin, extract:
'The thing about Ed,' Kingston confides later, 'is all you've got to do is tell him the Stones did it. And the Stones did do open-air festivals, didn't they?'

It was an epic day. Skins and New Romantics came. Unusually, the stage was separated from the crowd by a shallow lake which acted like a castle moat or security barrier, or so the promoters thought. I came on with a makeshift fishing rod and started fishing.

'This is the first time we've ever played to a dirty pool of water!' said I.

Whereupon, a load of jolly skinheads, stripped to the waist in the sun, waded into the water to get closer, and started a trend. They thought it would be fun to throw scooped up silt and rotten leaves from the lake bed at us, and it was. These were extraordinary conditions and only an idiot would not have exploited them to the full. For some reason I went on, for the only time ever, in white-face Pierrot make-up. At Crystal Palace the opportunities for entertainment went far beyond the confines of the songs. Bob was the co-frontman, the other star in the band, and was very good at bantering with the crowd (as was Dick to be fair, when he could get a word in).

It turned out to be a hilarious show and a massive triumph. Sometimes only the cliche will do. Dear reader, we went down a storm. And then, of course, afterwards we're all on cloud nine, drinking and laughing, playing the pop stars with other pop stars and musicians, and with Sarah and Sue, and the fans, and Madness et al. I can count the number of unfriendly musicians I have met on two fingers (Peter Gabriel and Nick Lowe).

The best feeling in the world is when you've finished your set, gone down well, and the day is still young. For that is when a man has earned the right to get happily off his head in whatever way he likes. Later I watched Midge Ure with Ultravox singing 'Vienna' in the sunset from the back of the crowd and brimmed with pride at having been an integral part of the day's success. A review of the event said:

'Tenpole Tudor launched into their punky, jokey set. Loud and anarchic, their music is too formularised to take seriously at present. They're out there for a laugh and on those terms triumphed as much as anybody.'

A later review would say that watching Tenpole Tudor was like a car accident – appalling but you can't look away.

Only much later did I realise the source of all my crazed punk rock drive was a charnel house of rage from the torture I'd been forced to endure as a kid. The punk movement gave me and many others – and many far worse off than me – the opportunity to vent hurricanes of rage and fury amassed in infancy.

Expressing a sort of parody of anger, in a controlled environment, and entertaining others by doing so, was very cathartic and healing. Where else could free rein be given to such unbridled excess without being arrested, other than onstage? We were an enactment of chaos, not actual chaos. I was fearless on stage; once I challenged a bunch of skinheads to a fight then and there, and all at once! You could spend thousands of pounds for treatment at a psychiatric clinic in Harley Street and not get a tenth of the therapeutic benefit my troubled soul was getting from the Tenpole Tudor shows.

The joy of having a hit single is short-lived, soon augmented and then eclipsed by decisions, anxiety and preparations for the follow-up. There is always mental and physical pressure when your group is doing well.

We wanted 'Go Wilder' to be the next single but Dave Robinson wasn't keen.

'You don't want to be one-hit wonders,' he said.

He wanted it to be 'Wunderbar'. The damage had already been done to that song by my stupid decision to change the chorus and title from 'Fall About' to 'Wunderbar' but my pop sensibility told me that it was a catchier tune than 'Go Wilder' which, laudable enough though its message may be, seldom had the effect of making people actually go wilder when we played it – they bobbed about at best. So 'Wunderbar' it was, and yes it was a top twenty hit but with a completely different crowd. At a stroke we alienated our core fanbase of twelve-year-olds who thought it was silly (it was) and deterred others who may have been beginning to take an interest by making them think that Tenpole Tudor was some kind of novelty act or comedy band. It was a catastrophe which did untold damage, one of many times where we missed having a proper manager to guide us.

Up until we signed to Stiff, I had been the de facto manager; arranging rehearsals and gigs, liaising with the club promoters and the band, writing the songs, doing the art work and fronting the show. This became an unsustainable workload for me. And though now Jos was nominated manager of the band, it was Stiff who arranged our schedules and plans.

When we were filming the video for 'Swords of 1000 Men' in the oldest barn in England with the Sealed Knot battle re-enactment society, it suddenly occurred to me that someone ought to take a photograph of us dressed as knights. There was a bloke with a camera and we got him to take a few shots of us there and then. One of these became the best Tenpole Tudor photograph of all, and the replacement cover shot for the single. That opportunity could have so nearly been missed through inattention, and was the sort of thing you need a manager for.

I used to try and think of everything all the time, but you can't do that forever.

The biggest struggle was the constant pressure to come up with new songs. I could never relax when I got home, feeling obliged to pick up the guitar and cast around for song ideas. Songs were our units of currency and I was betting on myself to be able to coin some more. If Jagger/Richards or Lennon/ McCartney could write songs under pressure then so could I. But it was difficult, I am fussy when it comes to songs and wasn't going to put my name to anything sub-standard. My way of songwriting is the long way. If a tune or a riff still hasn't bored me after a thousand plays it passes the exam.

Phil Lynott

When we went to re-record a shinier, more single-worthy version of 'Wunderbar', Phil Lynott was at the same studio and I bumped into him in the studio kitchen.

He was lovely and couldn't have been friendlier and we made instant friends like kids in a playground. He was recording his solo single, 'Old Town (This Boy is Cracking Up)', with its lovely piano arpeggios. He took me to his studio to have a listen. It is absolutely brilliant, and a plea for help, like Lennon's 'Help!'. In turn, I invited Phil to our studio to listen to 'Wunderbar' which we were really pleased with. He said he liked it.

14

Fame

Tenpole Tudor had only been going for a couple of years, and were still mainly playing the first tranche of songs we'd written. The success of 'Swords of 1000 Men' promoted us to a level where our inexperience and lack of musical knowledge were exposed. We would always entertain on one level or another but as a band we hadn't really learned our craft or paid our dues.

Bob Kingston, a natural star with a singing voice of gold, was going out with Kim Wilde and one Thursday evening he and Kim unexpectedly called round to Albany Street. They had been in Regent's Park and wanted to watch *Top of the Pops* as Kim was on it that day. Bob had forgotten I had no TV so I suggested we go upstairs to ask Liverpool George. George's amazement, when he opened his door and Kim Wilde walked in to ask him ever so sweetly if she could watch herself on his television set, was utterly priceless; a fairy tale moment. I daresay he's dining out on it still.

Kim was nice and friendly. But I later heard she'd said I wasn't 'boyfriend material' which stung a bit.

Around then, I was walking along Oxford Street when Nick Heyward, wearing a nice jumper, introduced himself. He said he'd got a band together called Haircut 100 who were going to play 'pure pop'.

'Great!' said I, never having made a secret of my love of pop music, and wished him well. It was nice to feel part of the pop scene as well as the punk.

Further up Albany Street lived Martin who had a group called The Regents. Months earlier he'd played me a demo of his song,

'Seventeen', and I had played him 'Wunderbar'. Both songs made the Top Twenty. Perhaps Albany Street runs along a ley line of creativity.

One day near Gordon Square a policeman beckoned me over. He asked if I was responsible for 'Swords of 1000 Men' and when I said I was, he congratulated me and shook my hand. That was a great moment. Now even the cops are on our side! Stewart Copeland, drummer of The Police (and yes, I'm name-dropping; but isn't that the whole point of an autobiography, to drop as many names as possible?) told me his band used to get away with loads of offences, because no cop wanted to be the man who'd busted a member of The Police!

'Joe Strummer' was an alter-ego, like 'Eddie Tenpole', stage characters, and not exactly real people. I'd met Joe a few times by now and would bump into him walking around Notting Hill, invariably with a girl on his arm. People hailed him, he waved back like Stallone in *Rocky*.

'Alright Joe?'

'How ya doin'?' said Joe, in a New York accent. He was a great performer.

It's nice being greeted by strangers in the street; it makes you feel you belong. Unlike Jagger, Bowie, or Stewart, you could talk to the punk rock 'anti-star' stars. 'The audience is more important than the band', Malcolm McLaren often said.

The last time I saw Strummer, and the best I ever saw him onstage, was at the Brixton Academy with his Mescaleros, shortly before he died. I loved The Mescaleros: their music took you places the Clash never could.

That night he had something of the Dean Martin about him and was utterly mesmerising. At one point Joe held his mic stand configured in a way I'd never seen: over his shoulder like a bazooka gun, which blew my mind. How simple! How effective! How...how come I hadn't thought of it?

I went to the dressing room afterwards which was full of people but there was no sign of Joe. I asked Mick Jones where he was.

'He's there!' said Mick, pointing.

And I saw that one of the nondescript people, sitting on a bench, in a grey T-shirt was indeed Joe Strummer.

This is quite a common phenomenon with great performers after a show; they've left their charisma on stage for a while, and can seem underwhelming backstage in the dressing room. Joe was as gracious as ever and stood up, and I told him: 'There wasn't a dry eye in the house, Joe.'

By now I was recognised a lot and was always in the music papers, and I had to be more alert. I had people in the pub helpfully telling me that our third single was better than the fourth, and telling me what we should have done. But I could hardly complain. Having worked very hard to become a pop star, it was entirely logical that when I walk into a pub, people are going to talk to me about it. You try to be magnanimous and obliging to the degree that courtesy demands but it was a shock to learn that never again in my life would I ever be allowed to talk about anything other than Tenpole Tudor. So, if I felt depressed, I'd stay indoors.

Constantly busy on the promotional rounds, one cold snowy winter's day a small private plane was hired to transport us and Alvin Stardust to some Euro TV show. Alvin was a friendly, gentle chap, and an anxious flyer. We teased him mercilessly on the flight by singing Buddy Holly songs. He was a good sport. We also met Suzie Quatro and she was friendly too.

The most exciting encounter I ever had at an airport was bumping into Boney M. I love their singles. We were from opposite ends of the pop spectrum, exotic to each other, and equally pleased to be meeting. We posed together for a photograph. Pop stars have a type of glamour punk stars don't, and to meet such pop royalty in the flesh was thrilling.

I could have done with a mentor; someone older and wiser to offer guidance. But the deal when you become famous is you make your own mistakes and you soon learn that no one in the business cares about you personally. The pop star is totally on their own. How they deal with it is part of the spectator sport. The dream climax for the tabloid press is a spectacular crash-and-burn.

The public on the other hand, not unreasonably, assume that having set yourself up on a stage you know something they don't. They look to you for help and don't imagine that you need any.

I continued in the slipstream of my adopted mentors the Stones as best I could, following their star in my imagination. I can see that to some readers my fan talk about the Rolling Stones might seem like the most frightful drivel, but their example, you can't deny, has proved to be the most reliable guide as to how best to comport oneself in the hard world of rock and roll.

'Wunderbar' came out and charted getting to number sixteen in the UK. My proudest possession (before my wallet was stolen) was a press cutting from the *Record Mirror* of the Top Twenty one week, showing Tenpole Tudor at number sixteen and the Rolling Stones at number fifteen, with 'Start Me Up'! How close is that?!

Journal: 14 July, 1981
We've done Top of the Pops again and by the second time it's become routine.

Jim Honeyman-Scott told me that when The Pretenders got to number one with 'Brass in Pocket' he felt a terrible sense of anti-climax. Becoming number one, his life's ambition, was underwhelming: nothing happened. It was simply a statistic. In my journal I complain about feeling lonely, rather a lot. It felt weird to be lonely as well as in the pop charts. I lacked a confidante. I wasn't in contact with my friend Pete in those times. He had joined Prem Rawat's Divine Light Mission and we lived in different worlds.

Tenpole Tudor went on *TOTP* twice more, did the constant round of interviews and photoshoots, plus much flying to Europe and back, to mime on TV shows. There was little opportunity for any social life outside the group. We were always together: in the van, studio, airport, aeroplane, dressing room, on stage, everywhere.

'Wunderbar' gave us the only number one we ever had, in Belgium, and we'd flown over the day before an early TV show appearance in Bruges. In the morning a Belgian driver picked us up from the hotel too early to have breakfast so I'd have to wait until we reached the TV studios.

When we arrived, I was told there was no breakfast. I said that anything at all would do: I wasn't fussy, but obviously I couldn't go on national telly to front a performance of the Belgian number one hit single with no breakfast at all now, could I? When they tried to insist that I would jolly well have to, their inhospitality angered me. If this is how they treated the band at number one, I wondered what on earth they did to the poor bands who were at only eight or nine. We were good boys, me Bob, Dick and Gary; we worked hard, we were punctual and reliable. We never saw the need to smash a hotel room, and were generally pleasant to those we met. But expect me to do a TV show without any breakfast? Fuck off.

Eventually a ham roll wrapped in cling film appeared and we did the show. We were treated like caged animals. Perhaps they were scared of us; but why? We were no scarier than Slade or Status Quo or Wizzard – and they're not scary. I always assumed people could see through the manic Tenpole front to the nice and cuddly real me underneath, but came to realise that some people thought it was real and that I really was that hooligan nutter on stage, which is so depressing. Come to think of it the Tenpole character was very similar to the one I played at the RADA audition. The whole point of acting is to make it seem real.

My brain was beginning to rebel against having to think of the group for every second of every day, of every month, of every year with every single conversation only ever about the group. I don't expect the gripe to elicit sympathy and nor should it, nevertheless it did become boring, and added to the attractions of solitude where I could gaze into the flames of the blaze I'd made in the marble fireplace – and consider the situation.

Seeking inspiration and needing stimulation outside the microcosm of Tenpole Tudor and because I could afford a ticket,

I went to the Colosseum to see the English National Opera company. *La Traviata* blew my mind.

The point of the ENO is that they sing in English instead of Italian, German or French. I don't know why they bother, you still can't make out the words, but you don't need to. It's the same with the Clash: Joe Strummer's singing was largely unintelligible on stage but you knew exactly what he meant.

In the same spirit of discovery I went to see a ballet for the first time; *Swan Lake* at the Royal Opera House, Covent Garden. I wore the same leather jacket I'd worn the previous evening watching the Anti-Nowhere League at The Lyceum and nobody batted an eyelid – I liked that, it made me know I was in a civilised place.

But, unlike the opera, this particular ballet show was disappointing; it didn't draw me in at all. My seat was in the back row of the stalls by an area where people drank in the interval, and where Freddie Mercury was pacing about, having a heated argument with one of his team and not taking his seat any time soon. I observed him, looking behind me before I sat down. It felt entirely normal to see Freddie Mercury at the ballet, after all where else would he be? That night I strolled home to Regent's Park along deserted pavements and grand architecture feeling very privileged.

15

Let the Four Winds Blow

We were reminded by Stiff that, according to our contract, we owed them another LP by September. This was a shock; we had hardly paused since the making of the first album a year earlier. And we didn't have many new songs ready. It is never ideal to have to force songs out, like eggs from a battery chicken, but we had no choice.

It was decided to record our second album at Genetic Studios, Goring, a pretty place halfway up a hill and in a secluded forest. We were billeted for five weeks at The Miller of Mansfield, a fine sixteenth century inn. Alan Winstanley was the producer.

When we first visited Genetic studio, the Human League's Phil Oakey was sitting astride a spanking new motorbike, with gleaming chrome and polished red – newly delivered by his record company as a birthday present. I made a mental note not to hold my breath waiting for Dave Robinson to give me a motorbike. They'd just finished making their *Dare* LP including 'Don't You Want Me Baby' among other hits. Genetic was owned by the renowned producer Martin Rushent and he excitedly told me the future of pop was the synthesiser and that the electric guitar is dead.

Hearing a new song develop in the studio, when you are the boss of that three-minute kingdom and can order it anyway your imagination sees fit, fuelled by knowing the song is pretty good already, and trying to make it even better before it is set in stone for all time, is one of life's supreme joys.

Every day I had a six-mile run preparing for the tour that followed the recording. I set off as Autumn dusk approached and imagined I was Bambi gambolling through forests. I overlooked the panorama of the misty autumn valley with plumes of smoke rising from distant cottages with twinkling lights.

At the end of a hard day's work we would return to our billet at The Miller of Mansfield for drinks, before steak and chips and a bottle of Bordeaux for dinner.

Our presence at the ancient inn was a magnet for the youth of the area and we were happy to chat to all and sundry with the fire blazing in the hearth. Over time we got to know some of them well and made friends. There were lots of girls taking an interest as well as blokes, which made a nice change. And it was the easiest thing in the world to invite girls upstairs to our timbered rooms, and dear reader, we did.

A week into our stay at the Miller of Mansfield, a new landlord took over. He was young, ex-army, highly-strung, very public school, and in behaviour and manner, I swear, was exactly like John Cleese as Basil in *Fawlty Towers.*

We were courteous to him as we generally were to everyone, but it soon became clear that he disliked the scruffy youth that we were attracting, and the sight of us all sitting round the ancient fireplace, drinking and smoking tobacco, irritated him. Rockers in the saloon went against the Olde Worlde image the surroundings suggested and that he had envisaged. And our dress certainly wasn't in code either. We were the antithesis of the English gentry, the tweed-jacket, checked-shirt crowd he'd pictured when buying the place. But because he was new, and because we were well-behaved, he had to put up with it for the moment. But he simmered with mounting resentment.

About two or three weeks into our stay at the Miller of Mansfield I returned one evening to find there had been some trouble. I don't know what. A couple of lads had been barred. Our new friends sketched the scene breathlessly outside the pub before I went inside.

As soon as the landlord saw me, he exploded. For some reason, he saw me as the root cause of all his troubles.

He shouted:

'You can do better than that Tudor Pole!!' and then he lost his temper completely, lunging at me.

I fled upstairs with Basil Fawlty in hot pursuit and managed to get to my room and lock the door behind me.

He started banging on the flimsy two hundred-year-old door shouting again:

'You can do better than that Tudor Pole!!' – as if we were still back at whatever godforsaken boarding school it was he went to.

As he was exactly like Fawlty he was more alarming than genuinely terrifying, because you knew he was mad. Nevertheless, it was a close-run chase, and he banged the door with great force.

I was standing on my bed in full battle mode, holding my guitar by the neck like a weapon and ready to repel boarders. Crash bang! The flimsy door splintered and gave way.

I shouted at him to keep out, but he burst into the room. It was only when he saw me ready to whack him over the head with the guitar that he at last stalled his charge.

I talked him down from his rage as best I could, assuring him of my innocence. The fact is that he was totally unsuited to the job of a publican or hotelier and I can only hope that he is happier in what he is doing now. Still, at least he gave us stories to tell, and we gave him a credit on the album sleeve, to the 'Mad Miller of Mansfield'.

Pete Townshend

One day I was recording the lead vocal of a song. I had done three takes and was on my way back to the control room to have a listen. I pushed the thick padded door and found, to my irritation, that there were three strangers there – a woman and two men.

'Alan, why are these people here? I don't like members of the public in when I am trying to sing.'

He didn't reply and fiddled with a knob on his desk. There was a peculiar atmosphere. I glanced at the woman, who was about forty, and in peripheral vision became aware of one of the men staring intently.

I panned over to him, and two big blue eyes drilled into me. Blow me down, it was Pete Townshend.

'Oh wow! Pete! man!'

We shook hands and I got Alan to play him 'Throwing the Baby out with the Bathwater'. It sounded good and Townshend was most encouraging. He told me 'well done', and 'keep it up'. This friendly welcome from one of the kings of rock and roll made me blossom with delight.

Pete Townshend showed up again, I heard, at a local pub, interrupting Gary and Dick's game of pool when he kept falling over the table. He was out of it on heroin and booze. Gary had to chide him:

'Oi Pete! Keep off the pool table!'

Townshend was going through a difficult time, of which, dear reader, there are many in the life of a rocker.

At the end of the five weeks, we invited the villagers up to the studio to listen to a rough cut of what we had done and had a party; Pete Murphy of Bauhaus showed up. For the cover photograph we hired suits of armour and drove into the heart of Wales to a ruined castle perched upon a rocky mountain.

Tenpole Tudor Winter Tour 1981

Back on the road, we were a professional crew getting on with the job with all hands on deck to keep up with the unremitting work schedule. An efficient tour is similar to a military operation. But we weren't the jolly musketeers we once were.

It was when we played Loughborough that Sue and I got together – and even now I cannot hear the word Loughborough without getting a pang. Seismologists, Volcanologists and the Meteorological Office were baffled, having never before recorded such tremors on the Richter scale outside the San Andreas fault line. It took us both by surprise. She told me it was Bob she used to fancy. That night a bond was forged as strong as any crusader castle whose ruins last forever. Everybody needs somebody to love.

Lochem Festival, Holland

The Lochem festival in Holland was a big affair. The Clash, Saxon, Bow Wow Wow, Kirk Brandon's Spear of Destiny were on the bill and it was great to meet everyone. Me and Kirk swapped stories of our training methods.

On the day the real surprise was Saxon, a long-haired, heavy-rock act. They used every trick in the book with Biff Byford egging the crowd on:

'Let me hear you say yeah!... yeah! I can't hear you, YEAH!'

'Are you feelin alright?!... yeah! I said, are you feeling ALRIGHT!!!'...YEEAH!! I can't hear you!'

And so on. It was unabashed old school hard rock entertainment at its best and they could not have been better received by the roaring crowd.

After Saxon's triumph I returned backstage to socialise in the heightened buzz. The Clash were on next, and taking their time about it; smoking spliff and huddled together in a corner in deep consultation. They faced a hell of a challenge; how were they going to follow that!?

We wished them well as they filed past us to the stage which was about seven or eight feet off the ground, with a wooden security fence a few feet in front of it. They ambled on and, ignoring the audience, started with a chilled-out dub reggae groove, which went on for some time. They played another song in a similar vein, their backs to the audience. The crowd began to sag when the third number was more slow-paced reggae.

Half way through it, Joe stopped the band and turned to the audience. 'Hey, people!'

Pin drop.

'We've come here to play for you. Why is that barrier there?'

Joe points to the fence in front of the stage.

'There should be no barrier between us! We are *you!* and you are *us!*'

The crowd needed no second bidding. They stormed the fence and tore it down. The atmosphere was electric. The mob surged right up to the stage, the Clash start 'White Riot' and everybody goes mental.

We'd been on at 11.15 in the morning and made little impact at Lochem so I was determined our headline show the following night in Bocholt Barn in Belgium would be a success. Now, dear reader, it was such an un-punk thing to do I had to pluck up courage, but I went on and said:

'Hello everybody let me hear you say YEAH!'

I was amazed when they roared back the loudest 'YEAH!' you've ever heard, like they'd been rehearsing it all their lives. When we got to the third 'Yeah' I was only partly joking when I said I still couldn't hear them because they were shouting so loudly I'd become half deaf.

Later on, I said:

'Hey people! We are *you*... and you are *us*! There is no barrier between us! We are ONE!'

They loved it. There was no physical barrier to tear down but they got the message all right. Bocholt Barn was one of the most powerful concerts Tenpole Tudor ever delivered.

David Dorrell wrote a review of us at The Zig Zag Club which ended:

'I took my leave numb and headless thanks to the block and axe that Tenpole calls pop.'

One thing that used to slightly puzzle me was that although I was in the music papers all the time, and the charts some of the time, not only did no one know the first thing about me, no one seemed in the least bit curious to find out. I was yet to learn the pop star is simply a cipher. Nobody cares who you actually are; you could be anybody. In essence all that matters is the sound of the record and the look of the photograph.

Gaz's Rockin' Blues Club

The best club of all time, and still going strong at St Moritz Club, Wardour Street is 'Gaz's Rockin' Blues Club'. In those days it was based in Meard Street. Expertly run by Gaz Mayall, son of John, he has an encyclopaedic knowledge of all the best old rock and roll, swing, ska, black rhythm and blues bands from the fifties and sixties. When they are DJ-ing, Gaz and his colleague Ska V Goldsmith make it utterly impossible not to dance. I was always made very welcome at Gaz's club and given a big hug upon entering by Juliette Cowan the lovely hat check girl.

I was in the French House one Thursday evening when in walked Robert Plant with a couple of voluptuous foreign beauties; it turned out he had been recording nearby. He was always a friendly chap and greeted me warmly once again. Come closing time Plant asked whether I knew of anywhere to go, to carry on the night.

'Yeah, Gaz's Rockin' Blues!'

'What's that?' said Planty.

'I'll show you,' I said.

It was all of a two-minute walk. A couple of hours later in that oasis of music and joy our eyes met across the bar and he gave me the thumbs up.

16

Rumblings

In Tenpole Tudor the atmosphere in the van was now a lot less jolly than it once was. There was resentment growing about the fact that I had more money than them, having written our first two hits.

The next single, 'Throwing My Baby out with the Bathwater', based on one of Gary's riffs was credited to us all, but that was not to be a chart hit (although it became such a live favourite it's been played at every gig for forty years since). There was a riptide of discord developing and murky undertows.

There was no love lost between Gary and me. Dear reader, we had nothing in common. There were things I did that annoyed him but as he would never say anything I never found out what they were, so could not address problems. He was all gum-chewing, surly 'passive aggressive'.

Gary was the odd one out in the group and would have been far better suited, as he later admitted, to being a professional footballer. I would always room with Dick, and Gary with Bob. Gary was a bit of a plotter and a manipulator, and Bob was under his influence to an extent.

The whiff of discontent grew imperceptibly. It could be ignored at first and no one wanted to start a row so nothing was out in the open. But this meant small irritations festered; if something had been said at the time, the issues could have been nipped in the bud. The end result was a building avalanche of resentments and grievances. In a band the human chemistry has to be right – otherwise you're fucked. Which, in fact, we were.

Now when I turned up at our Halligans HQ there was no warmth, just a few muttered 'alrights' in almost a parody of passive aggression. No cause or reason was ever given and now I felt like an outsider in my own band, how did that happen? I had no ally apart from Dick, to an extent, in the slowly growing air of antipathy.

Finland

At the end of April 1982, we flew to Finland for four gigs in a row. I felt very tired onstage at Helsinki as I went through the gymnastics I thought were needed to whip up a storm. I was fairly fit but not Olympian ultra-fit like Mick Jagger, which you need to be. He is so fit that even if he feels tired or not in the mood, he has such vast reserves of residual, super-athlete energy that no one in the crowd would ever suspect it.

Finland is all pine trees, lakes and snow. White, grey and green is the only colour scheme. All the Finnish women are green-eyed beauties. You could order Reindeer steaks or Bear from the menu. We never saw a pub or a bar and yet everyone seemed to be drunk.

We drove on snow to the second gig further inland, to play in a large barn-like edifice in the trees by a frozen lake. In the middle of the lake was a small island with a cabin on it which was our dressing room.

At the end of our set the only place to retreat, to be out of sight of the audience while we waited for the encore, was behind the amps. Outdoors was sub-zero. Indoors it was cold enough. The crowd were all dressed for the polar conditions, but the sweat was starting to freeze on our scantily-clad bodies. Encore over, we hurried back to the cosy island cabin to the sauna room. It was an enormous relief to sit there, pouring with sweat, drinking whisky and cooking a sausage on the hot coals. Dear reader, this is not the way to behave in a sauna – as I was told by a Finn in no uncertain terms.

The next show was even more extraordinary; we went on stage to be greeted with a sea of screaming girls as if we were in *A Hard Day's Night*. It was a hell of a buzz, which thoroughly energised us, although after about twenty minutes of screaming you could see how it could eventually become tedious. It was clear that Bob Kingston was the main focus of their attention. I couldn't feel jealous as he was such a natural star. That's how he got the job in the first place. If you were making a film about a young rocker, Bob would be perfect casting. But with me the role was more of a performance, and one that was becoming increasingly ill-fitting. I lacked the degree of narcissism and self-love which you need to play the frontman role on a regular basis.

As I grew more and more tired, the burden of the job became heavier. The banality of so much of it and having to answer questions like, 'So tell me, how did the band begin?' for the umpteenth time drove me nuts. I got Bob to do the interviews in Finland. He is a showbiz natural. The rest of us watched a TV interview he did somewhere abroad and he was most entertaining with his charisma, cocky wit and mascara.

After one of the Finnish shows, driving through snow in the night, and unable any longer to ignore the poisonous atmosphere in the van, I pleaded with Gary that we talk about the situation and try to sort things out. He told me to shut up. When I persisted, he said, 'If you don't shut up, I'll punch you in the face'. The others kept quiet.

From which, dear reader, I could only infer that people didn't want to make things better. Gary and Dick are both Librans, a sign allegedly denoting diplomacy and dislike of confrontation. But some things are essential to confront, especially the mounting problems that we had while travelling together here, there and everywhere in a small van.

To be fair to Gary, he also had a difficult start in life. Once on tour near Hungerford, his home town, we called in to see his mum who made us tea. Gary gave her our new poster, a very large one featuring the first album cover, and she unrolled it on the kitchen table. Seeing our heraldic lions again, now fifty times larger, and remembering how there was only just enough yellow left in the felt-tip pen to colour in the original artwork, I was marvelling at how much yellow that heroic little felt-tip did eventually yield, and told Mrs Long the story, hoping to amuse.

'Ooh, aren't you clever!' she said contemptuously. She completely missed the point and seemed to think I was boasting. I was shocked and hurt, in equal measure, by that unexpected bolt of hostility. There is a nasty, somewhat prevalent provincial characteristic, and perhaps the worst of the English faults, that doesn't like to see another person doing well – and thinks it better to take them down a peg or two rather than to praise the achievement.

Meanwhile our fifth single was to be released, the title track of our album: *Let the Four Winds Blow.* When you are in the middle of the merry-go-round of being in a pop group it is easy to get caught up in the minutiae of it all and lose sight of the bigger picture. The pretty boy look was all the rage in 1982 with Duran Duran, Japan and Wham sweeping all before them.

Bob had abandoned his classic original rocker-with-a-quiff biker look and wore shiny suits from Johnson's, King's Road. At the photo session for the single cover, we went all out for the heavily made-up, androgynous image, and ended up looking like a bunch of transvestite rent boys.

Dave Robinson roared with laughter when he saw the results. He tore the photos in two, told us not to be so ridiculous and said he would direct the photo session himself. He had us smeared in grease and dirt, posing as a bunch of pirates aboard the deck of a captured whaling ship. He was quite right: it was a much better picture.

Ibiza

When the band were offered a two-week holiday in a villa in Ibiza, all expenses paid, though with no fee, as such, in return for playing a single show in a castle atop a hill, it seemed too good to be true. Dear reader it was.

To go on holiday with someone is to find out all about them. Only when you've been on holiday together do you know whether you are truly compatible or not. It was a lovely villa in a lovely place but I was still stuck with the same four geezers in the same unpleasant social dynamic as in the Holloway Road.

Fortunately, in Ibiza I bumped into a friend and neighbour from Albany Street, John Barratt, heir to the Sherbet Fountain fortune, (irrelevant I know, but do not such details lend colour to a story?). At a hillside bar, with the glittering sea below, I confided in him that I wanted to escape what had become an intolerable situation. It was good to have someone to talk to.

In my carping about the other band members I am not so much including Dick Crippen. In real terms I got on with him the best and we often made each other laugh. One day in Ibiza, Dick and I were invited to spend the day with a wealthy young Dutch couple, to sail on their boat and hang out at their villa. I think he was a cocaine smuggler. They were certainly coke fiends and the boat ride was disappointingly brief; they couldn't wait to get back to the villa to take more drugs. He was becoming overwhelmed by her insatiable coke-fuelled sexual demands, he said.

The Tenpole Tudor concert in the Ibizan castle was very good. We delivered as we always did. We upheld our end of the bargain to pay for the holiday. But in our hearts, we knew that the band was running rapidly out of steam.

17
The Crunch

Shortly after Ibiza we played The Lyceum on 8 August, with 999, but we failed to connect with the audience at all. Being weighed down by my thick leather biker's trousers didn't help. I know part of me is clever and yet I can be very stupid sometimes.

The latest single, 'Let the Four Winds Blow', had failed to chart and the vibe in the band was by now truly rotten. At one point I suggested we do a rock and roll version of 'Donna e Mobile'(women are fickle) from Verdi's *Rigoletto*. That didn't go down well.

'Fuck off, Ed, we're a rock and roll band,' said Bob.

When talk of a North American tour supporting the Clash came up, I told them there was no way I was doing it while everything in the band was so shit. Cruising along Route 66 bathing in Gary and Bob's animosity, no love in the air? Mmmmmm. Nice! Dear reader, that would have killed me.

I was convinced the band were plotting against me. They were being secretive and shifty which no amount of exaggerated nonchalance and insistent gum-chewing could disguise. There's a bumper sticker caption: 'Just because you're paranoid doesn't mean they are not out to get you.'

In November I bought an *Evening Standard* and in Patrick Moore's horoscope for Sagittarius, it actually said: 'People are plotting behind your back.' Aagh.

We had one last Tenpole Tudor 'Christmas Show' booked at The Marquee for 21 December, 1982. In late November I went along to The Marquee Club one evening, as you do and I was greeted inside the door by the owner who said,

'Hello Ed, I'm very sorry to hear you've cancelled your gig on the 21 December.'

'What!! But we haven't cancelled it.'

'Your manager Jos rang up today to say it was definitely off.'

Shock begat realisation, which begat anger which begat defiance which begat resolve, which begat determination.

'Listen mate, watch my lips, listen to the horse's mouth: I am Ten Pole Tudor and I say we are playing! Even if I have to go on with a cold rice pudding the show goes on! I *never* cancel! OK?!'

'OK,' said the guv'nor, 'I hear you Ed. It's on. Good.'

When I spoke to Jos the next day, he told me that Gary and Bob had told him to cancel the Marquee booking as they definitely weren't doing it. And now, for the first time in ages, I knew where I stood, I could see the lie of the land at last, and lo, I was galvanised.

I rang Dick and told him I was going to do the show anyway and asked whether he would care to join me. Dick, made of nobler stuff than the others, agreed: 'I'll do The Marquee with you, Ed, but then that's it.'

'Don't worry, Dick; we all know that's it,' I said.

Also rehearsing at Halligans were The Helicopters whom I liked. I offered Mick O'Donnell and Paul Martin, the guitarist and drummer, a hundred pounds each to spend the next two weeks learning and rehearsing the Tenpole Tudor set with me and Dick.

Of course, they agreed and now, at last, after months in the doldrums the wind filled the sails, my spirits soared, the skies were clear and I was captain of my ship again.

I'd first met Mick O'Donnell the year before in The Castle, where the bands went after rehearsals. An engaging character, we hit it off right from the start. He was friendly and funny, which is all I ask of anyone, and we made each other laugh. Mick O'Donnell's family had emigrated to Islington from Limerick in the 1950s when he was a boy. He can play any style of guitar as well as anybody and has done so every weekend of his life on the Irish Pub circuit.

(After playing with Tenpole Tudor for years he hated being asked if he was the original guitarist, for as soon as he said no, people would walk away. I told him to say he *was* the original one as that's what people want to hear. There have to be some rewards for being in the group for twelve years).

Paul Martin the drummer was every inch the Holborn boy, born and bred, with generations of London skullduggery etched into his classical features. He sold fruit and veg in the Ridley Road market in Hackney with his dad and had all the gifts of a cockney barker. He was also a very funny man. Dick and I rehearsed Mick and Paul up to pace for the show. I was galvanised by adrenaline and the determination not to be thwarted by the backstabbers half the band had revealed themselves to be. We all rose to the challenge and there was a happy atmosphere in the room, which is the only atmosphere in which either me or my music works. I was in a state of delayed shock and I didn't try to process what was going on, there was no time; we had a show to do! If there's a show coming up, I can think of nothing else.

I went along to the *Melody Maker* offices and delivered a hand written press-release, sealed with wax, to pre-empt any rubbish Gary and Bob may have been about to put out.

'Tenpole Tudor has not broken up, for I Edward Tudor Pole, am Ten Pole Tudor, the rightful king of England in all but fact.

On Dec. 3rd 1982 I parted company with my old band quite amicably. Their continuing interest in the traditional rock and roll format contrasted with my burning need for a more imaginative and creative way of working. Not a man to be phased by a crisis, the Marquee gig on Dec. 21st will still go ahead. The show must go on. Dick Crippen and I will present a show with new people – a Christmas party with surprises about the story of Tenpole Tudor past, present and future.

Within a forest dark and grim, born of wolf and witch,
The future king of England lay, screaming in the ditch.'

This farrago of overwrought nonsense shows my state of mind, although it was a lot less far-fetched in those fairytale times where Adam Ant was Prince Charming, and I was pretender to some other imaginary throne, than it may seem now. But for us early exponents of punk, when punk was what we wanted it to be, because we were making it up as we went along, our days were numbered.

The 'second wave' of punk was sweeping down from the north to depose dandies like Adam and me, and in the swiftly moving world of pop music punk rock was suddenly very old hat. Now it was all pretty boy synth bands where every record had the obligatory fake-sounding snare drum turned up ridiculously loud.

The punk scene didn't die, it simply went underground, with second-wave punk flourishing up north. Punk rock traditions survive everywhere north of the home counties, particularly in Yorkshire, the North East and Scotland.

Meanwhile my tutor from RADA, Malcolm McKay, had written a play about the Sex Pistols which had a run at the Theatre Royal, Plymouth and then a few nights at the Hackney Empire. The band in the play featured my old RADA colleagues Kevin McNally as Sid Vicious, and Rick Cottan as Johnny Rotten. We asked them to support us at The Marquee in character as the 'Sex Pistols'. This was before the prevalence of tribute bands and the crowd were most bemused, though they certainly weren't complaining.

There were queues down Wardour Street and the place was packed. Tenpole Tudor went down the proverbial storm. Most of the people didn't even notice the personnel change, Mick O'Donnell having similar hair and build to Bob. We hadn't rehearsed 'Wunderbar', but right at the end when we'd played everything else, and the crowd were shouting for it, Dick and I decided to do it anyway, for a laugh.

Mick, normally very adroit at playing along to songs he's never heard, was flummoxed by this very early oddity, but it didn't matter: we were teasing him. That it was a riot of jolly dissonance mattered not, Mick had more than passed the audition, the night was in the bag, and we had unequivocally triumphed. How the crowd roared, and we were all ecstatic. It was one of our best gigs ever. Afterwards, on the way back to drop off the gear, we bought Kentucky Fried Chicken as usual from the Charing Cross Road branch near Centrepoint.

When I woke up the next day I was on my own; the fruits of all my dreams and labour gone rotten.

Bob, Dick and Gary announced they were going to call themselves 'The Tudors' which was a bit rich considering there ain't a Tudor among 'em! This was the second time that Gary had been party to ousting me from a band. Memo to self: don't work with G. Long and not expect to be betrayed. At the same time, I couldn't help thinking they were mad to have got rid of, surely, their most talented member.

I formed a Cajun band with Mick, Paul, Bill McCabe on accordion, Rick Cotton on violin and Andy Allen from The Professionals on bass. We called it The Hayrick Band and did a few shows, including at The Hammersmith Palais supporting Gary Glitter, playing Cajun and jigs and reels, which got everybody dancing, along with the old favourites. When I mentioned our new direction to Shane MacGowan, who was just about to start gigging with The Pogues, he was most indignant: 'But that's what I'm doing!' he said. And when we had a residency at Dingwalls he came to every show anxiously hoping we weren't going to become too successful and steal his thunder. He needn't have worried. When our single 'The Hayrick Song' failed to chart I was dropped by Stiff Records. The fact is, and Robinson knew it, I was exhausted. After five years of unceasing, high-pressure work, mentally and physically, I was deeply tired. My predominant reaction was relief to be out from under the yoke of the corporation, and the unceasing toil of its demands. This was a terrible time. Something inside me died. I would always be a musician but the band breaking up was when I lost any further desire to be famous. I didn't enjoy being a pop star and I never knew who I was meant to be playing.

PART THREE

18

Freedom

Having a meal in the Double Six cafe early one evening in Eversholt Street, next to Euston Station, as was my wont not having a kitchen, a young chap approached me.

'Hello, my name's Johnny and I've just finished at RADA. Is it true that you went there too?'

I told him yes it was true, and we chatted awhile. He was an amiable fellow and I was happy to accept his invitation to go for a pint, little knowing how that fateful five-minute walk around the corner was going to change my life.

The Cock Tavern was not a pub I knew, being tucked away in Phoenix Street, a back road of Somers Town, next to Chamberlain House council estate, where Johnny and Kath lived. It was a redbrick, nineteen thirties edifice currently squatted by every type of character imaginable. We walked into the large pub filled with an assortment of punks, anarchists, gypsies, exotic teenagers dressed like pharaohs, Irish men in old suits, Scotsmen, pale youths with nineteen thirties haircuts, old London couples, local fishwives, cabbies, builders and lots of dogs: a rich tapestry of London life.

The pub was run by an Irish lady, who was generous with her credit to the motley clientele until their next dole cheque arrived. There was a happy, humming atmosphere and a jukebox and a pool table and I instantly felt at home. Johnny introduced me to his girlfriend Kathy, a beautiful hat maker, dressed in a pink and purple colour scheme. She was most welcoming, and I rather fell for her.

After a few pints we went the short distance to the estate, calling on Johnny's neighbour Sean Poe. He was sitting in his virtually furniture-less room wearing an elegant powder blue suit and listening to a Miles Davis record. He told me he played the saxophone and we talked about music. He asked me whether I could lend him a fiver. Well, I could and I did.

Sean introduced me in turn to Nick Bodge, a South London ex-skinhead/mod, scooter-boy. Nick Bodge's flat contained two greyhounds and a whippet, two bikes and his gorgeous girlfriend, Lynn. Nick made me laugh with tales of how, when there had been a bit of a riot in the block not so long ago, where the police had been called, he'd been on the roof of the flats in a Nazi uniform lobbing petrol bombs down into the yard below. It was the level of gleeful relish at his own villainy that made me laugh rather than the villainy itself.

Sean Poe was with us when we went back to the Cock. Now I met Steve Organ, an earnest, handsome Irish lad who immediately began discussing a film idea he had and his ambitions to be a cameraman. Sean and Steve also introduced me to Matt Fisher, a talented musician and the epitome of charm. The air was blue with tobacco smoke, the lights pale red, the walls dark nicotine cream. The jukebox played 'From a Jack to a King' amidst the hubbub of chatter and laughter.

I had already fallen for Johnny's girlfriend, Kath, an eccentric bohemian type, and the issue of a Scottish aristocrat and a barmaid from Bristol after closing time. Kath was full of life and fun, a girl who could purr with pleasure in a sea of chaos.

Naturally I kept these thoughts to myself as she was Johnny's girl and he was my new instant best friend. Johnny was full of actorly swagger and looked like a Dutch painter in his lopsided leather beret.

I was very grateful to him for he introduced me to a fascinating new scene where lifelong friendships would be made, band members found, many adventures shared, and a whole new world of fun to be had. The great thing about it was that no one talked to me about Tenpole Tudor or treated me differently. These people had artistic dreams and ambitions of their own, and my chart success was now a distant three-year-old memory.

The next thing I knew was waking up in a strange room, fully dressed, with the sun streaming through the window. The birds were tweeting outside and I was content to lie there. I reached under the bedclothes for the cigarettes in my jacket pocket to enhance this moment of pleasure.

Johnny poked his head round the door, bade me good morning and said, 'Do you fancy brekker?'

After bacon and egg at the Double Six, Johnny, Kath and I strolled down via Russell Square and the British Museum, to Covent Garden where Kath had arranged to meet a woman to photograph her hats. We were still rather drunk from the night before and invented a song which became the theme tune of our nascent bender. 'I am a hunter, hunter catches prey, we put seven eggs in a box today.' We sang it periodically, lustily, loudly and merrily.

'Hello London!' Johnny exclaimed optimistically in full actorly mode. I too slipped into a stock stentorian, actor-manager type which is such fun to play and was so scorned at RADA (they thought it meant you weren't serious). Continuous drinking can improve your diction once you've drunk your way through the slurred stage. Keith Moon spoke like Noël Coward when he was drunk (Keith Moon spoke like Noël Coward) and I was speaking like some old buffer. Kath carried her hats, and Johnny had a black and white mongrel dog he was looking after.

We passed a Burton's where they were selling dinner suits for ninety nine pounds ninety nine so I bought one, plus a shirt and bow-tie. I changed into it and dumped my old clothes in a bin like Jack Reacher. It was symbolic: I was becoming somebody new in a brand-new life in a brand-new world.

Quite apart from which, when one is on a bender one must be suitably dressed. One of Kath's unusual green felt hats completed my new ensemble. The sun was shining and I was making myself up as we went along. Whole areas of my personality long dormant when in the band were now coming to the fore. I felt completely uninhibited for a change.

We greeted groups of tourists most effusively, and welcomed them to London, which went down well. We had nothing but goodwill to dispense. I had some money in the bank and would periodically withdraw fifty pounds in one-pound notes (so it seemed like more) to maintain our cashflow. My new friends had very little money. But now they did, so all was well.

Covent Garden was sunny and we loitered in the piazza waiting for the hat photographer. After years of ambition-fuelled travail in the grimy world of rock and roll, I knew almost nothing of the real world and now I had playmates who were from it, to show me around. It was fascinating.

'We put seven eggs in a box today!'

A young blond spiv in uniform, one of the security guards, came up and asked us to keep the noise down.

'My dear fellow,' I said, fleshing out my toff act, 'we are simply enjoying the delights of this fine piazza! Allow me to introduce you to my friends: Gilbert Montmorency Banboxenbury. And Katherine Clanricarde Ffilpingtonsonton.'

'How do you do?' said Johnny, genially extending his hand.

'Just keep the noise down alright!' said blondie, retreating rapidly.

I was happy. Pretty girls were walking along and an Indian summer was upon us. A very smart young lady with her well-groomed companion came along and I said, as if to a long-lost friend, 'I say, it's Tracy isn't it?!'.

'No, you fool!' her companion said without missing a beat, 'It's Davinia!'

It seems to me to be a civic duty to amuse people along the way as you proceed through life; if everybody's happy, then technically we're in heaven. Another man, with the face of Henry Cooper and the voice of Richard Burton, came up to me, eyeing my green headpiece with evident disapproval.

'What on earth is that ridiculous hat?'

'It's an Albanian Gipsaw hat,' said Kath, 'and look at these ones.'

She started pulling hats out of her sack. We amused him and he told us he'd spent eight years in prison for shooting a fellow officer in the leg when in the guards.

The photographer turned up and Kath tried to enlist me as a model for the shoot. The photographer wasn't in the same mood as us and much less impressed by my new suit than I was, which admittedly was more like a bouncer's uniform than something you'd wear to the opera.

'Why are you in evening wear?' she said. 'It's not what we want.'

'My dear madam, I sport evening wear because I have neither the time nor the opportunity to change before this evening comes about, and as a doyenne of fashion you will know what a sin it is to be improperly dressed at that time of day. I am merely early. Early is fine. It's being late that is the unforgivable sin, would you not agree?'

She was not amused, and I could tell she didn't like me. Not wanting to spoil Kath's chances of becoming a famous milliner I retreated to a nearby pub for an 'Admiral's Judder'.

The pub was crowded with office workers and tourists, and I noticed an old woman, somewhat dishevelled, sitting at the only otherwise unoccupied table.

'Hello madam, do you mind if I join your table?' I said.

'Not at all dear.' She has a Dublin accent, long grey hair, missing teeth and a grubby print dress. There are two full plastic bags under the table.

'Do you know, dear, you're the first person I've spoken to since I've been here. When I speak to people, they ignore me.'

'How very rude of them.'

'That's what I thought,' she agreed. I bought her a dry sherry and sat down at the table as she launched into a tirade against the Maidenhead police who had recently arrested her for being drunk and disorderly.

'They wouldn't give me any water, I kept asking for water and they wouldn't give me any water. I hate them. I was so thirsty.' She lowered her voice to conspiratorial volume: 'I had to drink my own ewe-rhine.'

'Good grief!' I said.

'I asked the lady policeman for some water, and she said I was filth!'

'That's out of order!'

'I know. It's terrible; it's awful. Don't ever go to Maidenhead.'

'Well, thanks for warning me, I shall give it a wide berth from now on, don't you worry.'

'It's a terrible place. They were so cruel to me at the police station they wouldn't give me any water.'

'Really?'

The woman eventually got off that train of thought going round its track. She then pulled out a grubby letter and asked me to read it to her. It was from someone in Hastings and had contained a five-pound note when it was sent – a long time ago judging by the state of it. She told me she had a son whom she never saw, and that she loved the opera.

'So do I!' I said, happy to find common ground. We were discussing our favourite, *La Traviata*, when Johnny and Kath came into the pub to fetch me. Their number now included Gerard MacArthur and Poric, two other actors fresh out of RADA and new to the world of unemployment which is the actor's lot. They were also squatting at Chamberlain House.

I introduced them all to the Irish lady after which she told me I was her favourite. We left her to her poverty and another dry sherry, and went to the French House in Dean Street. The pub was at its heaving best; everyone smoking, drinking, talking, laughing, and as I approached the bar a gorgeous girl said, 'Oh Tenpole, hello! I love you.' She had a thick Scouse accent, 'I'm Margi Clarke, Jamie Reid's girlfriend!'

Jamie Reid, you recall, was the Sex Pistols' art director who came up with the kidnap demand style of their logo as well as all the other artwork.

Her painted eyes shone like a thousand watt bulb as did her bright red double-decker lipstick smile. I returned the greeting with much pleasure but then her face clouded,

'Oh Tenpole, I thought you were one of us!'

'What do you mean? Of course I'm one of you!' I said before realising she was referring to my accent, which was exaggeratedly posh by this stage of the bender and going up a social notch with every gill. If nothing else my whole life has been a demonstration that you can't and shouldn't judge a book by its cover. Caspar John, my brother's father, once said to me: 'It doesn't matter how much scrambled egg someone has on their shoulders, take a man as you find him.' Which is very good advice.

Margi was soon mollified though and drinks all round were bought. We found seats in the left-hand corner and Margi said, 'Hey Tenpole, have you or any of your mates got a thick cock? I've had a couple of kids and I've got a big cunt (coont). And if it's not thick then I can't feel it: it's like throwing a sausage down an alley. Me mate said I should get myself a vibrator, but then I said I'd get ever so lonely, but she said, "Well, you could always have the radio on!"'

This was one of her party pieces I suspected, so glibly was it delivered, but no less amusing for that. She told me how much she loved Jamie but that his chronic alcohol habit wasn't helping their love life. Margi was the image of vivacity. I loved her rendition of an old Edwardian Music Hall song:

'Part your hair with a brick. A brick will do the trick. A glass facade, wafer-thin, a brick will put it in.'

Of course, I fell in love with her – I was falling in love all over the place.

We went on to a Chinese restaurant in Gerrard Street. By now we were drunk and I had to write out the cheque three times before they believed it was in English. It was all flourish and no legibility. Again, I ended up at Johnny and Kath's, fully clothed and fast asleep. And so the bender continued. We sallied forth daily on a perfect level of bright-eyed lucidity, infused with energy and enthusiasm for the day's fun and drinking adventures.

I read once of an old Edwardian character who in 1902 had gone into the Post Office and asked to see a sheet of one-penny postage stamps. He gazed at the sheet for a while before pointing to one of the stamps in the middle.

'I would like that one please!' he said.

I told the story to Johnny and Kath and they urged me to re-enact it at the main Post Office by Trafalgar Square. But times have changed since the Edwardian era, and when I said to the man behind the counter, 'I'd like the stamp fourth row down, third from the right please,' he told me where to stick it – and it wasn't on an envelope.

For years I'd been away from the real world so didn't have a gang of local mates. And I had lost Sue as well. We hadn't enough in common and she ran off with Max Splodge. Despite knowing it would never have worked out between us the pain of the loss was acute. But now all that was being wonderfully blotted out by this new adventure.

I longed to embrace Kath and cover her with kisses. She had an original way of looking at things, an amusing turn of phrase, and we made each other laugh with our verbal flights of creativity. I felt the excitement of a man fresh out of prison. In the band I felt inhibited from being other than a limited part of myself.

'How are we going to get off this bender?' was the rhetorical question of the hour. Wandering back to Albany Street I got into bed and fell asleep, and dreamed of Sue.

We met up at the Double Six for breakfast. The cafe served decent grub and was run by Chris the Greek, an affable chap. I wasn't very hungry and when Chris came up to take my order I asked for a bowl of custard with a chip in it. He chuckled, thinking I was joking. I told him I was serious, I really did want a bowl of custard with a chip in it. OK it was a mad spontaneous whim but it's nice when whims are indulged. He came back a few minutes later with his notepad and pen.

'OK Eddy, what do you want?'

'Chris, I've told you what I want. I want a bowl of custard with a chip in it, *please*. What's the problem? OK, I know it's not officially on the menu but it would be no trouble for the cook to prepare now would it? In fact, it could hardly be simpler! Well, could it?' Chris looked deeply uncomfortable.

'Look Eddy, I canter give you a bowl of custer with a chippiney!'

'But why not?' I argued, becoming irritated, my patience not being infinite before breakfast and being a practical man, 'You've got chips and you've got custard, what's the difficulty?' But Chris was not to be budged, there was something about my order he couldn't accept. I made a final sally.

'Chris, I will pay any price for this dish.'

He shook his head.

'£3? £5? £10! Chris, I'll give you TEN POUNDS if you indulge me just this once?' But despite the blizzard of bribery, he was adamant.

'Well OK Chris, it is your cafe,' I conceded, 'but as a matter of interest, at least can you tell me why you won't serve me a bowl of custard with a chip in it?'

He looked left, he looked right, he moved his head nearer to mine, and said in a most confidential manner:

'Look Eddy, if I give you a bowl of custer with a chippeney, then EVERYBODY wanna bowl of custer with a chippeney.' Entirely satisfied, I backed down and ordered a bacon roll. To understand is to forgive.

Later on, I had to go home to pick something up and Poric came with me. He was a gentle, amusing Irish lad. When we got to my room, he very soon had his penis out and urged me to have sex with him. This caught me utterly by surprise; I wasn't tempted to take him up on it at all. The telephone rang with perfect timing like in a play. I picked up the receiver as Poric scrabbled at my flies. It was Kath.

'Hello Kath, Poric's got his cock out and is scrabbling at my flies!' I said.

'Well, tell him to get off, and put it away,' she said, in the tone of voice you would use to explain to somebody how to walk across a room.

'Get off Poric, and put it away,' I told him, obediently.

It must have taken a bit of nerve to commit himself so unequivocally to his seduction attempt and, the moment over, I was most keen he shouldn't feel embarrassed, or think that the atmosphere between us would change and go weird. But all was well and we strolled back to the pub along the backstreets of Somers Town, by the Euston Road.

By now our number included a girl called Alice. She was self-assured, serious, nice – and drunker than us, not having spent the last few days developing a measure of immunity to alcohol. She also had beautiful breasts.

After a few more drinks, later that evening, Alice, Poric and I wandered into one of the flats, I'm not sure whose, and there was a large room with bare boards and a full bath of hot water in it. It seemed to double up as a kitchen, as there was a sink and sideboard and a dog bowl on the floor too.

Poric suggested that the three of us get into the bath together. Because Alice agreed, so did I. How lovely to be with a bare Alice in the bath I thought, and Poric being gay would be no competition - perfect. Alice said that me and Poric had to get into the bath first, so we did, and Alice was kneeling by the bath like mother. I told her to hurry up and join us as agreed, splashing her a bit. And then I had to tell Poric in no uncertain terms to lay off my cock. He was beginning to become tiresome, he'd had a lot of whisky. Alice squirted a large glob of shampoo onto my head thus enforcing a hair wash –is there a word for this type of assault?

My head thus be-sudded, she let me unleash her breasts and soap them. What happy joy. The heat of the bathwater, and the moment, prompted my nose to spontaneously bleed and I watched in wonder as my blood rolled down her soapy bosom. But as it soon became clear she wasn't going to actually join us in the bath I got out and into the towel she held for me.

Then Poric got out of the bath, and being very drunk he slipped and landed on the China dog bowl, a jagged shard of which cut deep into his buttock causing much blood to gush.

Taking command, I told him to get on all fours and asked Alice for some water to splash onto the spurting wound so that I could see, however fleetingly, the extent of the injury. It was a deep wound.

'Am I alright? Am I alright?' cried Poric in panic.

'Nothing that a few stitches won't cure, old chap,' I said, my nose still bleeding, trying to be reassuring in a Jack Hawkins type of way, and splashing another glass of water onto the spurting wound for another glimpse of the gash.

'Oi! What's going on in there? Open up!' said voices from outside.

Alice unlocked the door and some irate people entered led by the person whose bath we had commandeered. They saw me half naked with blood on my face, kneeling behind the completely naked Poric on all fours, his buttocks pouring with blood.

'Call an ambulance! There's a perfectly innocent explanation for all this, you know,' I said to the frowning, dubious, mistrustful-looking faces of these strangers.

They took over the first-aid ministrations and I got dressed. Once Alice and I knew that Poric was in safe hands and help was coming we decided to beat a retreat.

'Let's go back to my place,' I suggested. She slurred agreement as we got to the stairs but I failed to catch her in time as she toppled down the seven carpeted steps and smashed her head onto the wall. She lay still for a moment, but then started talking happily enough. She was drunk. The chap whose bath we'd used now reappeared and eyed the scene.

'What the hell do you think you're doing?!' he said to me angrily as if I had pushed her down the stairs, 'Look, I think you had better leave immediately.'

I thought so too, although I couldn't for the life of me see that I'd actually done anything wrong. But that night I seemed to be in the eye of a negative force field which made strange things happen around me. I went home alone to bed. That was the end of that bender though the friendships made during it lasted for years.

Now bereft of an objective for the first time in my life, my navigational skills no longer required, I abandoned the driving seat of destiny and let fate take over the wheel for a while. I lay on the bench seat in the back and slept.

Beginning with *Absolute Beginners*, the doors of the acting world were now being held open for me, as if by magic. The path of least resistance was to walk through them. I had to do something. Dear reader, I ran away and joined the theatre.

19

Absolute Beginner

Absolute Beginners was my crossover plank into acting. Julien Temple, riding high on his directorial debut with *The Great Rock 'n' Roll Swindle*, was now preparing to turn the Colin MacInnes book, *Absolute Beginners,* into a musical and direct it. I was the first person he cast, as Ed the Ted.

The focus required for an acting job allows no thought of anything else and this was the perfect antidote and anaesthetic to the slow-release horror-pill of the band's breakup.

I was taken to Shepperton Studios to look round and marvel at the set-builders' recreation of the streets of Notting Hill in the 1950s. In one vast studio several streets of Soho had been built including Old Compton Street, Dean Street, Frith Street and Greek Street, all perfect in every period detail. From the coffee bars, the shops and their contents, the magazines, sweets, cigarettes, matches and newspapers on sale to the fag-butts in the gutter every detail was perfect. I was told it cost a million pounds to make.

Temple asked me to write a rockabilly song called 'Ted Ain't Dead' for the film, and I reworked a late Tenpole Tudor number getting Mick O'Donnell and Paul Martin to play on the recording. Alan Winstanley and Clive Langer produced it at Air Studios, Oxford Circus.

On my first day of filming at Shepperton Studios I was picked up outside 27 Albany Street, at 6am, by a large car.

'I thought you was going to be an African gentleman with a name like that!' said the cockney driver as I stepped into my first ever Mercedes-Benz.

'You're the only man I've met who thinks "Edward Tudor Pole" sounds African!' I said, sinking into the blue leather upholstered bench seat in the back and lighting up a Players No.6.

As we passed the playing fields on the approach to Hogarth Roundabout, we saw a solitary man in the middle of the vast green expanse with a tiny domestic lawnmower. It would have taken him a fortnight to mow the whole field we observed, roaring with laughter.

My approach to acting is to become the character, inhabiting it so completely I don't have to act. Playing a yobbo like Ed the Ted was very easy for me, him being a stock character I'd been aping from a very young age.

I was reunited with Irene Handl, who this time was playing my mum. We shot a few scenes together, none of which ended up being used. In one she woke me up in bed and chided me for sleeping in my clothes. In another, when the camera was on Irene and a door on the set annoyingly kept swinging open, I knelt on the ground, out of shot, to hold it shut, to be helpful.

'It wasn't like this in the fifties,' Irene told me, not impressed.

Temple had a vision of how the film should look and feel, which was far more of a British 1950s black and white style than it turned out be. Artistically he was often outvoted. American money meant American influence and creative input, a lot of it at variance with Temple's ideas. 'You need a star in da movie!' he was told, and so David Bowie was hired, who also wrote the title song. Ultimately, the box office failure of the film was down to too many cooks spoiling the broth.

I was introduced to David Bowie on set and he shook my hand in a friendly manner with the most perfect handshake. He had a standard dressing room like everybody else and wasn't demanding. I have always found that true stars are easy to work with. It's only the second-raters who play up.

I wasn't exactly getting on fabulously with Sue Love, head of the Hair Department, who took over two hours to fashion my quiff. My protestations that Ed the Ted would have used a bit of engine oil on a metal comb, and taken five minutes to do it, fell on deaf ears.

'You stick to the acting, I'll stick to the hair,' she said.

It was fun shooting the song 'Ted Ain't Dead' on the bomb-site. It was played all day long, in many different set-ups, with a host of extras, and Sue Love was watching along with everybody else. The next morning in the trailer her eyes were shining as she told me how much she loved the song. 'Did you write it yourself? I couldn't get it off my mind last night!' We were the best of friends after that.

The Notting Hill race riots were re-created over several night-shoots, and with buildings on fire and all the noise and action it was very real. Bruce Payne, as the racist teddy-boy ringleader, was frighteningly intense in his role and he was quite scary in real life too, making me feel quite nervous when we once shared a car going to the set. Making *Absolute Beginners* was an epic experience and I loved the fact that I was in company with David Bowie having performed a role in the film and composed a song for it. The film was a box-office failure. There was no story. Some said that Ed the Ted was the best thing in it but there are no prizes for being good in a flop.

I never understood why chart success should mean that I was now a capable actor, for it was that alone which opened the doors into that world, but I wasn't about to object.

Road

Soon after *Absolute Beginners* came out, I was invited to audition for the part of Scullery in a new play at the Royal Court theatre: *Road*. Jim Cartwright, a young, ex-drama student from Lancashire, had typed out this gem with one finger in his under-heated council flat whilst unemployed and sent it to the Royal Court.

The Royal Court loves to stage plays depicting dysfunctional working-class life, performed for the delectation of their voyeuristic middle-class audience, who relish the squalor and gory details from the safety of an expensive stalls seat.

I was delighted by Cartwright's writing which has a rare poetic beauty reminiscent of Dylan Thomas. I went along to the meeting more intent on telling them how great the play was than in getting the job.

Jim Cartwright, with his broad Lancashire accent, and clad in an old blue school raincoat was forthright, funny and charming, and openly thrilled that the Royal Court was actually producing his play. We would go out drinking together after rehearsals and Jim would sometimes crash at mine. Late one night, quite drunk, Jim and I were approaching home.

'Do you think it will do well, Ed?'

'What will?'

'The play?

'Of course it will, Jim, it's a great play!' I said and pulled one of the black railings up out of its hole from the front of the house. With its leaf-shaped head it was now a spear. We went up to my first-floor room and I painted the word ROAD in large red letters on the wall.

'Stand back!' I said, and hurled the javelin across the room. It satisfyingly embedded itself into the wall above the letters.

'Now its success is guaranteed!' I said.

Road is set in a northern town, and Scullery being a lairy jack-the-lad type was fun to play, and his sexual magnetism rubbed off on me. It was a promenade play where there were no seats, my job was to interact with the public and point them in the right direction. In the interval the auditorium was turned into a northern disco with a mirror ball and Serge Gainsbourg's 'Je t'aime' playing. Scullery, a charmer, approaches the prettiest audience member he can find and says, 'Fancy a dance love? (Funcy a dunce lov?)'

They would always agree and as we smooched to the slow, sex-charged record I steered the girl to a cupboard and whisked her inside, closing the door behind us. In complete privacy I would then ask for a kiss and they almost always agreed. One woman came home with me after the show. As this bit of business was hidden from sight, I couldn't see how on earth it helped the play in any way, but I wasn't going to make a pedantic fuss about it: I was amazed this delightful perk was even allowed. One night some people said to me after the show, 'We're from Preston; what part of Lancashire are you from?'.

Road got rave reviews and soon transferred to the main house downstairs and lo, there was Jim's name in lights outside the theatre. We gazed up at it.

*** *ROAD* by Jim Cartwright'. ***

'See Jim, I said it'd be a success!'

'By gum, I can hardly believe it!' he said, amazed and delighted. His joy was a joy to behold. And it really did seem like a fairytale come true.

And thus I was inveigled into becoming an actor. Michael Foster at ICM offered to be my agent. I made the cover of *Time Out* and went with the flow.

During the run of the play I was, after seven glorious years, (two in the basement and five on the first floor) evicted from my beloved Albany Street. On the advice of my accountant, three years earlier I'd bought a flat just behind the Rainbow Theatre for just such a rainy day; where Max Miller, the Beatles and the Stones, Bob Marley, and me, had played; where 'Who Killed Bambi' had been filmed, and where Jimi Hendrix first set fire to his guitar. But Finsbury Park was a hell of a step down from Regent's Park.

20
Alex Cox

In 1986, Joe Strummer was in something of a 'wilderness years' period. We were both on the set of *Straight to Hell*, an Alex Cox cowboy film in which Joe had a starring role.

'We're in our thirties now, we should leave the electric guitars to the teenage kids; it's a young man's game!'

I wasn't sure about that.

Mind you, Joe, a method actor, and a passionate performer, was in character. The film was shot in Almería on the southern coast of Spain, and on at least one night he slept in an old Buick in the desert instead of at the Gran Hotel, to keep it real. Alex Cox did the same.

Eric Fellner from Working Talent had raised a million dollars for Alex to make a Western as some light relief. He had just finished making *Sid and Nancy*, a harrowing film about heroin addiction and death. I had first met Alex when he gave me half a day's work playing a hotel manager in it.

I'd had to go onto the roof to tell Sid Vicious and Nancy Spungen there was 'no roof-service'. Gary Oldman as Sid was brandishing a toy gun, and we happened to be overlooked by the MI5 building. It wasn't long before the armed police arrived, which lent a certain verisimilitude to this bit of Sex Pistols dramatisation. The first time I met Oldman was backstage at the Royal Court Theatre.

'What are you doing HERE?' he said most scornfully, as if I had no right. I felt defensive: why shouldn't I be an actor? What did he mean?!

(It would be years before I understood, as Gary knew, that I did not belong in acting).

Alex then offered me the role of the Priest in *Straight to Hell*, but as I had just agreed to be in Steven Berkoff's play, *Sink the Belgrano*, a left-wing polemic on the Falklands War, in an East End fringe theatre, I had to turn Alex down. It was agony. On its own the Berkoff project would have been a welcome and absorbing job. But in my heart it didn't compare to being in southern Spain making a cowboy film with Alex Cox, Joe Strummer, Shane MacGowan and a host of other groovy people.

But good old Alex, as consolation for my distress, gave me a day's work, a cameo role, scheduled to be shot (as was my character) on the weekend of the first week of rehearsals for *Sink the Belgrano.*

Elvis Costello, who has made some great records, introduced himself to me at the airport and was friendly. When we arrived in Spain there were a few of us in the minibus for the three-hour journey from Malaga Airport to Almería, during which Costello told us all about himself and his music career like he was doing an in-depth interview. He didn't stop talking for the whole journey and I'd had enough of him by the time we arrived at the Gran Hotel.

By then it was evening and we joined Strummer at a seafront bar as the sunset flared, for seafood and red wine and to discuss life, music, and the film, con gusto.

Next morning we were out in the desert filming on a dilapidated cowboy film set once used by Sergio Leone. It was baking, boiling hot. I had a hat and a gun, and played a bad guy who was killed that day and died a gory death (I've forgotten the name of my role but I bet Alex hasn't).

We stayed in character all day long. There were plastic bins full of ice cubes and cold drinks which I drank constantly yet I never needed to have a piss, such were the dehydrating effects of the oven-like location. Courtney Love, aged fifteen, was in the film. She was annoying. Alas, I missed Grace Jones by a day. From dreary London to this sunbaked gun-toting cowboy reality, with no end of interesting people to meet, was like being in paradise.

This was a fantasy made real. And I knew the role: I'd been rehearsing it since I was a boy. Bang bang you're dead! I met people I knew would have been my best friends if only they lived nearby. At 6am next morning I was on the plane home, with a girl from Amazulu, seeing Almería receding out of the window. I wept like a child who has had his favourite Christmas present taken away on Boxing Day.

Xander Berkeley played the Priest instead of me and better than I would have done, it has to be said. He's a terrific actor, became a star and is always popping up in Hollywood blockbusters.

Nicaragua

The next year, Alex more than compensated for the brevity of my time in *Straight to Hell* when he invited me to play a war artist in Nicaragua for the three-month shoot of *Walker*, set in the mid-nineteenth century, and starring Ed Harris. The film was based on a true story about William Walker, an American soldier-of-fortune, who'd led an invasion into Nicaragua in 1840.

It meant turning down a revival of *Road* at the Royal Court but with the lure of three months in Central America with Alex Cox, Ed Harris and Joe Strummer to make a war film it was hardly a difficult decision.

Daniel Ortega, President of the Sandinista socialist party ruled Nicaragua then (as he does now at the time of writing) but in 1987 there was a right-wing Contra insurgency being fought in the north, sponsored by Ronald Reagan.

Alex's sympathies lay with the Sandinistas and Ortega granted us permission to film in his country, giving us the use of an army contingent to be extras, and a one-day loan of a helicopter. I think he thought it was going to be more of a Sandinista propaganda picture than it was. There were parallels in Walker's story to the situation at the time. The actual war zone was about fifty miles north from where we were based, but as we were being endorsed by the Generalissimo, Alex reckoned we'd be safe enough from bullets.

After over twenty eight hours of travel and several changes, Alex and Ed Harris were there to greet us as we walked down the steps from our propellor-powered aeroplane onto the primitive airstrip that was Managua Airport. Ed Harris had turned down a big budget film to take part in *Walker.* Customs was little more than a tin shed and the soldiers waved us through.

We stayed at the InterContinental Hotel, in the capital of Managua, which was one of the few buildings still standing since the earthquake in the seventies, when acres of the town were razed to rubble. The debris had now been cleared up but no new buildings built yet, so you'd walk down the road flanked by neat and empty rectangles of flattened earth where the houses and shops had been. Being a socialist country blockaded by the US, there was no money for construction work. Everywhere was poor and there were no advertisements as there was nothing to buy. We, however, lived like princes in our oasis of material comforts at The InterContinental.

Soon after arriving in Managua from the airport I was handed a fat roll of banknotes for daily incidentals. The currency was Cordobas. An old chap approached me and asked for some of it. Feeling generous, I gave him fifty Cordobas no less. He glared at me, spat on the ground and stormed off. I can still see his look. I had yet to learn that galloping inflation had rendered the banknotes much less valuable than they looked. I had given him about twenty pence not fifty pounds. I felt bad and sought him out in vain to make amends.

The first thing we did before the shoot began was go on a twelve-mile trek over mountains and through jungle as a bonding exercise and to get into character. For some of the Americans from Los Angeles, where nobody walks anywhere, it was testing. I was fit but what sorely challenged me was the thirst. Water is king in this kind of heat. Towards the end I would have fought anyone who tried to take the last cupful of water in my flask. At the finish was a huge vat of fruit juice and it took pints and pints to slake my thirst.

On Sundays we'd go to a beach and gambol in the warm wavy Pacific Ocean, before a meal of lobster and rice which was only a couple of quid. After a few weeks we tired of hotel life and moved into houses in Granada. I shared one with Strummer, who had long hair and a beard for his role. One afternoon when an impromptu football skirmish erupted in our hallway, I caught a glimpse of Joe the schoolboy in the competitive scramble.

We had tiled floors, the odd scorpion, and a maid to help. The cars had no upholstery on the inside of the doors, just bare metal. Journeys were carefully made, zigzagging around the chassis-destroying potholes in the road. Things much in demand by the locals were biros and shampoo. Granada was a small and ancient town, where the bullet holes from the original conflict could still be seen. It is extraordinary what a different atmosphere it gives a place when there are no billboards, placards or advertising hoardings to mask the architecture. You could be in any century.

Outside the main bar and restaurant on the square there was an old guard with a machine gun. He was an officious janitor type and kept shooing away the gang of street children (the main requesters of pens) whom I'd befriended. We swapped language lessons and laughter. My Spanish was very rudimentary unlike Alex's, who'd taught himself fluent Spanish before the *Straight to Hell* shoot. He has a brain that can crack a walnut at twenty yards.

One day, much to the annoyance of the guard, I invited six of the boys for a proper meal in the restaurant. It was a splendid affair and these raggedy lads, on their best behaviour, were the most hilarious and delightful company you could possibly want. The janitor outside with the machine gun, who could see us all through the open front, looked sour. In the context his weapon had about as much menace as a mop.

On the corner of the square was a lady cooking food. As well as no pens there was no paper in Nicaragua so your portion of rice and beans would be wrapped in a large fresh green leaf off the tree, which feels much better. Rum was everywhere, but the beer, Victoria, was more highly prized and often running out. Victoria beer is a deceptive drink; you would be drinking it happily, not remotely drunk, and then you suddenly keeled over unconscious.

Being a method actor, I wasn't playing an artist, I was an artist, and did several watercolour paintings as well as artwork for the scenes. On the first day I had a bit of a row with the Spanish props man when he told me I couldn't touch the art equipment I carried, it was just for show. Alex put him straight on that. A central rule of mine is never to fake it.

My girlfriend in London, Jemma, sometimes sent copies of *The Times* for me to read at breakfast, which is a rare pleasure in the tropics. Spider Stacy of the Pogues didn't approve of this 'Rupert Murdoch publication', Murdoch being, I was told, an evil arch-capitalist. It was the first time I'd ever heard of him.

I said: 'Great Scott man, if an Englishman abroad can't read *The Times* at breakfast without being harangued for it then something is seriously wrong!'. We both laughed and Spider and I became friends.

I don't approve of people telling others what to do whether they like it or not. The Royal Court was equally critical when I was seen with a copy of *The Times* on the premises. I didn't believe they were serious for a second or two but they were. It was the first time I became aware of, and felt the effects of, Socialist militancy.

Nobody talked politics in the seventies punk world, all politicians were equally contemptible if we ever thought about them at all. Westminster wasn't on our minds whatever sociology academics and journalists may say. It was the Falklands War that introduced politics into the brain of the punk rocker and general conversation.

In a review in *The Times* while I was working there, it said, 'The Royal Court is the most conservative theatre in London; its politics never change'. I quoted this to Simon Curtis at rehearsals, but he was unamused. A bad sign. Any person or belief system that can't take a joke against itself can't be first rate.

But this wasn't England. I was now in a socialist country at war with the Contras. If anyone can create a Socialist utopia Alex Cox can, and he did in Nicaragua. Under his leadership the *Walker* set was an egalitarian, non-authoritarian, fully working socialistic society. Of the Nicaraguans, Mexicans, Americans, English and Cubans employed on the film, everyone felt equally committed and involved. Alex led by example, was equally kind to all, and from the humblest seamstress across to Ed Harris, everybody loved Alex.

One day Spider Stacy appeared at breakfast looking forlorn.

'Me and Cheyne have split up,' he said.

'I didn't know she was here!' I said.

'She's not. We broke up on the phone.'

A few days later he was happy again.

'Cheyne and I are back together!'

'Hooray' I said.

This scenario was often repeated over the weeks and after the three-month shoot Spider's telephone bill for all the calls to London came to more than he was paid for the film.

Helicopter Incident

Towards the end of the *Walker* shoot Alex introduced a few surreal touches of modernity into the 1848 period settings, like a shot of a radio, or a motor car.

President Ortega gave us the use of a helicopter for one day and it arrived straight from the war front, with real bloodstains in it.

The army pilot, in battle fatigues, needed all his skill to prevent the helicopter's rotor blades from clipping the architecture as he landed in the square, which was barely wide enough to receive it.

The scene was a group of us actors covered in fake blood, some carrying guns, running into the helicopter, fleeing the enemy. What was meant to happen was that, after we were on board with the door closed, Alex would cut the shot, let all the actors out of the helicopter, and then film it flying away.

The pilot looked exhausted, nervous and wired. In the take, as we piled into the aircraft one of the actors, replete with epaulettes and playing a General, ordered the pilot to take off immediately. So convincing was the actor (which is the whole point of acting) that the pilot, straight out of a war zone and trained to obey orders, could be forgiven for obeying him.

The noise of the engine became even louder as the wobbling craft began to rise up into the air, the cabin vibrating. I was thrilled by the pilot's misunderstanding, and to be airborne. My first helicopter ride! But most of the other actors, especially the Americans, became fearful and started to panic.

'Oh, my gaahd! We're all gonna daaah!'

I was surprised by this display of feebleness, had they no sense of adventure? But actually, actors are quite weedy: Norman Mailer got it right when he describes them as 'those flamboyant timid creatures'.

The three months filming in Nicaragua was a fabulous adventure. One Sunday I was with Luis Contreras, a devilish-looking Puerto Rican actor who specialised in playing baddies. At our Sunday table under the palms by the sea, Luis and a soldier on leave from the battle front were talking; I was trying in vain to follow the conversation.

'What's he saying?' I said.

'He says he trusts you but he doesn't trust me.'

21

Acting with Rex Harrison

A couple of months after returning from Nicaragua I was put up for the juvenile lead in *The Admirable Crichton* by JM Barrie, at the Haymarket Theatre Royal, starring Rex Harrison and Edward Fox.

When you have an agent, you go where you're told for auditions. You play your part to assist the machinations of fate. As I crossed the road on my way to the meeting, I noticed a scrap of tabloid newspaper in the gutter with 'GO EDDIE!' on it which, of course, I took to be a good omen; you look out for good omens on the way to auditions.

The director, Michael Rudman, was Texan; another good sign. I tend to get on well with Americans, who are generally amenable to my type of Englishness (he was married to Felicity Kendal). I was up for the part of the Honourable Ernest Woolley, an upper-class Edwardian twit; a role I considered within the ambit of my capabilities.

I felt at ease with Rudman. He plainly had no knowledge of my punk rock career, the world of music being as remote and far away from theatreland as Alaska is from Sri Lanka, and I knew not to mention it. After all, I was in effect a defector, on the run from that world to this. Experience had already taught me that if ever Tenpole Tudor was mentioned at an audition, I wouldn't get the gig. Without illuminating the context I told him I'd recently performed forty two one-night stands in forty seven days, which impressed him as intended. He got the message I was professional and capable of hard work. So I had a recall with some of the other hopefuls including Susie Lindeman who was to be Tweenie the undermaid. She laughed at all my lines as we read the scenes together, which could only have helped me get the part.

Having been an actor for a year or two, I was now to tread the boards alongside two acting legends, Rex Harrison and Edward Fox, in the West End! It seemed too good to be true but there was little time to marvel. The gut-churning, adrenaline-fuelled, heart-hammering thrill of hearing the news was soon supplanted by gut-churning thoughts of the enormity of the challenge.

I'd had very little acting experience. Whipping up a storm on a punk rock stage is not exactly a training ground for a 1902 Edwardian comedy with Rex Harrison, a film star since the nineteen thirties and one of the best light-comedians Britain has produced.

Rex Harrison on stage was utterly realistic and made it look easy; you could never tell he was acting. With bravado and bluff, I'd blagged the part, but would I be found out as inadequate? Could I pull it off?

Rex Harrison at eighty one was rather ancient and the plan was to tour the provinces first, in a series of one week stands, so he could learn his lines which he found hard to retain as any octogenarian might, before the three-month run in London at the Haymarket.

At the read-through on the first day of rehearsals I was greeted warmly by Lisa Jacobs, a beauty. She said I must share a cottage with her, Lucy Aston and Martin Clunes when we went on tour. I was delighted by this show of hospitality and have loved her ever since. Clunes played my sidekick – a man of few words.

At the first rehearsal in a scene with Edward Fox where I'm meant to be sleek and debonair whilst doing some adroit business with a footstool, my inexperience showed, and I was two left feet as we blocked out the scene.

Early on the third day of rehearsals I got a call from my agent telling me not to go in as Edward Fox had resigned from the show. There was no further explanation. All of a sudden the whole project was in doubt.

My heart sank, but after all I had said to myself I'd thought it too good to be true, so shouldn't be surprised that it was.

Nevertheless, it seemed such rotten luck; and I could have done with the five hundred quid a week. Aagh.

I wrote a letter to Edward Fox hoping it wasn't my ineptitude that had put him off. He wrote a sweet one back assuring me my acting had absolutely nothing to do with it.

We soon found out that Edward Fox and Rex Harrison strongly disapproved of Michael Rudman's stage plan which had two sofas back-to-back in the centre of the drawing-room. Edward Fox, a stickler for correctitude, maintained no Edwardian household would have the sofas thus configured.

'What does an American know about Edwardian England?' he drawled disdainfully, sounding just like Edward Fox. Such was their combined star power they had the producer, Duncan Weldon, who had invested thousands, over the proverbial barrel.

'Either Rudman goes or we go,' said Edward and Rex. And so, Michael Rudman was sacked. There's always drama in the theatre.

Enter Frith Banbury to the rescue, to take over as director: Banbury was another ancient, a director of the old school, and with a terrific pedigree (he directed the original production of Terence Rattigan's *The Deep Blue Sea* in the 1950s). He clearly knew what he was doing.

'The way you're delivering that line will get a laugh,' he said to me at rehearsals, 'but there are potentially three laughs to be had in the line,' and he would point them out and explain how to get them, giving me precise lessons in technique, and more practical advice than ever I had at RADA. He was great.

Edward Fox, whom I'd always admired in films for his quintessential Englishness, was perfectly nice to work with, and a complete professional. He was like he seems on screen – plus a touch of the fifth form schoolgirl.

I drove Lisa and our luggage in my Rover 80 P4 up to the rented cottage in North Wales, to be shared with Martin Clunes and Lucy Aston, near the Theatre Clwyd (cloo-id) in Mold where the play was to begin its tour. We were invited to a local dignitary's grand house for a reception where some of us got drunk. At the end of the evening Martin, a superb and fearless driver, drove us back to our remote cottage in his Citroen at high speed most expertly, along twisting country lanes. When we arrived, we noticed the hatchback rear door of his car had been up and open throughout the journey. Whether it was the alcohol or my faith in his driving, or both, I do not know, but I felt no fear for our lives and nor did I need to.

Martin Clunes was fun to be with, and very funny with his improvised clowning of an evening at the cottage, with Lucy's dog as his sidekick. I was madly in love with Lisa Jacobs but she was in love with her bloke Steven Macintosh (and they're still together today), and Clunes fell in love with Lucy Aston, who would go on to become his first wife. We all got on well and had much fun. We also played the Bath Theatre Royal, and The Yvonne Arnaud Theatre, Guildford, before coming to London

Like all dedicated stage performers of an advanced age, Rex Harrison conserved every ounce of his energy for the show. You would see him backstage, a stooped old man, shuffling along, being steered to the wings by his dresser, to await his cue. Just before it came, he would lift his head, straighten his back, shed twenty years, and stride on stage with a twinkle in his eye, his voice as clear as a bell.

'Ah Lord Brocklehurst, you're here at last!'

In the entire run of eight shows a week Rex Harrison only ever missed one performance, a matinee. The reason he gave was he was saving his strength for the evening show.

There are lots of Rex Harrison stories, not all of them salutary, but he was always fine with me and a consummate professional, a quality that ever elicits my admiration.

Over the course of the run, Edward Fox would at times get very upset when Rex would muck about in the island scene, and come off muttering to himself and shaking his head with disapproval. Rex once proclaimed, 'Look here, I'll do it how I want. Believe me, if I'm not having fun then nobody else will be'.

Our production was Rex Harrison's final West End appearance and also the last time a call boy was ever used in a London theatre. A call boy being he who runs up and down stairs to give every dressing room the calls: half hour call, five minutes, beginners please.

I was now a West End actor in an Edwardian reality, dressed nightly in white tie and tails and playing my part with conviction. I could not have been more hidden from view in the music scene had I run away to Costa Rica.

When it came to the grand opening night in London, Rex forgot one of his lines, and I managed to steer him back on course. Afterwards he thanked me for preventing him from 'getting egg on my face'.

I shared a dressing room with Martin Clunes and Steven Pacey, another good man, who played Lord Brocklehurst. Robin, our dresser, helped us into our costumes and attached our collar studs etc. He was amusing, camp, would bake 'his boys' a delicious cake every week and was full of stories – like catching Ralph Richardson rogering actresses in his dressing room.

At the beginning it's a sort of glorious party you never want to end. To play a leading man in the West End who makes the audience laugh was immense fun. I had fifty three potential laughs and knocked them off like a sharpshooter. There was one bit of comic business which always got the biggest laugh of the night by far. I won't trouble you with the details but you learn to fine tune it to maximum effect. As I rose up, they laughed. As I reached the sofa the laughter grew; and when I was halfway along the back of the sofa to the door they burst into applause as I exited the stage. Although it brought the house down every time you get used to it, and I'd be annoyed if the applause started too late, when I was at the end of the sofa, for instance.

You get to know the doorman, the fly man and the usherette. The play takes over your whole life when you're in it, and it can all be very cosy. The price you pay is not having any life outside it. My girlfriend Jemma felt somewhat sidelined.

Once the Queen Mother came; it was her favourite play. Her presence caused much excitement all round and the laughs were louder than usual. The only guests whose presence electrified the show more than Her Majesty were when Sarah and Sue came, my charismatic punk rock friends, with their vivid, peroxide, spiky hair. They sat bang in the middle of the stalls, like beacons, and laughed raucously from the off as if it was the funniest thing they had ever seen.

It was extraordinary being onstage or backstage that night and hearing the almost hysterical gales of laughter, verging on the unhinged and five times as loud as at any other performance. It is almost unknown for punk rockers to be seen at West End theatre shows and it was undoubtedly the girls' presence that caused the excitement. The girls set the level of laughter, and this particular West End audience jolly well wasn't going to be outdone in how funny they found the play by a couple of punk rockers. It was the loudest and best show of the run by far.

England is a funny old country with its two strands of society running in parallel, which seldom cross paths with each other. Interestingly, the play was about social distinctions.

Rex Harrison would sometimes forget the other characters' names. He quite often addressed Lord Brocklehurst as 'Lord Brocklebank', to our intense glee, and henceforth Martin and I called Steven Pacey: 'Pacebanks'.

After the play had ended its run, Steven was the first of us to get another job; again, in the West End. Out-of-work actors, Clunes and I thought it would be hilarious to alter his name to 'Steven Pacebanks' on the painted billboard in front of the theatre. Going to a lot of trouble and attention to detail, we made a stencil in the same font type, bought the matching shade of red paint and all the tools, and at two a.m. Martin drove us to the theatre, the plan was executed to perfection, and we laughed like rogues on the way home. However, we later found out Pacebanks was rather less amused. Although oddly he claimed to have no idea who could have done it.

Somewhere in the back of my mind I was puzzled as to why no one noticed the fact that a bloke who'd sung with the Sex Pistols was now in a West End play with the legendary actor Rex Harrison. Surely that was a story? What sort of person could do that?! I try to maintain a modest demeanour having learned it's the one which serves a man best in England, but I never understood why that feat of versatility wasn't noticed. Mind you it was only in the back of my mind. After all I'd given up my ambition for fame so why should I even care?

As the five months' work on *Crichton* approached its end, I told my girlfriend Jemma to hang on for just two more weeks until the run was over, and then she would have my undivided attention. We would go away on holiday and have a lovely time. The play ended on 3 December and she left me two days later. The day before my thirty fourth birthday. I was distraught.

The next day, in extreme misery, I went to the French House. I had to go somewhere. All my chums had evaporated along with the play. I stood at the bar with my scarf on, minding my own business. It was about 4 pm and the place wasn't busy and when a chap at the other end of the bar announced that it was his birthday, I was too sad to say 'Me too!'. I stared dead ahead looking at the optics. Woe, shock, perplexity in equal measure were buffeting about in my mind like a pinball.

In the early evening my old chum Johnny turned up and, very glad to see a friendly face, I told him all. He was most sympathetic and said I must join him and his wife for supper that evening. I thanked him and he went upstairs to tell her on the telephone. Minutes later Johnny came back looking sheepish and said he was awfully sorry but there wasn't enough food and the offer to dine was now rescinded. I was stunned. Icy quiet, I turned back to the bar and ordered another drink. Johnny went off for his supper.

And then suddenly, remembering it was also Sarah's birthday, I got hold of her on the telephone upstairs and she joined me. At last, I was with a true friend. We got drunk together and back at my place, about 2am, we concocted a plan to flee urban misery and go somewhere in the 1964 Rover 95 I had recently bought.

When an actor finishes a long theatre run he is surging with power and unused energy. We decided to drive through Spain and would leave the very next day – why not? We looked at the atlas. It was thrillingly feasible. We had nothing else on, a lovely old car, and with the theatre money I'd earned, could afford all expenses. The thrill of our forthcoming adventure trumped my sorrow.

The next day, having booked the ferry by credit card, we drove to Plymouth to catch it. Sarah was indeed a friend in need.

22
Meeting Clint Eastwood

With acting you never feel as though you're getting anywhere. At the end of a job it's always back to square one, a powerless place where all you can do is pray for a break. You don't know how long your time in the doldrums will be. It may be forever. Me talking about the work makes an actor's life seem fun. And it is fun when you are actually doing it. But essentially acting is like languishing in a dungeon for months and months in return for the occasional first-class adventure-holiday. What sort of deal is that?

One day I auditioned to be a pilot in *White Hunter, Black Heart*, to be made in Africa, starring and directed by Clint Eastwood. On a dismal late afternoon Mary Selway filmed me in an office in Twickenham sitting on a chair pretending to be having trouble at the controls of a faulty aircraft. I thought no more about it.

Then I heard that Clint liked my screen test and it was now between me and Tim Spall for the role. My advice to actors, which I knew then, is never to tell anyone that, for instance, you are up for a Clint Eastwood film and down to the final two. This will jinx it. And if you don't get the part, salt will be rubbed into your wounds when friends keep asking whether you got that part in the Clint Eastwood film.

In this case the role went to Tim Spall. Which was fair enough: he is a terrific actor. But the very nice and normally unheard-of thing, and one of the reasons why I love Clint Eastwood, is that as a consolation prize for coming second, he offered me five thousand pounds to do a day's work at Pinewood Studios playing a man in a suit with a couple of lines. It seemed like a lot of money, got me out of a hole and ameliorated the disappointment of not going to Africa.

It nearly didn't happen because the day scheduled for filming was the same day Tenpole Tudor was to play a gig in Shepherd's Bush. But as filming was due to end at 7pm I deemed it doable, if not ideal.

There were two scenes: the first one was me and three other businessmen talking to Clint. Or rather him talking to us, each of us having one line of our own. As we headed onto the set early that morning, me and the other English actors were giddy as nuns at the prospect of meeting the superstar in the flesh. And suddenly there he was, plain as day, looking exactly like Clint Eastwood and wearing a fine English tweed jacket.

He shook our hands somewhat distractedly. Our scene was the first one of the day, with him talking to us in a corridor. He delivered his speech, but never the same one twice; it was variations on the theme.

'Hell, I'm just an old derelict who can't remember his lines,' he said with breezy self-deprecation. We didn't mind! We all laughed as Eastwood, who understands actors, put us at our ease. When it came to my line he stood behind the camera and said, 'OK, I'll be your eyeline; say the line to me'.

Normally in that situation you'd be delivering the words to a chalked cross. I spoke them realistically enough. When a man is saying his line and looking Clint Eastwood straight in the eye, he can't help but feel happy.

Eastwood works efficiently, not doing many takes. The other scene was where my glorified-extra character sat next to Clint at a nightclub table while the focus was on the floorshow. In other words, hours of sitting around out of shot and waiting. Acting can be grindingly boring.

As the clock ticked on, pre-show nerves began to kick in. Eventually I approached the first assistant director and said that while I was happy to stay for as long as needed, and that my loyalty to Clint was absolute, I did have a gig that night and did he by any chance know how long it would be before I could go? He said he'd find out. Ten minutes later Clint Eastwood announced;

'OK everyone; get set up for Mr Tooder Pole's close-up. He's got a gig tonight.'

Then he came over, introduced himself in a friendly manner, and apologised for not having said hello properly before but he'd been busy. Clint has a lot of respect for musicians; he plays the piano himself, has composed music for his films and he made the acclaimed Charlie Parker biopic, *Bird*. As soon as he found out I was a musician I came into focus as an actual person. I was no longer an actor, the lowest of the low, no longer a blank waiting to be filled in.

'Mr Tooder Pole can be released after his close-up so make sure his car is standing by', said Clint. Before I left he shook my hand and wished me well. When Clint Eastwood tells you to have a good gig you have one.

For reasons I can't recall it was a secret gig for us. We were billed as 'Nine Stick Elizabethan' and supporting Becky Bondage. All her crowd were dressed identically and I apologised for not being dressed the same as them.

'...But as I was expelled from school for not wearing a uniform, I'm hardly going to start wearing one now!' I said, which got an audible belly laugh from Becky in the dressing room behind the stage, if from no one else.

I made it to Africa not long afterwards when Martin Clunes offered me a week's holiday at a luxury beach hotel in Mombasa, Kenya, provided I could leave the next day. A job had come up and he couldn't go. It would cost me two hundred pounds all in.

Thirty hours later I was on the east coast of Africa, just below the equator. The hotel was self-contained, luxurious, and the other guests were mainly romantic British couples. I chatted to the Kenyans in the hotel and after a couple of days, I was beginning to tire of being waited on hand and foot in the hotel compound, with its bars and pool and private beach; I wanted to see the real Africa.

When I asked at reception how long it would take to walk to Mombasa they said they'd arrange a taxi immediately and it took a while to convince them that I actually wanted to walk, and for them to tell me it took about forty five minutes. They neither liked the idea nor understood it. I noticed a dead Black Mamba snake on the ground just outside the hotel gates as I set off. Alive, they're deadly.

It was a lot more fun to be out and about, walking along the road in the boiling heat in my khaki shorts and sandals. Mombasa itself was a seething churning mass of Africans, a few Asians, and a cacophony of noise.

I bought some nail clippers at a market from a sun-bleached driftwood box. There was not a white face to be seen. It was an Indiana Jones film brought to life. The seller remarked on how happy I seemed. 'I am very happy, thank you, I am happy to be here!' I said truthfully, for I was.

I was pumped up with adrenaline and alert but knew my best protection was an open heart and friendly demeanour, like Peter Sellers in *Being There*. I went to an open-air bar and chatted to some prostitutes, politely declining their offers, ordering a round of beers and managing to carry the conversation onto more general topics, steering them back to being the friendly girls they were. As an actor I am no less of a prostitute than they are. We make a living by selling our bodies and by pretending to be what the client wants. That's why I've always got on well with the type.

I walked to the docks, with people everywhere, and with the dhows and other primitive craft it could have been almost any time in history. It was fabulous. One bloke came up and, to my delight, asked me whether I worked in Mombasa. This proved I didn't look like a tourist. That's real acting on a world stage. The whole point of acting is to be realistic, right?

On the walk back I picked up a stick. 'Why are you carrying a stick?' a man asked. I tried to explain by demonstrating that it was simply a stick to have and to hold and to wave about a bit, in a nonchalant manner. Like so, ahoo! Aha!

After that little holiday, thanks to Lucy Boulting the casting director, I went back to Kenya again to appear in an episode of *Young Indiana Jones*, filmed near Nairobi. Of course it was fabulous fun, much of it spent on horseback, riding across the plain. I met many Africans including a couple of Masai warriors roped in as extras.

'Why are you sitting with us instead of your own people?' some local herdsmen asked me one lunchtime out in the bush. I assured them they were far more interesting to talk to than actors, and hoped they didn't mind. They didn't, and they explained the local tribal differences. I loved being in Africa.

I once went to Barbados to appear in a musical about slavery on a bill which also included Luciano Pavarotti, but apart from an incident with Larry Adler's granddaughter, he being the greatest mouth-organ player in the world, and despite a most unpredictable twist in the tale, which discretion forces me to omit, there's no story beyond how much fun it all was.

Likewise, *Harry Potter and the Chamber of Secrets*, in which I played Mr Borgin, is only memorable for the initial cast read-through where I was sitting next to Ken Branagh. He talked to me nonstop listing all his achievements. This happens a lot – actors on set telling you how successful they are. Even when you're trying to be generous, there's only so many times one can say, 'Well done!' and 'That's terrific' before feeling and sounding somewhat hollow. I could never work out whether these people are trying to make me feel better or worse.

Sent to audition for a cowboy opera, *Horse Opera*, I wore a cowboy hat and took along my father's old blank-firing starter pistol. Behind the desk that sunny afternoon was Bob Baldwin the director, and Stewart Copeland the Police drummer, who'd written the music. BANG! went the gun, just in case they were falling asleep. 'Yes!' said Bob clearly delighted, and I was offered the part of the Preacher in a one-hour TV film, commissioned by Channel 4.

Stewart Copeland is considered to be one of the best ever drummers and some of his off offbeat rhythms I found tricky, but he is a good and patient teacher and I soon picked them up. The songs he'd written, with words by Jonathan Moore, were superb. No great song can give all its treasure away in a single hearing but because a *Horse Opera* soundtrack record was never made those great songs were only ever heard once in the single hour of transmission on Channel 4 at 8.30 pm, which is a terrible waste.

Michael Attwell was playing the baddie and I was happy to sit next to him on the plane to America (Tucson, Arizona to be precise), to play cowboys amongst the cacti in the broiling heat.

It was far too hot to sit by the pool and if you went to a shopping mall, you'd steel yourself for the walk from the air-conditioned vehicle across the tarmac to the store. It was a walk in an oven.

Jacob Marley, our flamboyant gay black choreographer, told me he had recently been hired by Mick Jagger to suggest a few new stage moves and naturally I grilled him for details. Jacob showed me the funny way of walking using the outside of his feet that he'd taught Mick, and sure enough when I next saw the Rolling Stones play Wembley Stadium there was Mick doing Jacob's walk.

On the permanent cowboy set, just outside Tucson, the locals were hired as extras to play background figures. Jacob completely won over these rednecks by giving them stylised moves, and choreographing them as if they were actors. They all rose to the challenge, had fun and were happy to do it. One of them said to me admiringly, 'Hell, normally all I get to do is cross the road.'

In Arizona it's usual to wear your cowboy hat indoors, while sitting at the bar for instance. We were stationed at a Ramada Inn hotel complex at the same time as the annual convention of Police Chiefs. I was given a law enforcement baseball cap.

Silas Carson, who played a native North American, was in the opera and we became friends. On a day off Silas and I thought we'd drive south across the border into Mexico in a hired car. On the map it didn't look as far as it turned out to be. After a couple of hours or so driving through the desert we realised we didn't want to spend the entire day on the road, so we abandoned our plan and turned round. There was a bag of weed on board so I was eager to ditch the motoring responsibilities.

After about an hour of driving north we were stopped by a police patrol car with flashing lights, checking for illegal immigrants. Silas gulped and hid the weed under his seat. Feeling supremely confident and telling Silas not to worry I got out of the car and strode towards the uniformed men in a friendly manner.

'Good afternoon, officers,' I said in my best Edward Fox English voice, 'How may I be of help?'

'My gad, listen to that accent!' they said, grinning from ear to ear.

Like any audience once you've got them laughing, they're on your side and as soon as I produced the morning's car rental document proving we hadn't come from Mexico we had a very pleasant chat with the policemen and told them about our cowboy opera. There was no question of them searching us and we parted on the best of terms. That's where acting skill comes in handy.

As for the work, when you are standing in forty five-degree heat in a ten-gallon hat with a gun in your hand, outside the saloon bar staring through narrowed eyes at the man you're about to kill, then no other reality exists and no acting is required. You *are* a cowboy.

But you don't need to go abroad to have fun, I've had some just as amusing laughs on a 141 bus.

For example, when a Jamaican lady sat next to me for a few stops until I had to get off.

'Excuse me,' I said.

She mumbled something.

'What did you say?' I said.

She said, 'I said I've just got meself all cosy next to you and now you're going to leave me!'

My elated apologies and promises to sell up and move next door to her so it would never happen ever again were eventually curtailed by the driver. For those few seconds what a fire we made. A great moment in my life.

On *Quills*, when Michael Caine learned I'd been to RADA he went, 'Oh, I say, old boy!', taking the piss in a friendly cockney way.

I was playing a lunatic in an asylum who couldn't act being rehearsed by another inmate, Geoffrey Rush as the Marquis de Sade, who was trying to get a better performance out of me in the subversive play his character had written. My lines were:

'I'm just a lowly cobbler, I have been all my life, so with this shoe I'm asking you, to one day be my wife.'

The job was to deliver the lines really badly. How could I fail? There's not a reader among you who wouldn't have delivered the lines to perfection. I was pushing how badly I could say the words, and weeping with laughter between takes. Michael Caine was also laughing, and during the takes, as he watched me through the cell door out of shot. Caine is a good fellow and was very kind to me.

I was in a few films with Geoffrey Rush, an unusually generous actor. In *Quills* I had a line which I didn't know how to say and asked his advice. He told me exactly how to deliver the line and at the premiere of the film it got a big laugh making me look good. He is a superb actor.

One Wednesday I went to New York for a week to attend Andrew Seear's wedding on the Saturday. I stayed at the infamous Chelsea Hotel and checked in with my guitar, delighted to see the sign: 'This hotel Welcomes Musicians'.

I had no contact number for Andrew, only the wedding chapel address. So, at something of a loose end, I bought a newspaper, rang up a music venue, Coney Island High, picked at random, and told them I was Ten Pole Tudor and could I play their club in the next day or so?

The manager grumbled that I should have given him more notice but agreed. He hired an amp for my guitar and paid me a hundred dollars. There were three other bands on but it was my solo Chuck Berry renditions which got them dancing. In the dressing room afterwards a man comes in and says in broad New York: 'My name's Luigi Babe, I used to manage Johnny Thunders, I want you to play my club on Tuesday night and I'll get you a band.'

They don't hang about in New York. The Tuesday show with a band after the wedding would have been better if someone hadn't spilled beer all over my guitar just before we went on, but afterwards I spent the night with a lovely girl who would have become my girlfriend if I hadn't had to fly back the next day to another reality on another continent. America truly is the land of opportunity.

I went up for *Withnail and I* and it became down to between me and Richard E Grant for the title role. The right man got the part. I am more like Withnail in real life perhaps but Grant, who is a very nice chap, was much better in the film than I would have been. It would have been unfair for me to have got the role as I wouldn't have appreciated the acting career it led him to.

Just before the Crystal Maze came along, I was filming in *Princess Caraboo,* an eighteenth-century drama, which period influenced my choice of costume in the game show.

As the director was quite grand and well-connected he had real aristocrats to play the guests in the ballroom scene instead of normal extras. Jerry Hall was there too and us being mere commoners, naturally, we hung out together.

I clearly remember a young nob, Edward St Aubyn, dressed as a hussar, proclaiming that all he wanted to do was to live in a hotel and do nothing but write all day. As some of you know, Edward St Aubyn has since become one of our greatest living authors.

23

An Actor's Life

If, in the course of a year, an actor is cast in a theatre play in the provinces for eight weeks, then a four-week job on TV, then a part in a Hollywood film for, let's say five weeks, then he is considered to be doing well.

The actor will talk about his work at the family Christmas get-togethers and his fascinated aunts will press him for details – 'So tell me, what's David Suchet really like?'

The relatives are thrilled with the vicarious excitement of Lionel's glamorous life, and very pleased with his success. And they shall certainly tell all their friends to watch *The Bill* next March when his episode is due to be shown.

'He plays a criminal suspect, my dear.'

The actor will go home much cheered, the heartfelt encouragement ringing in his ears. But if you do the maths there are still thirty five weeks of the fifty two in a year when Lionel isn't working. The unemployed actor, which is almost a tautology, has no option but to eke out whatever he earned from the last job most frugally, not knowing how long it's going to have to last.

Actors live on dreams and hopes and no money. Their most convenient remedy is a few drinks to paper over the precariousness of their position. The actor never tells you about those mornings when he picks himself up from the floor at 4am, having drunk himself unconscious, before going to bed. What else is a man to do but embrace oblivion under those circumstances?

As a musician you can make things happen, but the poor actor is at the very bottom of any food chain. He is literally a nobody which is why he is waiting and wanting to pretend to be somebody in the first place, in order to be anyone at all. Most of the time all he's being is depressed. The actor can ring his agent, hope and pray, and scour *The Stage* for auditions. The actor is a desperate person and something like a beggar.

Some actors have honed their I'm-the-nicest-most-charming-person-you've-ever-met act to perfection. It's an extra skill which could tip the balance. I can admire the artistry of it but believe me dear reader, no one is that nice. I'm not saying I'm never nice, but no one's perfect.

The actor is a wretched creature and over the years becomes hollowed out by hope disappointed, and riddled by self-doubt, until in the end all that's left is a brave face masking years of sadness. The actor's sense of self-worth is degraded over time and he becomes pathetic, and grateful for crumbs.

For how can an actor hold his head up in his own estimation knowing he has chosen to be unemployed in order to wait around hoping for the opportunity to pretend to be somebody else? What sort of fatuous occupation is that for a serious man?

In the actor's defence, making a film when it does come along is the most terrific fun, made all the more so by the contrast to the life it's replaced. Suddenly you have status, a luxury hotel, chauffeur-driven car and are surrounded by people whose job it is to be nice to you. When early one morning you find yourself in the African bush, donning a 1904 military uniform before getting onto your horse, it is hard not to consider that all is well with the world.

But in all the film adventures, enjoyable as they were, there was always the niggling thought that I was essentially idling. I was enjoying a fully paid adventure holiday – it wasn't work. I was making money but wasting my time.

I couldn't bear the realisation that my two options in life were to be either unemployed or some kind of gigolo. I knew I should be pursuing music but couldn't see how to do it now I had a mortgage and all the bills that people in the real world had to pay.

The actor's job is to be available and ready for acting work at all times, so I couldn't fire the band up in any meaningful way because, if an acting job did come up, I'd have to take it and thus have to cancel gigs: an untenable position.

Although we never let too long go by without Mick, Paul, Sean, Matt and I doing a quick thirty-date Tenpole Tudor UK tour, these laps of honour round the club circuit, though great fun at the time, only netted each musician about three hundred and sixty eight pounds at the end of the tour. We called them the Purple tours after Paul Martin our drummer explained the name Deep Purple. It's short for deep purple helmet.

Driving in the West Country after a show once, the police stopped our van. Barney the driver is sober so we are OK. When told the name of the band the policeman, with his West Country burr says, 'What! Not ooh arr ooh arr ooh are ay?' The very same, said Barney.

When we played Barrowlands in Glasgow in the nineties, the crowd were starting to drown us out with chanting:

'Ya fuckin English bastaards! Ya fuckin English bastaards!' over and over. I was forced to stop the band mid-song, and said, 'Look here! I may be a fucking English bastard, but Mick on guitar is a fucking Irish bastard! and Matt on bass is a fucking Jewish bastard!... And YOU, you're all a bunch of Scots shiters!! (roars of laughter)... So NOW where does that leave us? Eh?!... To ROCK 'n' ROLL! ... 1-2-3-4!'

And in came the band.

After the tour it would be back to the enforced idleness of an actor's life. I daily ran along a disused railway track, followed by one hundred press-ups and a pint of banana milk in a hot bath, followed by an hour of scales on guitar, at the very least – even if I wasn't in the mood to play creatively, so that something was salvaged from the day, from the bleakness of an actor's demoralising, paltry existence. Dear reader, the guitar has been a lifelong friend and comfort.

Then, if a couple of days on a TV job came along to play somebody in a suit-and-tie much less interesting than I am, I'd have to do it for the money.

To be trapped is a state most vexatious to a Sagittarius. The fact is I am not an actor but a musician, which is a completely different animal. I was like a cow in a field of sheep looking over the hedge at all the cows in the next field, wondering how I could get across.

It became ever more odious and absurd that I had to undergo such unemployment and misery simply for the occasional and dubious pleasure of speaking other people's words in other people's productions, like some kind of midwife – for the amusement of a comparatively small and privileged section of society that I neither belonged to nor cared about. Acting is very difficult to do, and those who can pull it off convincingly I greatly admire, but it is an essentially frivolous occupation, like tightrope walking or conjuring.

Three months into *The Rocky Horror Show,* after a cast change, I asked why Linda Davidson had better billing than me on the new poster. It's the sort of thing actors think about in a long run of eight shows a week.

'Because she's more famous than you, she's been on *Eastenders,*' said Robin Lefevre, the director.

'But I've been on *Top of the Pops!*' I said.

'That doesn't count' he said. Why not?

Later I bought an evening paper in Trafalgar Square and the vendor, who looked like he hadn't got a home let alone a TV, said, 'Alright Tenpole 'ah's it goin?' This made me all the more aware I was in the wrong job and should be doing music. I wanted to be entertaining people like him and his mates; people who appreciated and understood me!

Quite often when I turned up on a film set or a TV studio to play a man of few words, the crew, the gaffers, sparks, carpenters etc., being generally working-class, thus knowing about the Sex Pistols and Tenpole Tudor, would greet me with a warmth not usually extended to actors. This would irritate the producers.

Recalled for a screen test at Shepperton Studios for the part of Brains in *Thunderbirds* all the crew were standing in line to shake my hand and say hello. I felt like the Duke of Edinburgh as I walked along greeting each in turn. It was ever so pleasing and lovely but yet again twisted the dagger of discontent within my heart. It was my music they liked, not my acting. Had I betrayed these people and my audience by pursuing acting instead? Dear reader, I had. For years, I was tortured by this dilemma, but I couldn't see a way out.

Escape

My escape from the acting trap began when I went up for a small role in Mike Figgis's remake of Terence Rattigan's *The Browning Version* and was offered a part for which the going rate was fifteen hundred pounds. I decided to make a stand and told my agent to demand three thousand pounds.

'They won't pay that, Ed.'

'Michael, I'm worth three thousand pounds! Tell them I won't do it for a penny less, and call their bluff. Come on, man, you're the agent! How am I meant to get ahead?'

'It doesn't work like that, Ed,' he said.

But by now it was a matter of principle. Much as I needed the fifteen hundred pounds I wasn't going to back down. And nor did I. I called their bluff and they told me where to go – and it wasn't to hair and make-up.

Nevertheless, I felt a certain grim pride at having stuck to my guns for once instead of cravenly relenting in the end. And I swear it was making this small stand that changed my luck.

Soon afterwards I was sent to audition to be the new presenter of *The Crystal Maze*, a TV fantasy game show, to replace Richard O'Brien. This was to be the gift from providence which rescued me.

PART FOUR

24

The Crystal Maze

'I'm a very lucky driver, you know,' said the man who drove me to an aircraft hangar near Harlow which contained the *Crystal Maze* set. He mentioned other hopeful auditioners he'd driven to successful outcomes in his time. I like these promising signs on my way to auditions, as I've said, but I didn't feel particularly nervous: I'd never seen the programme and in snooker terms it was a shot to nothing.

They said I was the only one who made them look at the screen and they offered me the job. At first I wasn't sure whether to accept, wondering if it would be seen as 'selling out', but all the punks, skins and bikers I asked and all the crazies on the street said without hesitation I should do it. And, after the production company assured me I could write my own words and design my own costume, I took the job, having no further reason to say no.

I instinctively played it as a character in a G A Henty book, like a Victorian explorer. I don't do satire and my character was heroic, intrepid, untiring, and amusing. When you're inventing someone to be you may as well strive for an ideal. I played it as I would have played Doctor Who.

I was well paid for *The Crystal Maze* which, in contrast to the pittance on which I'd become accustomed to survive, seemed like a fortune.

Each episode of the series in a freezing cold aircraft hangar took thirteen hours to film, and being the Maze Master no less I was in every shot like Schwarzenegger or Sly Stallone are. I was the star now so no more hours of waiting around for the last shot of the day. Fuelled by copious amounts of food and already fit I was happy to be riding this beast and giving of my best. All the crew were top people and thus fun to work with. I would then have a day's break, resting up in the hotel and writing my script for the next day's episode while they filmed the contestants' hands, feet, and close-ups in cutaway shots. It alternated like that for five weeks.

Every other evening I went downstairs to have a jolly dinner with the next batch of contestants. They too buzzed with excitement and my job was to keep them happy. I was possibly the only true friend they had and I hated hearing the sarcastic remarks about some of them from the control room in my earpiece. I asked the producer to close the feed that allowed me to hear them mock my team.

So many gloriously funny exchanges with the contestants in between the games never made the final cut that I complained to the director.

'If we put those in Ed, there wouldn't be enough time for all the games,' he said.

'Well, have one less game, and make a funnier programme!' I replied, to no avail. They weren't interested in developing The Ed Tudor Pole Show.

My case for the contestants' defence I feel honour bound to make, and the reason why some of them seemed so thick, in not seeing what to do to get the crystal, when the viewer at home is yelling at the TV in frustration, is that in real time they have about twenty minutes waiting around, while the crew set up the lights and cameras inside the game cell before they play. That's twenty minutes of thinking about the eight million viewers who'll be watching them – twenty minutes to become a complete nervous wreck.

The people had to pass an intelligence test to be considered for the show and were arguably too similar in character, but I was on their side. After twelve hours together we were a nicely bonded unit. It took five weeks to record a series of fourteen episodes, and I enjoyed it all immensely.

The day after my first series on *The Crystal Maze* was completed in 1993, on a miserable, rainy, grey, cold December day I strode into a humble travel agent in North London opposite The Rainbow Theatre and said:

'I'd like sun, sea, sand, palm trees and heat! Money no object! Where can you recommend?' as if auditioning for Toad of Toad Hall.

While the woman behind the counter looked on her computer a shabby Irishman in an old coat entered the shop carrying a tray of socks. 'These socks are very lucky socks,' he said to me, 'would you like to buy some?' As money was no object I bought three pairs of the thin acrylics on the spot, before the woman shooed him away.

A two-week holiday was booked in Goa for me and Kate, whom I knew loved India. We flew out soon after Christmas Day and found ourselves on a hot sandy beach under a deep blue sky by palm trees, while a capable woman rustled up some chicken noodles in a bamboo beach hut, to go with our cold beers before we had another swim in the warm Indian Ocean: we were in paradise. The sand reminded me of the Aztec Zone and sinking my bare feet into its warmth I'd quote a few Maze Master-ish lines to the sky, just for fun. This time it was the proper temperature for the Zone and I didn't need to pretend it wasn't bloody freezing Harlow.

The acting jobs, such as they were, ceased immediately as I knew they would. They don't give bit parts to game show hosts. The profession likes you to know your place and stick to your category. I felt greatly relieved.

Our son was conceived in India on Kate's birthday, the advent of whom made everything better for everybody. The Irishman wasn't lying; they were very lucky socks. And to think I could so easily have had an unlucky driver on the way to the audition, or missed the Irish sock-man by minutes...

'Show me the child for the first seven years and I'll show you the man' or something like that, the wise man said. We were in the fortunate position of having the *Crystal Maze* money to live on and I could ensure that I was there for my son to see that his formative years would not be traumatic, as mine were.

Becoming a parent, a job I took seriously, forced me to engage my brain for once and do some serious thinking. Instead of spending all the time on drugs I had to unscramble my mind, marshal my thoughts and work out what I truly believed, in order to build an intellectual base camp from which to instruct the lad. Happily, no logical inconsistency or slack thinking on my part ever went unnoticed or unchallenged by the boy. You don't mind being bested by your own son. We laughed a lot and I didn't need to worry. The nearest I got to shouting was to murmur: 'What I just said but ten times louder' – virtual shouting. I thoroughly recommend it.

I could talk about the joys of parenthood until the cows avoid a cliché, but shall desist on the grounds that to parents among you it's familiar territory and to non-parents the topic is of limited interest. But it was fatherhood that turned me from a boy to a man.

25

John Michell

My father was cagey about his father, my grandfather, Wellesley Tudor Pole, and seldom mentioned him. Dad lacked the traditional impulse to pass on tribal stories to the young. And, as a boy, whenever I asked about WTP he fobbed me off.

Dad's lack of enthusiasm may have been because when growing up his father was never around. Dad's early development definitely suffered from the lack of a paternal influence. His mother misguidedly tried to make up for it by spoiling him rotten.

I knew WTP had written a number of books on matters spiritual and paranormal. This included, during the First World War, *Private Dowding*, a book he claimed was dictated to him in a psychic trance, by a soldier who had just been shot dead in the trenches.

The dead Dowding's spirit begins the account by looking down at his corpse as he slowly rises above it, and then tells of what happens next at an interim stage. It's a plausible tale but I think us mortals are not meant to know what happens in the afterlife before we're done with this one. Nowhere is speculation more idle than when pertaining to the hereafter. We'll all find out when we 'die'.

In 1909, the young WTP had a vision that there was something of great spiritual significance to be found at St Mary's Well in Glastonbury (the town, not the rock festival in Pilton). He was in Bristol at the time and unable to get away, so he wrote to his sister Katherine telling her to go and have a look in a certain well. Katherine went to the pond by the spring and, taking off her shoes and stockings, waded into the water and with her foot felt something solid in the silt. It was a blue glass bowl or chalice, an unusual object that no one could accurately date or identify.

The story reached the newspapers and there was speculation that this chalice was the actual Holy Grail, the cup that Jesus drank from at the Last Supper, supposedly brought over to England by Joseph of Arimathea, a disciple of Jesus. Mark Twain was quoted as saying how extraordinary it was that after all the quests through the ages for the Holy Grail by Arthurian knights and other heroic characters, it should be found by some 'ordinary' Englishman.

Though the Grail theory became discounted, the mysterious chalice allegedly had a 'remarkable spiritual resonance' and an 'aura'. Years later in the 1960s WTP founded The Chalice Well in Glastonbury, as a peaceful place of reflection where the bowl is kept, and whose spring water is said to have healing properties. You can visit the Chalice Well and its garden today, and in special cases stay there. That was about all I knew of Wellesley Tudor Pole then.

In Glastonbury town in the mid-nineties, one very hot afternoon, I was at an ill-advised and excruciatingly embarrassing solo appearance to play some songs to a dozen very elderly people standing up, at the Somerset Rural Life Museum, which exhibited hoe-blades, scythes and plough-heads through the ages. I had been hired by a local Somerset radio DJ in a loud suit whom I disliked at first sight when I arrived, when it was too late to escape.

Standing about in the small museum miserably ill at ease, putting on as brave a face as I could muster and wondering what on earth I ought to play to these elderly folk, a raffish chap in a hat approached me – a Scot named Jamie George. He said he was there out of curiosity to see 'Wellesley Tudor Pole's grandson'. Jamie and Frances lived above the town towards the Tor, and Jamie invited me to their party that evening.

That party turned out to be a seminal occasion: like the first time I walked into The Cock Tavern twelve years earlier where I also met a new crowd of people who would be significant, and lead to years of friendships and social fun.

Frances Howard Gordon and her dogs welcomed me into the house. She could see I was a bit freaked out, and poured me a glass of wine. She sat me down in the kitchen, passed me a joint and told me she'd been a Mod in the early sixties, and in the live audience of the *Ready Steady Go* TV shows when the Stones and Beatles were on it. Frances was kind to me and I loved her immediately. She led me outside to meet everyone. It was a jolly crowd, half what you might call 'New Age', a bit older than me. This was the original 'flower power' generation, those in the vanguard of the post-war social revolution in the sixties, and the first to grow their hair, take drugs and help to change the face of society; the generation I'd admired from a distance as a short-haired boy. Old hippies, if you will, intellectuals smoking pot, alongside a host of teenage friends of their daughter.

They asked me to play the guitar and something wonderful was improvised on that full moon night; a flight of joy expressed in music, impossible to repeat and which amazed me as much as anyone else. Credentials unequivocally established, the rest of the night was spent in chatting to people, as cosy as a kite. It could be said that my grandfather Wellesley, my connection to whom being the sole reason I was there, had introduced me to these new friends from beyond the grave.

Shortly afterwards, they invited me to join one of their walks for the summer solstice, over hills and plains, taking in stone circles, barrows and 'sacred' sites. Frances said that John Michell was coming. She tried to describe him and I inferred he was a hippy type I wouldn't particularly like. Wrong!

When I met John Michell, I felt a shock of recognition. He was exactly as I'd imagined the perfectly mannered, aristocratic guest to be at the tea with the Queen my mother had tried to teach me to imitate for when that occasion might arise. He was my type of ideal Englishman vividly brought to life.

He was most friendly and in erudite tones and without preamble, he started telling me all about my grandfather. For instance, in 1918 in World War One, at the Battle of Haifa, Wellesley Tudor Pole persuaded General Allenby to let him lead a force to rescue Abdu'l Bahá, founder of the Bahá'í religion: he had been imprisoned by the Turks, who were about to execute him for his 'heretical' views. WTP's raid was successful and Abdu'l Bahá was liberated from prison. Wellesley took him back to the family house in Clifton, Bristol, where Abdu'l and his kin sheltered for some months. After that, my grandfather and this inspirational religious leader became lifelong friends.

In World War Two, WTP founded 'The Silent Minute', a daily event at 9 pm on the BBC's Home Service when the country was encouraged to pray for peace and victory – the fact of everybody doing it together greatly adding to its power. Adolf Hitler, known to be superstitious, was said to be spooked by 'The Silent Minute', a force to which he had no riposte.

Fantastic things happened to WTP, like the time he lost a precious ring in Egypt – until two years later when it inexplicably appeared on his desk in England one morning.

My grandfather is remembered still by followers of the Bahá'í religion. In 2018, on the hundredth anniversary of the Battle of Haifa, all his descendants who could be traced, including me and my son Henry, were invited to the House of Lords to join the Bahá'í elders and Indian nobility at a reception to remember and honour my grandfather for saving Abdu'l Bahá's life a century earlier. It felt great to be basking in another family member's glory for a change. He died in 1968 and I only met him twice but I am proud to be his grandson. A spiritualist, his message was a Christian one and you could say WTP was an activist for universal peace and love.

John being the teller of my family history identified himself as the 'tribal elder' I'd hitherto lacked. I recognised him as such and loved him from the start. John Michell taught me an awful lot. He taught me to be happy, for a start, and never uttered a sentence that wasn't both enlightening and very funny. Being with John was like hanging out with Socrates or Aristotle.

The summer solstice walk had John pointing out the site of an Iron Age settlement, indicating the salient features so eloquently you could see it. And later on, he'd point to where a Bronze Age village had stood, and explain the difference between the two. This stuff was all new to me and I lapped it up.

As we strode across the land and across the day, and not wanting mere ignorance to prevent me from contributing to the general erudition, I pointed out the site of a 'Cornerman's cottage', making it up as I went along.

John pounced upon the game and contributed many more 'facts' about Cornermen and their ways. We fed off each other, the ideas leapfrogging to ever more inventive creation. By the end of the walk, we had enough material to write the definitive door stopper Cornerman history book. We became friends.

I was often at John's flat in Notting Hill and grew under his guidance. With John I was free to be the very truest version of myself, without slant or affectation, without tilt or taint. I was his humble pupil, sidekick and mucker— and, vitally, I could make him laugh. With John there was freedom to discuss big ideas, however extravagant they might seem. With John there were no forbidden topics of conversation and it was a joy to be in the company of someone with an intellect so vastly superior to my own and yet so eager to give me the benefit of it. Aware of my privilege in having the rewards of one of the finest, most erudite, minds in England for company, I could not but feel at home. He often talked about Plato: what joy! Who else was going to teach me about Plato, and the universe? And who else would take the time to do so?

He talked in gentle tones and smoked roll-ups to which he'd sometimes add hash, but never so you'd notice, and not for passing round. He liked a drink as much as the next man and was never less than sharp. John had the energy of a professor and was always among the last to go to bed at the Glastonbury parties, if he went to bed at all. Despite the vast difference in our intellectual capacities, there was a resonance and connection on some deep level. He once described me as a simpleton but it was not meant unkindly, or in a way that implied it mattered. I've been thinking about this. John wouldn't lie so I suppose I must be a simpleton; albeit, in my defence, one made not born. Does the fact I wasn't offended prove him right? Only a lie can offend.

John had been to Eton and Cambridge and was very conventional, he told me, until he took LSD in 1966, aged about thirty, which dramatically expanded his mind and led to revelations about the nature and geometry of the universe. He perceived the world anew, seeing the patterns of creation, which led to his explorations.

With his book, *The View Over Atlantis*, John was able to bring ley lines to wider public attention. He saw there was an order to natural things, known and understood by the ancients, and could prove his theories with geometry and equations. It was John Michell who advised Michael Eavis precisely where to place the Pyramid stage at the first Glastonbury festival in Pilton in relation to ley lines running across the area to ensure the best cosmic vibes for the music. He also claimed to know the exact site of King Solomon's Temple, as revealed in his book, *The Temple at Jerusalem: a Revelation.*

His family seat for centuries was Stargroves, a grand country estate in Hampshire. Stargroves became unsustainable as a family home after World War Two and Mick Jagger later bought the place.

Around the time I made friends with John Michell when my son was about two, John had recently become acquainted with his own son, Jason Goodwin, aged thirty three, for the first time. I think I received some of the rewards of John's newly aroused paternal instincts due to better proximity.

John Michell lived in an attic flat in Powys Gardens, Notting Hill and was part of the set of aristocrats who befriended the Rolling Stones when they took off in the nineteen sixties. Christopher Gibbs, who was very grand, and was present at the Redlands drugs bust with Mick and Keith and Marianne Faithfull, would sometimes come over. The lady who lived on the ground floor at Powys Gardens was the actual 'Lady Jane' who inspired the Rolling Stones song on *Aftermath.*

I loved being with John at the flat, surrounded by his Merlin-esque paraphernalia; his papers, his geometrically-patterned watercolours, and fascinating old books like *Things Not Generally Known*, published in 1898 and containing priceless information such as how many tons the planet weighs. He often assured me we live in an ordered universe, and once proved it beyond doubt on the back of an envelope, using a triangle, a circle and a square. It was so unassailable, so simple and so reassuring. But, as with dreams, clear as it seemed at the time, when I tried to pass on this proof I could never recall what, at the time, were unforgettable details.

John was a philosopher with an irresistible urge to enlighten those around him. To be on the receiving end of his teaching made me deeply happy as well as expanding my outlook.

John would sometimes order a shepherd's pie from a traditional butcher in Notting Hill, and one evening he invited me round to share some. The other guest was a lady he introduced as Liz. The three of us had a pleasant enough meal and later I found out 'Liz' was the Chatelaine of Sudeley Castle, which had been in her family for centuries. John had asked me round as protection against any pass he feared she may have been about to make. John, born into that world, and imaginable by her as a 'Lord Emsworth' type, happily pottering about her castle grounds, wanted none of it. 'I just couldn't live like that' he said, as he poured wine into my glass.

The upper classes are very insular and necessarily self-protective, whose world, like Hassidic Jews for instance, is impossible for an outsider to gatecrash. However, being John's companion, I was welcomed by his friends, and most happy to find that once I was in their circle, which is the hard part, I was afforded the same degree of intimacy as the others in the room.

Proper good manners is making the guest feel truly at home. Mere displays of politeness are very amateurish, and actually rather bad manners. The difference lies in the degree of intimacy afforded. Proper good manners are letting the guest in behind the iron curtain of 'politeness' and giving them your heart.

Rosie Hall, Jerry's sister, came to live at John's for a while and kept house for him. She was friendly, attentive and funny, with a lovely Texan burr like her sister.

We became friends and she would feed me fruit, nuts and water in the Rover, with John in the back, as we drove to Glastonbury for a Burns Night party, for instance. Many times, I drove John to Glastonbury parties at Jamie and Frances's. Chris Jagger, Mick's brother, had recently moved to the area and it was great meeting him. He's got a sort of Cajun band and has an encyclopaedic knowledge of old music blues and twang. We both played at John Michell's seventieth birthday party in the Assembly Rooms in Glastonbury and roadied for each other. John always said he thought Chris was the more talented brother.

Occasionally, John would have parties in his small Powys Gardens attic flat, the atmosphere elevated, relaxed and glamorous, and would include Jerry Hall, who was always fun. Everybody loved John Michell. All good parties are roughly the same. It wasn't because George Tsatsos was a Greek billionaire in the concrete business, and a great artist, that I liked him, it was because he was friendly and funny.

One evening John, Rosie and I went to Jerry Hall's Richmond mansion for supper. I walked into the large drawing room and blow me down there was Bill Wyman, on his own, sitting by the fire. My heart gave a little jump but I was determined not to be tongue-tied. We shook hands and I asked him if he remembered nearly wearing Dick Crippen's leopard skin jacket on *Top of the Pops* (this was when Dick was playing with King Kurt). This opening gambit worked, and Bill was friendly and easy to chat to although keener to talk about cricket than music. A veteran of the celebrity charity match scene and, like Jagger, mad keen on cricket he told me with pride how he's bowled out various star England players in his time. But mostly he wanted to talk to John Michell about antiquarian matters. So elevated did I feel in John's company it made me take having supper with a Rolling Stone not exactly for granted but par for the course of general delights. Under John's tutelage I flourished. He showed me that to be happy was a natural state. I would go home and try to pass on these pearls of wisdom to my son in ways a three-year-old could understand. And the laughter of understanding rang also in our house.

By the time Henry was seven, and set fair, my job mainly was done. He was bonny. The *Crystal Maze* money was gone and I needed to find work. It seemed as though all avenues were closed. The last attempt at forming a band was with Darrell Bath on guitar, Ade Emsley on bass and Sam Woodward, Edward Woodward's grandson, on drums. It started out promisingly enough, but matters weren't helped when Emsley, a great player, decided to leave, and that Bath was an addict as well as a virtuoso guitarist, and the band petered out.

An unemployed man in the house is irksome and Kate told me to 'get a life' which was good advice but what could I do? Later on, more helpfully, she said, 'You could always do a gig with your guitar and earn fifty quid'.

26

The Fifteen Year Solo Tour

In 2003 I was alone at home one night aged forty eight, at a very low ebb, my domestic life awry, no career prospects, and rather drunk, when something made me take an old videotape off the shelf of 'Ed Tenpole', playing solo in Sunderland nine years earlier at The Ropery in 1994. Never in a hurry to watch myself on film I hadn't got round to seeing it yet.

The man on the video maintained a steady beat on guitar, locked in the groove. He sounded like he was playing two guitars at once, he held his nerve and the rhythm took hold. It was swinging, and I was impressed. There was a nice rapport with the audience and every song worked to take it higher. At the end Jimmy Nail's drummer and bass player, fresh from chart success with 'Crocodile Shoes', joined me on stage for some Chuck Berry songs and the 'Swords of 1000 Men' climax. They were as tight a rhythm section as ever I've played with. It's funny how performers can forget how good they are, in a similar way to long-term couples forgetting how nice it is having sex with each other – until they do it again.

I was jolted awake by the video. There was no denying the evidence of my eyes and ears: this chap was good. Here was the obvious answer to my problems. If I could be as good as the bloke on the video, I'd be very good. And seeing as he was me in the first place albeit nine years ago, this was achievable.

I telephoned Big Steve there and then to request a solo spot at the music club he held in a pub in Camden every Sunday afternoon. Big Steve is a country music singer and songwriter in his own right and a likeable, approachable bloke.

'Of course you can play, Ed,' he said. Like God.

Come the gig, there was no actual stage in the sunlit big-windowed afternoon pub in Camden, with cables across the floor and kids running about, but it went very well, with much comedy mileage got out of the children. There are many ways in which a solo gig can succeed although solo is a misnomer: 'collaborative-group-effort-with-the-audience show' is more accurate.

Some ex-RADA colleagues also came along that afternoon. A couple of weeks earlier there had been memorial celebrations at The Old Vic for Hugh Cruttwell, our much-loved RADA principal, and I'd mentioned the gig. They said they remembered me playing solo at freshers' balls at RADA in 1974-75, in the pre-punk era, when I wore a leather jacket and modelled myself on a surly Keith Richards.

The next event was the first gig proper, of what turned out to be a fifteen-year solo tour, and the first day of never being out of work again. It was 3 October, 2003 at The Betsey Trotwood pub in Clerkenwell. It went very well, details of which were soon upstaged when a young Cambridge graduate 'pulled me', as she put it, and took us to paradise for the next year or so. This was an intoxicatingly happy turn of events which I took as an unequivocal sign I was on the right road at last.

Subconsciously, I had deliberately burned my bridges to the acting world so that the only way out, and the only possible way of making money, was by playing the guitar. The solution was to do what I was best at. And thus, my expeditionary determination was set

Darren Griffiths from Crucial Talent became my agent and with other contacts emerging I discovered I was still in demand and playing guitar became my regular work. From then on, I got as many bookings as I could, all over the country, very happy to be working hard, head down, and earning money. I played somewhere in the kingdom every weekend for the next fifteen years.

Now I could carry all my own equipment, and on a good weekend, after hotel, travel and commission expenses were deducted, I could take home a few hundred quid, put food on the table and we could just about manage. The next weekend's show was always waiting to yield more cash. I was released from the tyranny of the Tenpole Tudor set list and developed a new show with new songs. (Although I've always got to play 'Swords', and 'Who Killed Bambi'). People initially missed the weight of the band, and some folk always will, but I could amuse the mob, and get them singing, and my line was there were 'enough crash-bang-wallop merchants around as it is without me adding to the racket'.

When my son got a three-quarter bursary to a good school I had to find what worked out to be sixty pounds per week for five years, as our share of the fees. So being a responsible parent, it was my duty to ensure I always rocked the house to great effect so the venue would always have me back again, so I'd always have the weekly sixty pounds. That's punk rock.

I played in every city, market town, and every other sort of town, every week (or nearly) from 2003–2019. Clubs, pubs, theatres, ballrooms, Butlins, church halls, converted cinemas, concrete 02 Academys, open-air festivals, scooter festivals, biker festivals, the village hall, year in year out. I was under any media radar but working every day. To my delight I discovered there was plenty of love and goodwill remaining for the Tenpole Tudor brand, especially in the Midlands, the South West, Yorkshire, the North East and Scotland; less so in the home counties.

Quite early on this epic tour, I went to a Pizza Express in Richmond, Surrey, to take on food for that night's gig at a nearby club. In the entrance I bumped into Pete Townshend and his girlfriend Rachel Fuller who were also going to eat. He was very friendly and gave me a hug and introduced me to his girlfriend.

'Tadpole, I didn't know you were still going!' he said. I told him I most certainly was and invited them, of course, to my show. We went to our respective tables to eat, and a little later Pete came up to mine and handed me his work and home telephone numbers written on a piece of paper.

'You can use my studio any time you like!' he said.

I was overjoyed, and bucked up no end to be thus honoured by rock royalty, as you can imagine. I took him up on the offer and we went to Townshend's fabulous studio on the banks of the Thames. It's a beautiful room with natural light, and he employs a recording engineer on permanent standby for when he or his girlfriend are struck by the muse and feel the need to record.

With Mick O'Donnell on bass, Ali Byworth on drums (who played for The Godfathers) and me on guitar, plus Pete's resident genius called Miles operating the desk, we laid down three tracks, two of which can be heard on *Made It This Far*[2].

With the horror of my time as an actor indelible in my memory, with all its misery and bleakness, poverty and squalor, I was deeply proud to have a full-time steady job at last. I was now a professional singer. In my own value system, I've made it. I play the guitar to create banknotes, an astonishing alchemy which never ceases to amaze and delight.

In the hours, weeks, months and years of the twenty-first century, playing guitar week by week, my playing skills improved as well as my posture. When a new song idea came along, I could play it at the next show and find out immediately from the crowd's reaction whether or not it was worth pursuing. Music hall rules apply: if they aren't singing along by the second chorus you know it's no good. The last thing the world needs is another well-crafted average rock song.

All gigs are congregational acts and if the tune is good enough the crowd are happy to be a mass choir and sing the songs. Singing makes the participants happy. Quite often at the end of the set the support band comes onstage for 'Swords of 1000 Men'. It's quite easy to play.

In Leicester once, when I was about fifty four, there were three bands on before me. I was chatting to the bottom-of-the-bill band

2 Gazing into the fire one evening I knew I needed an album to sell on the road to promote my act, but that's a major undertaking, like building a house, a daunting project and expensive. A minute later I realised if I mastered and edited the best of my demos recorded over the previous twenty five years I *did* have an album. *Made It This Far* might be the quickest album ever made.

in the dressing room who had just come off stage. They were teenagers and their excitement was infectious.

I invited them to come onstage with me at the end to play 'Swords' and they said they'd love to, not letting the minor detail of them not knowing the song stop them. They didn't know 'Swords' as they weren't born when it came out.

'It's easy!' I said and showed them how it goes.

They got the gist soon enough in the tiny back room and with them twanging on their unamplified electric guitars, the drummer clacking his sticks on the back of a chair and me singing, we had a little rehearsal, competing with the racket coming from the hall a few feet away.

When they joined me onstage an hour and a half later, even more fortified with beer, the lads gave it a jazz tilt; which was much more fun than trying to copy the record as normal people do. The first time they actually heard 'Swords of 1000 Men' was when they were playing it themselves live on stage. People always dance to that song however it's played.

The most enjoyable part of the day is the drink after the show. In Rotherham once, weary after the gig and sitting on a bench in the bar at The Cutlers Arms, the bloke beside me said, 'I can't believe Eddie Tenpole's sitting next to *me*!'

'Aha! So tell me, who do you think I should be sitting next to?' I asked, far more amused by the question than he was.

Later on, at 2.45am in an eighteenth-century pub bedroom, leaning out of the window having a smoke and looking at the moon, the wine finished and all quiet in the market town but for the hoot of an owl, I smell the dewy countryside, the smell of England, and am perfectly content. On a northern branch line railway station, the next morning, the sun beginning to pierce the mist, I hear the jolly laughter from the family on the opposite platform, a sound less common down south. And it makes me happy.

Another time, walking down the road to the station in Wigan on a Saturday morning, the road sweeper waylaid me and we had a most amiable chat about the old days. Two old boys in our fifties, we parted the best of friends, and equally content. Now I'm at home all over the country. Once the bloke serving at the buffet bar on the train gave me a free drink because he liked my music but that's very rare. Another time when changing at Darlington, the station master delayed the North Eastern Express to King's Cross to take a 'selfie' on the platform with me.

'Don't worry, lad,' he said, 'you won't miss the train 'cos it's me who tells it when to go!'

I can take this sort of thing all day long. These kind gestures make a man feel connected to the country as a whole, and having played across the land, and been up and down it so many times and talked to so many people and heard every accent, and overheard hundreds of family groups on the train, I feel as though I know everybody now. We're all one big happy family, if we only but knew it.

I was in a Midlands town supporting Sham 69, after a soundcheck at a venue where the communal dressing room's ceiling leaked and I was waiting outside in the rain for a taxi to the hotel to check in, and feeling somewhat down to say the least. Suddenly, a shaft of sunlight slashed the sky and a rainbow appeared, which I took as a very good omen. And then the taxi arrived! Even better. I got in, and on its radio, I kid you not, was Judy Garland singing 'Somewhere Over the Rainbow'.

In Scotland, at a rough place north of Glasgow, a chap backstage, Davey, was telling me how late one night in the Highlands he accidentally ran over and killed a young deer in the road. He may have been in a state of shock but was compelled to sing 'Who Killed Bambi' to the corpse. The police turned up, saw him imitating my absurd rendition of that song in *The Great Rock 'n' Roll Swindle*, and arrested him on the spot, refusing to believe he wasn't under the influence of excessive drink and drugs.

Another time I was invited to Glasgow, not to play but to watch *Gamers*, a Scottish film in which I took part. I decided to wear a kilt, my non-specific tartan one from the Hayrick video. It didn't cause much comment; in fact, no one mentioned it at all, until eventually one Scotsman asked me why I was wearing a kilt.

I answered along the lines of, 'Well, you know, "when in Rome do as the Romans do", what!'

'Aye,' he said gently, 'but have you nae noticed, no one else is wearing a kilt?' Later on, it was time to leave and fly back to London. Approaching the airport an American lady tourist waylaid me and said, 'O my gaahd! At last! (liest) A gen-yew-wine Scotsman! Do you mind if I take a photograph of you, kind sir?'

Well, of course, I didn't mind. This was a whole new experience: I wasn't Ten Pole Tudor, I was a Scotsman, and very happy to be one! I've never grinned more happily for a photo. All the world's a stage, dear reader, and there's a lot of joy to be had in the public arena.

In Edinburgh once I walked into a tobacconist and serving behind the counter was a traditional-looking be-turbaned, bearded Sikh. He saw me and loudly exclaimed, 'Och the noo, it's Tumple Tewdah!' in a broad Scottish accent.

Hereford

Supporting the Sex Pistols Experience I was about to go on stage in Hereford in 2014. The hall was rammed to well over the legal capacity which, in the face of popular demand, the verger decided to overlook. The much-needed extra money would go towards repairing the church roof.

That suited us. It makes for a better gig when the place is properly packed; the legal limit never seems full. Yet for some reason I wasn't in the right frame of mind, I had been distracted by conversing with interesting characters from the other bands backstage and wasn't fully focused when I went on.

I faced a sea of white males, aged fifty plus in T-shirts, jeans, boots, balding and beer guts. Perfectly amiable, there was nothing wrong with the crowd, only my mood. After a couple of songs, I said peevishly,

'How come there's no black people here?! After all, I'm playing the black man's music!' ...as if they could do anything about it.

At which point, as if by magic, and I swear it's true, a black woman climbed out of the crowd at the front, and up onto the stage. She then put her arms around me and gave me a beautiful hug and a kiss. Flabbergasted, and filled with love, I was almost overwhelmed. It seemed like a miracle. The crowd must have thought it was staged. Everything was fine after that.

One rainy evening in Newcastle, on my birthday, outside an Italian restaurant, in the dark, awaiting a taxi to take me over the river to Gateshead for the gig, I was smoking a cigarette and, as usual before a show, feeling anxious and low. A lovely girl walks by and says,

'Are you Ed Tudor Pole?'

I say yes and tell her it's my birthday, whereupon she takes a tangerine from her bag and gives it to me along with a kiss. The taxi comes and takes me to The Black Bull where I'm greeted by everybody singing 'Happy Birthday'. The lovely Geordies yet again reminded me that I may be many things, but I'm neither alone nor forgotten. It occurs to me that this appreciation existed before I became aware of it, so it stands to reason I can walk down any road knowing it's out there, without needing proof all the time. Just because you can't see something, like God, for instance, doesn't mean it isn't there. So, logically, I can never legitimately feel lonely again.

Fifteen Year Tour Weekly Routine: On the train home Sunday morning: elated with post-show euphoria and happily tired. On Monday I'm knackered. On Tuesday I become normal, and then on Wednesday, startled by the imminence of the upcoming gig and suddenly feeling its pressure, I pick up the guitar, go to the rehearsal studio and practise hard. Friday and Saturday playing and Sunday on the train home elated which is where we began: every week it's Groundhog Day like most jobs are, but once or twice a week I'm required to be stretched to the fullest extent of my powers, like an athlete.

The word got out that my show is good and I was invited to support other bands on their tours, like Hayseed Dixie, The Damned and Stiff Little Fingers. The road crews love me; I only need a microphone and a hole for the guitar lead. And the bands love me, I warm up the crowd good and proper; and I love it because I'm on a massive stage with an onstage sound man giving my guitar tone plenty of bollocks to a large crowd out front. Who could ask for anything more?

The Damned and I travelled in a huge coach in one section of which were shelves of curtained-off coffin-sized sleeping compartments. We could do what we liked after the show as long as we were back on board by 2am to set forth for the next venue when the motion of the coach and hum of the engine soon sent everyone straight to sleep (apart from the crew in the onboard bar of course).

A few hours later the coach was parked up behind the next venue in another town. Every morning I'd open the coach door to seek breakfast not knowing what I'd see, transported Tardis-like to a different locale, and every day was a day off, all the travelling done. It's the most efficient and enjoyable way of touring. Jed is the Damned's merchandise girl, she has a Gothic look and is very good at selling. She said she'd sell all my merchandise – and she did.

'Give us this day our daily envelope,' I said each morning as she handed me a manilla one, filled with cash.

I was compering The Rhythm Festival one year. Geno Washington turned up in a bit of a state. As well as the anxiety of being just about to go on stage, he discovered he'd left his spliff behind which became a base camp for rising panic. I understood his state of mind so, an expert on pre-show nerves, I nursed him, by building him a spliff for starters. I did as I would be done by, and helped the champ to the starting block. He drank white wine, and we talked, or rather he talked while he pulled his mind together to the necessary pitch of performance, like the pro he is. He went on to be utterly brilliant that day. I also met John Mayall, and Dr John the Night Tripper who was very considerate and kind to me.

For thirty years I'd been using my guitar, a Fylde (named after a piece of North West English coastline), and by 2011 it was very battered having survived decades of tours, stage invasions and the like. It had holes in it and made Willie Nelson's acoustic guitar look slightly scratched.

However, although out of true, the guitar had a superb tone and I loved it too much to replace; I learned to bend the neck to hit the correct notes. Backstage at the Electric Ballroom in Camden once, when I was supporting The Blockheads, and just as I was about to go on, one of the guitarists of that fine group noticed my guitar.

'What do you call that!?' he said scornfully, judging a book by the cover. I went on and played one of the best shows ever. The sound-man was superb and I was on form. I did the work of four men and the crowd roared their approval. The Blockheads bloke, to be fair, ate humble pie afterwards admitting that, yes, appearances can be deceptive. The remark I've heard most often in my professional career is, 'I never thought you were going to be *that* good!' Why is this? It either means I was truly exceptional or that their expectations were low. Or both. But which, dear reader, which?

Once at a Halifax pub, The Shay, I was upstairs, miserable, anxious and waiting to go on. It was 11pm and the punk band in the large bar below was making the most infernal noise. If they like that sort of racket, how are they going to like me, I thought. And then a little boy aged five entered the kitchen where I sat with my cup of tea. He saw my guitar and said,

'Your guitar's broken.'

'It's only a bit broken.'

'I can mend it for you!' he said.

'Can you?' I said, perking up.

The boy ran off and came back with a roll of Sellotape. With great concentration, tongue sticking out, he taped over the worst of the holes on the guitar as I held it steady for him. It is moments like that which make it impossible not to believe in God. Or was it the karma back from helping Geno? Anyway, a classic example of Yorkshire hospitality.

Feeling fully restored, I thanked the little lad, told him to go to bed, and went downstairs to play my set of tuneful songs to great effect. In the morning, I watched the boy playing with his big toy lorry in the vast sitting room above the pub. He kept checking I was still looking on.

'Dad, can Ed come again?'

But by now, a couple of hundred gigs into the fifteen-year tour it was becoming apparent my guitar had become too bent out of true to be any longer viable. I had to face the facts and stop being so sentimental. Sometimes you have to put the dog down. I was thinking this, sitting backstage in the dressing room at the Shepherd's Bush Empire after a show with the Damned, when a bloke noticed the make of the guitar.

'Hey, a Fylde! I know the man who makes them! Roger Bucknall. Do you mind if I take a photo to show him?', he said, and I thought no more about it. At the next gig I used a different guitar for the first time in thirty seven years, (a Guild) which felt most weird.

The very next morning there was an email from Roger Bucknall MBE, the man who has been making Fylde guitars since the 1970s, saying he'd seen the photograph of my guitar and that he could restore it. That it came the very next morning after using a guitar which wasn't a Fylde seemed extraordinary. Needing no second bidding I took the guitar and the train up to his workshop in Penrith in Cumbria and he marvelled at its condition. Roger took it apart, replaced the front of the guitar and set it up into perfect tune. Then he stuck the original soundboard onto the new one as a 'veneer' so it still looks the same – including a bit of the little boy's sellotape.

Chas & Dave

To actually see Chas & Dave play live was a total revelation. They were so massively better on stage than you could possibly imagine if you've only heard their records or seen them on telly. They were pure rock and roll and drive the crowd insane. Their twin harmonies are sublime, the tunes irresistible and Chas Hodges was a piano genius to rival Jerry Lee Lewis. He was also a great soul and gospel singer.

Chas said they'd always liked Tenpole Tudor when we met for the first time at the Amersham Arms in South London where they'd asked me to support them. Backstage in the dressing room Chas was telling me how Jerry Lee had taught him to play the piano, '...although he didn't know he was teaching me. I was his bass player on his UK tour in 1963, and I was watching him closely.'

Chas Hodges had been in the music scene since the early 1960s. In 1962, just before they got famous, The Beatles were booked to support his band The Outlaws. But, come the gig, Beatlemania was kicking off and they had to let the Beatles go on last. He was also in Head Hands and Feet in the seventies. A supremely talented musician and lovely bloke. Now here he was regaling me with stories and I was spellbound. I was all agog and Chas, who loved to keep an appreciative audience happy, kept the stories coming (you too can enjoy them in his autobiography).

Suddenly someone said, 'Ed, you're on!' and I jumped out of my skin.

Chas's stories had carried me far away from the focused mental preparation so necessary to live performance. The place was packed and I went on stage like a scalded cat. It took me two key changes and three tempos before I managed to produce an actual song. Chas and Dave attracted a cockney-type crowd, which is ideal for me as the more working-class the audience the better I go down.

And then Chas and Dave came on, and altered my world as they comprehensively and utterly rocked the house with a show of Rolling Stones-like depth and epic proportion. Pure rock and roll, country and soul.

When Chas Hodges died, I was invited along with a host of stars to play at his memorial concert at the Shepherd's Bush Empire. Joe Brown of the Bruvvers and Gary Brooker of Procol Harum were there, and Eric Clapton too. I was chuffed to bits to be on the same bill and to meet these legends I first heard as a schoolboy. At the big finale everyone was on stage for a mass singalong: a teary-eyed rendition of 'There Ain't No Pleasing You'.

And now, dear reader, never mind the same bill, I was on the same stage as Eric Clapton, four feet away. Anyway, I was impressed. Walking off stage at the end when I said, 'Wow, it's not every day you're on stage with Eric Clapton!', I didn't realise Eric was right behind me.

He said 'Oi oi'. I turned round, and there he was. We shook hands and had the briefest of chats – I've got the photo somewhere. Also through that concert I'd met Chas's daughter Juliet Sutton who accompanied me on piano that night, and when I ever need a piano player Juliet's the one to ask, being a chip off the old block and a great player herself.

The Sex Pistols Experience

When Darren first told me there was a Sex Pistols tribute band who wanted to play with me, I was adamant in my refusal:

'I don't work with tribute acts, man, I'm nothing if not real!'

Now consider. It was easy for me in 1977 to join the punk scene as it was on the doorstep. But how does a man get involved if he lives in a sleepy northern seaside town? Like Dave Twigg, for instance, a drummer from Bridlington, two hundred and thirty three miles away from the capital, whose one desire was to be in the heart of the music scene drumming to packed houses like the groups he reads about in the music papers and sees on telly. He played for a number of local bands going nowhere and had to get a proper job. He couldn't help feeling disadvantaged by geography. When in the twenty-first century tribute bands became commonplace, Dave Twigg, ever open to opportunity, had the brainwave of forming a Sex Pistols tribute band. If you are going to copy something, copy the best. He is blond, plays the drums, and so he could be 'Paul Crook' he thought: one down and three to go. And lo, the Sex Pistols Experience was born.

He formed the band and on the phone, on the drums, on the computer, social media, at the wheel, and backing vocals too; he managed the band and booked the tour and drove the band, in the van, day and night, hotel reservations made, the band was always paid. Dave was indefatigable in his efforts to gain ever more gigs and greater recognition for his brainchild 'The Sex Pistols Experience'. He worked week in month out, year in year out.

I was won round by how great they were. Nigel the bass player, with the help of half a bottle of vodka, could turn himself from a gentle pipe-and-slippers type of chap to an utterly convincing strung-out-on-drugs Sid Vicious. And Nathan Maverick, a natural frontman, played Johnny Rotter. Remember that John Lydon was imitating Laurence Olivier as *Richard III* at his initial audition for the Sex Pistols which Shakespearean lampoon remains the template for the traditional punk rock singer to this day. You cannot play Johnny Rotten without humour. In Croydon Rotter sneered at the crowd with withering contempt:

'So how come you 'aven't got a tube station, eh?'

You can intellectualise all you like but when the hall is packed, the band is rocking, the singer in total control and the audience transported, it's as rock and roll a show as a rock and roll show has ever been. Constant exposure to the Sex Pistols songs made me realise how good they are. 'EMI' for instance, is Mozartian, musically speaking. The crowd certainly experienced the Sex Pistols.

Over the years I did many shows with the Sex Pistols Experience, always got paid, and there was always the big cherry-on-the cake 'Swords of 1000 Men' finale to make everyone's night. They played a great barnstorming version with every showbiz trick in the book we could think of to maximise its impact. In fact, I have sung 'Swords' many more times with them than I did with Tenpole Tudor. They took me to Bucharest and Dubai, and we played in some great venues like the Buxton Opera House. It worked very well and the double bill provided a splendid night's entertainment, which is all it's about but I rationed my gigs with them as it was an easier ride for me and a man needs the challenge of do or die.

Game of Thrones

The day after the Buxton Opera house we played the Worthing Pavilion ballroom on a Saturday night, and the next day I was on an aeroplane to Dubrovnik for a day's work on *Game of Thrones.* The casting director, the lovely Nina Gold, thought of me for the 'Street Preacher'. The money was good and Wilko Johnson had done a cameo role for the series, as the Executioner, so there was a 'rocker precedent'. I agreed for old times' sake. It was a one-off and looked like a piece of cake.

That evening, I was installed at a luxurious, modern, five-star hotel near Dubrovnik and they said I was free to relax and recuperate for a couple of days with nothing on apart from a wardrobe fitting one day and a Hair-and-Make-Up meeting the next. Feeling utterly exhausted from the rock and roll exertions of the weekend, where you pretend to be younger than you are, I was jolly glad to hear it.

On Monday in glorious sunshine, I lazed by the pool and ordered a cocktail. I waved across the water to other actors doing the same. Tuesday was another lazy day by the Adriatic. I had lunch with a fight coordinator who was also a singer. His image was Pop star as Action-Man, which is an interesting idea.

Back at the hotel I went over my lines yet again. In the balmy evenings we dined like kings and partied on the snazzy soft-lit terrace, all white linen, to the gentle tones of an elegant lounge band. I made friends with Rowan Atkinson's 'Johnny English' stunt-double. With the drinks and the company and the luxurious ambience it was enjoyably glamorous.

On Wednesday a wig fitting.

Thursday was the filming day and in a chauffeur-driven Mercedes-Benz with cream leather interior I was driven to the ancient mediaeval part of Dubrovnik where the actors (including Peter Dinklage and Jerome Flynn) and I were given a beautiful area in which to hang out and be waited on hand and foot, with snacks and refreshments throughout the day apart from the infrequent occasions when we were actually required on set. It was all exciting to me but I couldn't help noticing how glum the other actors seemed, and faintly bored. Yet here they all were, at a career highpoint, starring in the world's most popular TV series and earning bundles of dosh.

To be fair, acting does become a bit tiresome, week in week out, lounging around for hours before you film a couple of lines and then break for lunch; then ditto in the afternoon before being whisked away in a luxury car back to the privacy (isolation) of a luxury hotel suite, all of which perks, I assume, are provided to compensate for the tedium of the job. Most actors don't work enough to find out how dull screen acting actually is, as well as being very difficult to do well.

Having had plenty of time to prepare, I played my role to the director's satisfaction and by Friday I was ready to leave the party: I'd had enough of the hotel and all the poncing about, and by then the gig in Southend the following day had commandeered my thoughts.

On the plane home, whilst happy to have had a pleasant five days paid holiday in a Croatian film-land fantasy, I was relieved to be getting back to work. I had to gear up. You don't want to play Southend half-cocked: you don't want to play anywhere half-cocked.

Next Saturday afternoon I was having a smoke outside Fenchurch Street Station before the Southend train departed, and near me was a bloke talking intently on a mobile, his little boy in a buggy beside him. I caught the eye of the lad and gave him a cheery sort of a nod whereupon he burst into floods of tears. His father, distracted from the phone call, looked down at the boy, looked at me, and then looked back at the boy. Without missing a beat he said to the boy in his cockney accent,

'Don't worry about him son, it's only Ten Pole Tudor' as if saying 'it's only the Postman', and then went back to the phone call. That he made no eye contact with me was what made it comedy genius.

The pandemic ended the fifteen-year solo tour and the break from it, I do admit, gave me a welcome respite from the unceasing toil that is a working musician's life. And then I wrote this book. (See page one, chapter one). And then it's back on the road again.

All my life I've said as long as the Stones are still going, I've got eleven more years. I'm not so sure about that now...

Ruminations

Music has led me the long way round, via notoriety, and constant touring, into realising I am a valid member of general society and I exist. This may seem obvious to you, but for most of my life I've felt more like a spectator than a participant; an outsider.

On the tour, happy to ply my musical trade like a normal working man, I was pleased to see familiar faces wherever I went, on an expedition great in miles to seek not the source of the Nile but the source of happiness. And I did find it.

There's the old trope that people go on stage to gain the love of the audience as compensation for some essential lack of love in their own lives. And if they do become successful, however much love they are given by the public, it's never quite enough. I may conform to the first part but to say the friendship I've been shown throughout the land over the decades has not been enough, with all the appreciation and hospitality given, would be most ungracious and quite untrue. It's been the kindness and the welcome of the people in the country at large which mended and restored a broken heart. And in the main I've been happy ever since; so when I say I love the people I really do. The fifteen-year tour provided the redemption, and the happy ending without which this book could not have been written.

I worked for The Prince's Trust in the nineties and at one of their parties Uri Geller accused me of not wanting to be famous. I was taken aback by this insight, but on reflection I think he may be right. With fame there's too much attendant anxiety and zero peace of mind. Anything that steals a person's freedom to walk along the road unmolested is surely their enemy. It is far more fun to be a real man in the real world, believe me, than some kind of icon, or demi-god. Normal life is where it's at.

What makes people happy is human interaction, having a friend or two, and belonging to a community. That and having something to do: the human is designed to work. And there you have it, people: the secret of life.

Had I gone for massive fame it would have killed me as surely as it did George Michael – and for similar reasons. Stardom cuts you off from the human hubbub of real life and it's the isolation that kills; being ultimately alone in a house of empty rooms. My keen instinct for survival, honed in infancy, could see that danger a mile off, but obviously a rock and roller needs a *bit* of fame otherwise there would be no one at the shows, and you wouldn't be reading this book. Hmmm...it's all a question of degree. Meanwhile I shall keep on playing the guitar as long as I can.

Dear reader, it's been intimate sharing my story with you. Does it matter that now you know everything about me? I think not. I have observed that us humans are remarkably alike; and that love is always in the air at the best concerts.

Malcolm McLaren was right, the audience is more important than the band.

The End

THE FIFTEEN YEAR TOUR

2003-2019

THE FIFTEEN YEAR TOUR DATES 2003-2019

Gigs 2004

February 5	Bilston The Robin
February 13	Cartoon Club Croydon
February 22	Dublin Castle
March 2	Islington Academy
March 6	Ipswich The Station
March 20	Brighton Prince Albert
April 1	Chiswick The Duke
April 23	Bristol
May 29	The Metro Oxford St
June 18	Little Wulfrun Wolverhampton
June 25	Glasgow
July 3	Kings Arms Acton
July 10	Real Music Festival Colchester
July 15	Morecambe
September 4	The Enterprise
September 10	Derby The Vic
September 17	12 Bar Club Denmark Street
September 23	Half Moon Putney
September 25	Llandeilo
October 2	Astoria downstairs
October 9	Hertford Marquee
October 23	Bull and Gate
November 3	The Plough Walthamstow
November 7	Wigan The Mill at the Pier
November 18	The Lion Inn, Blakey N. Yorks
November 19	Skegness The Farm
November 20	Leicester The Attic

December 4	Winchester The Railway
December 12	The Astoria
December 16	New Priory Hotel

Gigs 2005

January 15	Vauxhall Tavern
January 22	Gloucester Rugby Club
February 5	Berlin, Wild at Heart
February 11	The 100 Club
February 19	Nottingham
February 24	Oxford (John Otway)
March 19	Gloucester Welsh Harp
April 9	Amersham Arms
May 7	Tooting Green
May 19	Morecambe
June 10	Gillingham
June 11	Thames Boat trip
June 24	Garage upstairs
July 9	New Priory Hotel Hereford
July	Cheltenham Racecourse
July 15	Betsey Trotwood
July 16	Jailhouse Coventry
July 29	Badfest
August 22-27	Edinburgh Fringe
September	The Plough Walthamstow
September 25	Scunthorpe
September 30	Leicester The Attik
October 1	The Lamb Little Harrowden
October 13	Blakey Ridge
October 14	Hull
November 4	Barracuda, Stoke Newington
November 10	Gloucester Guildhall
November 19	Torquay
December 16	Swansea
December 17	Mau Mau Club Notting Hill
December 30	100 Club (Chas & Dave support)

Gigs 2006

January 14	Hertford Marquee
January 28	Burns Night Glastonbury
February 9	Southampton The Joiners
February 10	Howden North
February 19	Chepstow The Five Alls
March 4	Liverpool Cavern
March 5	Dagenham
March 11	York
March 23	Norwich
March 24	Croydon Cartoon Club
March 26	Tamworth
April 6	100 Club
April 8	Frome
April 14	Swindon The Vic
April 15	Skegness Butlins
April 18	Bournemouth
April 22	Hastings The Crypt
April 28	Hereford
April 29	Coventry Jailhouse
May 5	Kettering
May 6	Ace Café
May 18	Newcastle Trillians
June 17	The Plough
June 23	Pontypridd
July 21	Cardiff
July 27	Crewe Limelight
July 29	Acoustic Festival of Britain
September 30	Coventry Jailhouse
October 6	Milton Keynes The Pits
October 14	100 Club
October 25	Peebles Eastgate Theatre
November 4	Leicester Attik
November 11	St Albans The Horn
November 17	Derby The Vic

November 25	York
December 8	Amsterdam Milky Way
December 11	Eastney nr Portsmouth
December 16	Sheffield
December 17	Norwich
December 20	Hull
December 21	Southampton
December 22	Nottingham
December 23	Shepherd's Bush Empire

Gigs 2007

February 24	Winchester The Railway
March 19	100 Club (John Otway)
March 18	Knaresborough, Harrogate
April 7	Deal
April 8	Frome The Cheese and Grain
April 14	Kingston Kingsmeadow Live
April 15	Portobello Golds
May 12	The Coach House @ The Angel Hotel. Lincs.
May 17	Leeds Rio's
May 26	Strummercamp
May 28	Croydon
May 31	Glasgow Cathouse
June 1	Edinburgh Subway
June 2	York Fibbers
June 9	Watford
June 10	Mansfield
June 16	Sheffield Boardwalk
June 23	Kettering Sawyers
July 6	Barrow-in-Furness
July 27	Blackburn North Bar
August 4	Rhythm Festival Compere
August 10	Endorse it in Dorset
August 11	Bristol, Black Horse
August 31	Scunthorpe Crosby Hotel
September 1	Newcastle Academy

September 29	Dundee Hustlers
October 13	Ipswich Railway
October 26	Halifax The Shay
October 27	Lancaster Yorkshire House
November 9	Hemsby Speedfreaks Ball
November 15	Tappie Toories Dunfermline
November 16	Rosyth nr. Dunfermline
December 12	The Volks Brighton
December 18	Hertford
December 28	Kettering Sawyers

Gigs 2008

February 1	The Railway Hotel Southend
February 15	100 Club (supporting Eddie and the Hot Rods)
February 16	Leicester Shed
February 22	Bilston Robin
February 23	Gloucester Guildhall
March 2	Gateshead Three Tuns
March 8	Witchwood Ashton-under-Lyne
March 11	Oxford Henley
March21	Sheffield Boardwalk
March 30	Leeds Rio's
April 3	Newcastle Trillians
April 17	Electric Ballroom (the Blockheads)
May 17	St Anne's Castle Great Leighs Essex
May 23	Newcastle Academy
May 24 and 25	Acoustic Festival of Britain, Catton Hall
June 13	12 Bar Club Denmark St
June 27	Salisbury Winchester Gate
June 29	Glastonbury festival
July 3	100 Club
July 20	Chuck Berry (night off)
July 25	Kettering Sawyers
July 27	Sheffield supp. Dickies
August 2	Hartlepool
August 10	Rebellion Blackpool

September 6	Banbury
September 11	Wakefield
September 12	Kendal
September 13	Dudley JB's
September 21	Portobello Gold's
September 27	Crewe M Club
October 4	Stoke Newington Airport
October 11	Stroud
October 18	London Bridge Shunt
October 24	Doncaster Vintage Rock Bar
October 25	Halifax The Shay
November 7	Screaming Lord Sutch Festival LLantrwyde
November 29	Hamfest Milton Keynes
December 5	Bristol Thunderbolt
December 19	Newcastle Academy
December 20	Hartlepool Clarendon
December 28	York Fibbers

Gigs 2009

January 3	Brixton Hootananny
January 17	Southend The Railway
January 30	Glasgow Rockers Club
February 13	Shildon Civic Hall
February 20	Sheffield Casbah
March 6	London Bridge Shunt Club
March 19	Kettering Sawyers
April 3	Hastings Brass Monkey
April 4	Tunbridge Wells Kelsey Arms
April 11	Derby The Venue
April 12	Hednesford The Uxbridge
May 22	Acoustic Festival of Britain
May 30	Cardiff The Toucan
June 5	Poole Mr Kyps
June 12	Newcastle Carling Academy
June 13	Sheffield Red House
June 19	Screaming Lord Sutch Festival, Wales

June 26	Anglesea Scooter Rally
July 4	Barnsley Birdwell Club
July 11	The Pokey Hole
August 21/22	The Rhythm Festival
September 4	Harlow The Square
September 5	Rotherham Blues Club
September 11	Wigan New Tavern
September 13	Walthamstow Ye Old Rose & Crown
September 26	Crewe M Club
October 23	Hertford Corn Exchange
November 7	Holloway Road, The Gaff
November 20	Poole Mr Kyps
November 29	Swansea
December 5	Leeds
December 11	Newport
December 18	Salisbury Winchester Gate

Gigs 2010

February 5	100 Club
February 24	Aberdeen Lemon Tree
February 25	Inverness Ironworks
February 26	Banchory Wood End Barn
February 27	Glasgow ABC
February 28	Dundee Fat Sams
March 1	Edinburgh Picture House
March 2	Newcastle Academy
March 3	Wolverton Craufurd Arms
March 19	The Robin Bilston
March 20	Hull Piper Club (H.D.)
March 21	Sheffield Plug (H.D.)
April 3	Basingstoke Scooter Festival
April 10	Southend The Railway
April 14	Manchester Moho
April 21	Nottingham The Bell Inn
April 28	Hoxton Underbelly
May 15	Rotherham

May 18	Reading Sub 89
May 20	Falmouth Cornwall
May 21	Bristol Academy
May 22	Bristol battle ground skate park
May 23	Acoustic Festival of Britain Uttoxeter Racecourse
May 27	Leeds Academy
May 28	Glasgow ABC
May 29	Edinburgh Picturehouse
May 30	Aberdeen Warehouse
June 1	Nottingham Rescue Rooms
June 2	Cambridge Junction
June 3	Oxford Academy
June 4	London Shepherd's Bush Empire
June 4	Nottingham Rock City (H.D.)
March 5	Cleethorpes (H.D.)
March 9	Leicester Y Theatre (H.D.)
March 13	Deal Astor Theatre
March 17	Cambridge (supporting Hayseed Dixie)
March 25	Manchester Academy
June 6	Newcastle Academy
June 18	Kettering Sawyers
July 9	Weston-Super-Mare Decades
July 18	York
July 21	Covent Garden Poetry evening
July 23	Wickerman Festival
July 29	Bristol Thunderbolt
July 30	Bideford
August 8	Blackpool Rebellion Festival
August 21	Rhythm Festival
September 11	Swansea Harvest Festival Green Valley arts
September 24	Bournemouth Champions
October 1	Bradford Zulu Bar
November 5	Barrow in Furness
November 12, 13, 14	Bucharest Romania
November 19	Sheffield Red House

November 27	Stroud Valley Arts
November 28	100 club
December 17	York Stereo
December 18	Hastings The Tub
December 29	100 Club
February 27	Newcastle Riverside

Gigs 2011

January 29	The George Eastleigh
February 18	Bradford Rio's
March 4	Harlow Square
March 11	Barnsley The White Bear
March 12	Halifax Illingworth Club
March 13	Wakefield Snooty Fox
March 18	Shafton The Singing Man
April 15	San Paulo, Brazil Clash Club
April 23	Wolverton Craufurd Arms
April 29	Chagford, Dartmoor Jubilee Hall
April 30	Stockton on Tees Georgian Theatre
June 17	12 Bar Club (with the Roadholders)
June 25	Halifax White Rose Festival
September 4	Nigel's Party Ramsgate
September 8	Central St Martin's School of Art
September 10	Durham Punk Festival
September 16	Buxton Opera House
September 17	Worthing Pavilion Theatre
October 1	Southend The Railway
October 2	Exeter The Cavern
October 12	Reading Sub 89 (with Stiff Little Fingers)
October 14	Fife Rothes Hall
October 17	Bath Komedia (with S.L.F.)
October 21	5 Bells, Colne Engaine Essex
October 29	Warsop nr. Mansfield
November 11	Birmingham 02 Early Show (doors 6.00)
November 19	Nr Bury – Hark to Towler

November 26	Selby Riverside
December 17	Winchester The Railway
December 23	Crewe Box
December 31	Bristol The Fleece

Gigs 2012

January 14	Corby Park Leisure Centre
January 28	Guildford Boiler Room
February 18	Sheerness Ivy Leaf
February 25	Birmingham Ballroom
March 1	Bucharest Rumania
March 2	Poole Mr Kyps
March 3	Basingstoke Sanctuary
March 16	Cardiff Globe
March 17	Plymouth Junction
April 14	The Garage
April 29	Butlin's Minehead
May 12	Gateshead The Black Bull
May 27	Cumbria
June 2	Rotherham Trade Union Festival
June 15	Nr Swindon Summer Breeze
June 22	Glasgow Renfrew Ferry
June 23	Edinburgh Studio 24
June 29	Derby Queen Vic
July 7	Dunfermline Sinky's Bar
July 15	Nr Swindon Summer Breeze
July 20	Batley
July 27	Southampton Talking Heads
July 28	Bristol Thunderbolt
July 31	100 Club UK Subs
September 7	Southend The Railway
September 28	Dexters Dundee
September 29	Bathgate
October 13	Lancaster Yorkshire House
October 20	Wigan Maxine's
October 26	Carmarthen Three Salmons

October 27	Pontypool The Hog and Hosper
November 17	The Plough Norwood
November 23	Wakefield The Hop
November 24	Gateshead The Three Tuns 2
December 23	100 Club (early set, 7.00 pm)

Gigs 2013

January 5	Stoke Newington The Sovereign
March 2	Penarth The Windsor
March 8	Brighton Concorde + SLF
March 9	Nuneaton Queen's Hall + SLF
March 14	Manchester Ritz + SLF
March 15	Newcastle Academy + SLF
March 16	Edinburgh Citrus Club
March 17	Glasgow Barrowlands + SLF
March 19	Cambridge Junction + SLF
March 20	Norwich Waterfront + SLF
March 21	Leeds Academy + SLF
March 22	London The Forum + SLF
March 23	Nottingham Rock City + SLF
March 26	Exeter Phoenix + SLF
March 28	Bristol Academy + SLF
March 29	Wolverhampton The Robin + SLF
April 1	Bridport The Palace + SLF
April 3	Bedford Corn Exchange + SLF
April 5	Southend The Railway
April 11	Berlin SO3 + SLF
April 12	Hamburg Neuer Kamp 30 + SLF
April 13	Dusseldorf Zakk + SLF
April 15	Frankfurt Batschkapp + SLF
April 16	Munich Hamsa 39 + SLF
April 20	Dunfermline Slinky's Bar
April 27	Minehead Butlins
April 28	Cardiff The Globe
May 10	Bloxham Festival Banbury
May 26	Morecambe Nice'n' Sleazy

June 1	Acoustic Festival of Britain Uttoxeter
June 7	Manchester Three Minute Theatre
June 8	Wakefield Long Division Festival
June 21	Gateshead Three Tuns
June 28	Glastonbury Festival Shangri-La
July 6	Harlow The Square
July 11	York The Duchesss
July 14	Wolverton Craufurd Arms
July 20	The Penn Festival
July 27	Derby Rock & Blues Festival
September 1	Stroud The Queen Vic
September 29	Ipswich The Railway
October 4	The Garage
October 12	Barnsley
October 19	Winchester The Railway
October 24	100 Club
October 26	Bilston The Robin
November 30	Skegness Great British Folk Festival
December 6	Gateshead The Black Bull

Gigs 2014

January 10	Wakefield The Hop
January 24	Portsmouth, Wedgewood Rooms
February 28	Hereford FC
March 1	Birmingham Roadhouse
March 21	Basingstoke The Sanctuary
March 22	Harlow The Square
Apri 19	Shepherd's Bush Empire + T.M.T.C.Hang
April 23	Wolverton Craufurd Arms
April 24	The Forum + The Damned
April 26	Swanage Rock-a-Hula Club
May 2	Newport Riverside Tavern
May 3	Bristol O2 supping Buzzcocks
May 4	Newcastle Academy
May 5	Gateshead Black Bull PM Show
May 9	Belfast Voodoo Club

May 1	York Fulford Arms
June 14	Wimborne Folk Festival
June 20	Willowman Festival Yorks
July 6	Rotherham Festival
July 11	Reading + SPE
July 20	Penn Festival
July 26	Gateshead Three Tuns
August 2	Southampton Langley Arms
August 9	80s Rewind Festival
September 6	Nr Bristol Iron Acton
September 12	Wakefield Warehouse
September 15	Lowestoft
September 24	Spice of Life Soho Guest Spot
September 27	Southend The Railway
October 10	Wigan
October 11	Butlins Skegness
October 31	Selby
November 1	Keighley
November 2	York Fulford Arms
November 5	Bristol Motion
November 15	Northampton
November 28	Deal
December 6	Gillingham Beacon Court
December 19	Cardiff The Globe

Gigs 2015

January 7	100 Club + The Lurkers, 999
January 30	Coventry + SPE
January 31	Cheltenham + SPE
February 7	Corby
February 20	Portsmouth Wedgewood Rms
March 7	The Pipeline E.1. (Mayall)
March 22	Clitheroe + The Rezillos
March 27	Liverpool O2 Academy
March 28	Manchester O2
April 10	Dubai

April 11	Abu Dhabi
April 17	Preston Continental
April 24	Wolverton Craufurd Arms
April 25	Leamington Spa Assembly
May 1	Gateshead Three Tuns
May 24	Morecambe Nice n Sleazy
June 7	Rotherham Cutlers Arms
June 13	Fiddler's Elbow Camden
June 28	Leigh-on-Sea Folk Fest
July 9 &11	Norway Tonnesberg
July 17	Deal Hole in the Roof
September 11	Whitwell Community Centre Worksop
September 12	Wakefield The Hop
September 13	Derby The Hairy Dog
October 9	Newport Riverside
October 16	100 Club supporting The Professionals
November 6	Gateshead Three Tuns
November 13	Coventry
November 14	Keighley
November 27	Garage Holloway Road + SPE
November 28	Glastonbury Fair Giblet
December 4	Ripley
December 11	Harlow Square + Chas and Dave
December 12	Plymouth + SPE

Gigs 2016

February 19	Sutton-in-Ashfield
February 20	Scunthorpe Lincoln Imp
March 18	Cardiff Globe
March 19	Derby Hairy Dog
April 1	Liverpool
April 2	Sheffield O2 Academy
April 8	Clitheroe Keystreet
April 16	Southampton All Day Punk
April 23	Nottingham Scooter Fest
May 7	York Fulford Arms

May 14	Kingston Fighting Cocks + Department S
May 21	Brussels + Department S
May 27	Fiddler's Elbow
May 29	Bruton Shindig Festival
June 17	Sonic Rock Solstice
June 18	Buryfields Chesham
July 8, 9	Norway Pirate Festival
July 16	Stoke Underground
July 23	Southend Cricketers
August 18	Reading Sub 89 + The Damned
August 19	Birmingham Bow Wow Wow
August 20	London Garage
September 8	Swindon The Vic
September 17	Grimsby Yardbirds
September 18	Brighton
September 20	100 Club
October 1	Croydon
October 7	Glasgow Stereo
October 8	Inverness
November 25	Coventry
November 26	Northampton Roadmender
December 3	Banbury
December 10	Ramsgate Queen Charlotte

Gigs 2017

January 10	100 Club + SPE
February 18	Glasgow
March 4	Gateshead Black Bull
March 29	100 Cub + Jilted John D
April 21	Woking + Department S, Eddie and the Hot Roads
April 23	Wolverton Craufurd Arms
April 29	Birmingham Flappers
May 13	Rotherham Cutlers Arms
May 27/28	Merthyr Festival Doc Insane
June 2	Uttoxeter Acoustic Festival
June 17	The Wirral

June 23	Falkirk
June 24	Penicuik
June 30	Norway Odal Rock Festival
July 21	Ashington
September 1	Blackpool
September 8	Coventry + SPE
September 9	Watford The Flag
September 15	Reading Sub 89 + SPE
September 16	Sheffield Plug
September 29	Leicester Musician
September 30	Wigan Old Courts + SPE
October 8	Skegness matinee show 12.30
October 20	Wolverhampton Wall Heath
November 15	Norway Oslo
November 17	Norway Brumunddal
November 18	Norway Odalfest
November 24	Leamington Spa Zephyr

Gigs 2018

January 4	100 Club + Vibrators
June 2	Cardiff Globe
June 30	Norway Odalfest
July 6	100 Club
July 20	York Queen Victoria
July 21	Kirkhamgate Village Hall
September 3	Piccadilly London Crazy Coqs
October 5	Skegness Butlins Alt Rock Festival
October 19	Gateshead Cricket Club
December 17	Shepherd's Bush Empire for Chas

Gigs 2019

February 3	Hartford Cheshire The Salty Dog
March 27	O2 Islington Vive Le Rock Awards
April 12	Wolverton Craufurd Arms + Vikings
April 13	100 Club Tenpole Tudor + Vikings
June 1	Bristol The Fleece + SPE

June 15	Cardiff Globe
July 7	Sandwich Kent
September 6	Margate
October 4	London 229 Grt. Portland Street + SPE
October 5	Sheffield Punk Festival
October 12	Ashford
November 23	London Nell's Club + The Vapours
November 30	Preston Continental
December 6	Gateshead The Schooner

Gigs 2020

February 8	Whitby Steam Punk Festival.

The Covid Pandemic ended that tour.
Gigging resumed on 4 November, 2021 at The 229 Club, Great Portland Street and will continue as long as possible.